POEMS FROM PRISON

Billy Leland

To order additional copies of this book, contact:
Xlibris
1-888-795-4274
www.Xlibris.com
Orders@Xlibris.com

ISBN: 978-1-7960-9345-2 (sc)
ISBN: 978-1-7960-9335-3 (e)

Print information available on the last page

Rev. date: 03/12/2020

Contents

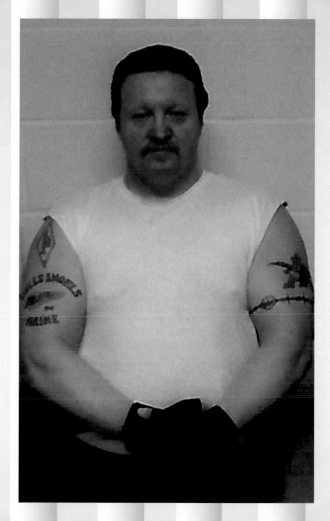

This is a picture of me after my arrest.

I was put in the Maine state prison in maximum security.

At this time, I had never stepped foot in a courtroom.

They put me in prison right off the streets with no bail.

Acknowledgement

I want to thank many people for believing in me and helping me since I've gotten out of prison. My family first and foremost. They have supported me and loved me through my life whether I made mistakes or not. I love all of you with all my heart. Thank you for always being there for me.

Next, I want to thank my good friend and best tech support guy anyone can ask for, Fred Peavey. He set me up in his home with an office and a computer giving me the chance to write my books. He was always there for me to show me the ins and outs of Word 2019. Believe me, I'm not the best of students at my age. But I'm living proof that you can teach an old dog new tricks. Thank you, buddy from the bottom of my heart.

I want to thank Wally Thurston for the cover design for this book and also the first book I wrote called, The Fall of an Angel. I couldn't have done it without him. Love and Respect to you my friend.

Last but not least, I want to thank all of you for wanting me to write this book in the first place. I started writing poems when I spent so much time in solitary confinement so I wouldn't lose my mind. Time goes by extremely slowly when you're alone, especially when you don't have anything to do. I never thought I'd be letting anyone read my poems but then Facebook came along while I was in prison and my good friend Christina Thurston started putting my poems on a Facebook page she made for me. I didn't even know what Facebook was until many years later.

I have to give special thanks to my daughter Tianna, her husband Ryan and my beautiful granddaughter Kiaira for being there for me day in and day out no matter what I was doing. I can talk to them about anything at any time. They support my decisions and give me constructive criticism when I need it. They may not agree with me all the time and I can't blame them. I continue to make mistakes but they aren't anywhere near as serious as in the past. I love you guys with all my heart. Thank you for always being there.

A special thanks also goes out to my other daughter Lynda Johnson for her excellent editing job on my books. She also gives me constructive criticism whether I want it or not. I love you sweetheart and always will.

There are others too. You know who you are!

Just Words

As you read the words I've written in this book, try to put yourself in a situation where you have no control over your life at all. You are told when to eat, when to sleep, when to shower, what to wear and where you can and can't go throughout the day. Every aspect of your life is controlled inside those walls. You can be searched at any time, day or night. If you're lucky it's only a pat down search. Strip searches are very degrading. You can be moved from one tiny cell to another anytime they feel like moving you. You can never get comfortable. Every phone call you make is monitored and recorded, if you can make phone calls at all. They can put a stop to your phone calls for no reason at all. If you can get through to your loved ones on the phone it costs them fifty times more because you have to call collect from County Jails and you pay for your own calls in Federal Prison with the money that is sent to you. You do have to have a job in prison but it only pays twelve cents an hour, hardly enough at the end of the month to make one phone call. When the food comes in to the prison it is labeled "Grade D, Institutional Use Only". The government buys the foods that can't be sold in the grocery stores anymore because of the age. I bet you never thought of where all the meats went after the expiration date ran out, did you?

You are locked into a cement room no bigger than a small bathroom in an apartment. Not only is this your bedroom, it's also your bathroom. The toilet is so close to your bed that your leg touches your bed when you are on the toilet. In this tiny cell you can't have anything at all on the walls. If you have pictures sent in from the people you love, you have to have them out of sight in a photo album that you purchase from the commissary. You are only allowed one photo album in your cell. Your mail can be thrown away at any time and they won't even notify you that you had mail. They open every piece of mail and read it and inspect it for contraband. In your tiny cell all day you hear big steal doors opening and closing with a big bang. It's very hard to get used to that and get sleep. You also hear the guard's keys as he walks through the prison. Some guards make it a point to be really loud and slam the doors as hard as they can. Not all guards do it but there are a lot of sadistic guards that work in prisons. They have no sympathy or compassion. You are just a number to them. A piece of shit in their eyes because you are in prison.

In these prisons you live with others that have no values. They will steal from you in a heartbeat. They don't value human life at all. There is no such thing to them as your space. These are guys that are mostly in gangs because there is safety in numbers. But you are alone, the feeling of loneliness in prison is something you can't even imagine. You never knew loneliness until you are put into one of these tiny cells for days, months and years. Depression sets in so bad that you contemplate suicide. It crossed my mind more than I can count.

So, to stay sane and kill an awful lot of time I began writing. I wrote letters, books and hundreds of poems to keep my mind busy. I wrote poems about anything and everything. The poems you will read will give you an idea where my mind was on the day's I wrote them. I'm glad God gave me the gift to write. I don't think I would have survived fifteen years not knowing how to write. You can't show your feelings in prison. The only one understood in there is anger. The rest you have to hide or you will be considered weak and the weak are prey. These poems allowed me to get my feelings out so they aren't bottled up inside me making me want to explode. I hope you can see the person I really am through my writing and not just think of me as a convict that broke the law.

I was asked many times to publish my poems. I really don't want to just put a bunch of poems in a book and call it a book of poems. I want to try to make you see how an ordinary guy can learn things he never thought he'd learn when put in a dire situation alone for so many years. I'm a guy that never played a video game, never watched much TV because I was always on the go. As an adult I was in three motorcycle clubs and travelled the world. I've ridden motorcycles in every state in America and many different countries. Then all of a sudden, I was locked up in a tiny cage and lost everything I owned. I thought my life was over.

When I first was locked up, I was married. I wrote my wife a lot of poems but they didn't do any good. She was in another man's bed within ninety days. I'm going to start out this book with some of the poems I wrote to her to try to keep her. As time goes on and I don't hear from her I realize trying to hold on is useless. No matter how many letters or poems I write to her she is gone. I don't know if she even reads them anymore. I finally give up and the hurt turns to anger. I wrote dozens of poems to her but I'm only putting a few in this book. With just the ones you are going to read you'll see what a sap I was for even trying. I think back on it and I realize what a fool I was. But it's just one more lesson I had to learn the hard way.

"I don't always learn my lesson,

But when I do, you can bet

I learned it the hard way."

Chapter One

I BELONG TO YOU

One time with you is not enough,
living without you is too tough.
My heart is beating just for you,
it knows what you can do.

The love that you have shown,
is the best I've ever known.
Your love is something new,
to make me feel the way you do.

You'll have me with your first kiss,
your lips are what I'll truly miss.
I open my eyes and I see your face,
and I feel your sensual grace.

You are so beautiful to me,
you are the one I want to see.
You're everything I prayed for,
and I will never want more.

Please believe me when I say,
I want you in every way.
God knows you belong with me too,
just like I belong to you.

Love Always,

Billy
....

As I wrote this poem, in my heart I knew it wouldn't do any good, but I was desperate and very lonely. My world has fallen apart and I was ready to give up on everything. I look back at it now and know that I was a fool for thinking that she would wait for me.

A LIFETIME TO FIND

I don't need a doctor now that's for sure,
I know he doesn't have a cure.
It wouldn't help if I had a private nurse,
I think it might make it worse.

I don't need a prescription for this pain,
drugs would drive me insane.
I don't need diamonds, or a pot of gold,
I'd still be sad, lonely and cold.

I don't wanna argue and I don't wanna fight,
and I don't wanna be alone every night.
I don't need a psyche telling me what to do,
There's only one cure for me and that's YOU!

I have been infected with a case of "love",
and you fit me like a glove.
I told you before and I'll tell you once more,
I love you so open up your door.

Believe me when I say all I want is you,
and no other woman on earth will do.
You have taken me a lifetime to find,
and I can't get you off my mind.

I have so much love I want to share,
can you please wait till I get there?
I'm not sure how long that will be,
but it will be worth it, you'll see.

Sept. 8, 2003

When I wrote this poem, I hadn't heard from my wife in two months and I had a suspicion that she was sleeping with someone else but I was so alone in solitary confinement I wouldn't let go of her. It was my birthday and I can remember it well after all these years. Some memories I can't forget no matter how hard I try.

As time goes on and my suspicions grow, my poems take a turn. Twenty-four hours a day in solitary confinement for weeks and weeks can get to you if you don't do something to keep your mind busy. It has been a few months since I've heard from my wife and my family hasn't got a clue what she is doing or who she's with. My mind is all over the place now. I'm so hurt because I know in my heart that she has someone else already. You'll see how my poems change from the loving ones I wrote to her.

2

You Forgot Me

I'm lying awake and crying,
in the middle of the night.
You knew how hard I was trying,
to make things turn out right.

Even when I do get to sleep,
it's broken and sporadic.
My heart lies here in a heap,
and my tears are automatic.

I never have any good dreams,
just a lot of nightmares.
People must hear my screams,
but nobody really cares.

Are grown men even supposed to cry,
or just when they're a baby?
I'm always asking myself why,
is my life over now maybe?

I've been up all night just thinking,
how it was to be free.
Through tears my eyes are blinking,
knowing that you forgot about me.

I wish I could say that I'm moving on,
but it's hard to do when freedom is gone.
So, I'm going to lie here in this lonely cell,
wishing that you would go to hell.

March 10, 2004

I knew what my wife had done to me at this time. She not only went to bed with the confidential informant, she was selling everything I owned as fast as she could. When she couldn't sell, she was going to the pawn shop in Brewer and giving them my jewelry. I lost so much because of her.

A New Start

Darling, please remember that I love you,
under these conditions there's nothing I can do.
So, baby don't be wasting your love on me,
it's breaking my heart, but I'm setting you free.

You've got a long wait and it just won't work,
taking away your happiness I'd feel like a jerk.
There are many men that would fall in love with you,
they can share your love the way I'd want to.

I'm no good for you bound by these chains,
it would only cause heartache and pains.
My love has to stop at this prison gate,
because now I live in a world full of hate.

I hope and pray you find true happiness out there,
I'm sure that you have love you want to share.
You deserve to be as happy as you can be,
And I can't give that to you now, can't you see?

It's going to kill me but I have to let you go,
I will always love you, I hope that you know.
So, I'm writing this with a severely broken heart,
as I set you free so you can get a new start.
10-20-04
Solitary Confinement

Our Dance

I'm know I'm never going to dance again,
the way I danced with you.
Because your love is etched in my memory,
and with that, I'll get through.

I've done a lot of things in my life,
and many times I've been wrong.
You don't believe a thing I said,
but my love for you was strong.

I don't know why you hurt me so,
because what I said wasn't a lie.
But still you broke my heart so bad,
it's a wonder I didn't die!

As this lonely time slowly passes,
I'm slowly forgetting all the pain.
I will always remember the good times,
like our dance in the rain.

I've finally accepted that our love is over,
and you've gone about your way.
I'm struggling to get through this way of life,
without thinking about you every day.

Time is a killer when you're locked away for so long. You have too much time to think and you always think the worst. I hope these poems don't bore you or sound too corny. It was my way to get my thoughts and feelings out in a place where feelings were not allowed. Nobody knew what I was writing and I never let anyone read them. It feels strange to me now as I am putting these in a book for anyone to see. I hope that they can help people see that there are ways to get your feelings out so you don't end up getting too depressed. I've seen firsthand what depression can do. Especially when there is no one to talk to that cares. It helped me get by fifteen years of loneliness and heartache. When I write these, I thought that someday someone would read them long after I'm gone and appreciate them. I often thought that my family would be the ones to read them and I wanted them to know how I felt and how I got through that long prison stretch. I also often wondered if I was ever going to see freedom again. Maybe I was going to die in prison.

Forget

She looks at me like I'm a stranger,
and being near me would put her in danger.
She doesn't know this is tearing me apart,
or realize how hard this is on my heart.

I can't take this heartache and pain anymore,
knowing that she just walked out the door.
I can see her now packing her things,
I know she pawned her wedding rings.

I used to cry about losing her at night,
and to get to sleep, I had to fight.
A lot of nights she showed up in a dream,
It hurt so bad I'd want to scream.

She would be the last one I'd want to see,
I knew she didn't care about me.
I was only hurting myself on the inside,
now she can take someone else for a ride.

Being alone will be so hard to forget,
I'll find someone else though, you can bet.
I just have to get myself out of this cell,
and stop living like I'm in hell.

"6-6-04"

I wrote this poem thirteen and a half years before I got out of prison. I didn't know at the time how long I was going to be in there. I never once gave up hope of getting out though.

Another Lover

My life has unlimited possibility,
but not for you to be with me!
When you left, it was no imitation,
now my love has a limitation.

I thought it was true love we created,
I went to jail, you never waited!
You said that we'd wait for each other,
it wasn't long before you found a lover.

Now there will never be a me and you,
if there was, you'd never be true.
Because faithfulness, you do lack,
So, I could never take you back.

Now I'm the lonely man that you see,
it started when you left me.
I don't understand, so don't ask me why,
when I think of you, I still cry.

I know the pain will leave me somehow,
I just wish it would be now.
I've given up on you as my wife,
I've got to get on with my life.

I'll just sit here writing on this hard bed,
keeping thoughts of you out of my head.
But my thoughts will hover and hover,
Picturing you with another lover.

Christmas Day 2003

Holidays in prison are the hardest. Missing the ones you love and not being able to get anyone anything for Christmas is hard. You can't stop thinking about the past and how happy you were. This was my first Christmas in prison and I never dreamt I would be spending so many others there.

Tears

I've cried tears of joy,
and tears of pain.
I've cried tears in the sunshine,
and tears in the rain.
I've cried tears for the strong;
and tears for the weak.
I've cried tears for the homeless,
and tears for the meek.
I've cried tears for my family,
and tears for the deceased.
I've cried tears for my thoughts,
and tears to be released.
Forty-Eight years of tears,
have burdened me with sorrow.
I will cry more tears tonight,
knowing I'll be here tomorrow.
All these tears I will surely hide,
you don't show tears on the inside.
You hide all feelings behind these bars,
but they will leave emotional scars.
It's hard not to show heartache and pain,
holding it inside drives you insane.
When you're as fed up as you can get,
you'll do anything to find and outlet.
I've seen inmates cry like they were dying,
everyone would see them crying.
I've cried a hundred million silent tears,
nobody has seen me in all those years.
There's one thing that I will never do,
and that's shed another tear over you.
I don't wish you any harm in this life,
but I'm over you as being my wife.

....

I wrote this poem long after my wife left. She was on my mind quite often. I slowly got over the pain and
heartache and got my feelings out in poems.

Do Your Best

I often wonder what happened in my life,
and why it was I didn't keep a wife.
I've been thinking hard and long,
wondering where I went wrong.

Some people say I'm a really nice guy,
I've lost everything and maybe that's why.
With everyone around me I was caring,
And I was always the one sharing.

I've been told I was way too nice,
Is prison changing my heart to ice.
I treated most things like it was a game,
thinking back now, that sure was lame.

Back then I thought life was hard,
now I'm watched by a prison guard.
I trusted too many and it put me in jail,
It was so bad I didn't get bail.

Prison is a place that's lonely and cold,
take it from me, you've been told.
Don't let your whole life slip by you,
always do the best that you can do.

You won't be in prison feeling this bad,
and you won't lose everything you had.
I am going to get out of here and start a life,
and find me a much better wife.

These are just a small portion of the poems I've written about losing my wife. I don't want you to get too bored reading them all. But you get the idea of how I got my thoughts and feelings out when I couldn't show that I was hurting and so lonely without a woman to write to and come visit me. I know life goes on and it's hard to wait for someone. It's not all her fault for leaving me. I was the one who put myself in the position to be taken away from society and locked up so far away.

New Home

I know I'm the only one to blame,
and I'm the one carrying the shame.
I'm sorry I broke your heart this way,
please forgive me, I pray!

I wish I could give you a loving embrace,
I long to see your beautiful face.
I want you, I need you, I love you dear,
I'd give anything for you to be near.

I'd be so happy just to see your smile,
and get a letter from you once in a while.
I look at your pictures and think of you now,
I wish I could just see you somehow.

With tears falling and loneliness at its peak,
my heart is feeling terribly weak.
You could motivate me with your heartfelt love,
It would be something I'd never let go of.

Now with pain and suffering I'm all alone,
I also know you've got a new home.
In my heart I hope its true love you've found,
but I hope I never see you around.

I'm not sure I ever want to see your face,
I'll never try to invade your space.
We've both got to find our separate ways,
I've thought about you too many days.

It's over now as you being my wife,
I hope your new home will be a happy life.
Even after all I've been through,
I only wish happiness for you.

I kept on writing poems and sending them to her even after months and months of not hearing a word from her or about her. She was with someone else by then.

Forgiving You

In life there is no in between,
believe only what you have seen.
Don't believe her just because she cries,
she could be filling you full of lies.

I thought love was guiding our way,
but she testified against me today.
Now I have prison as my new start,
starting out with this broken heart.

I've learned that being alone is really hard,
with nothing to do but walk the yard.
Walking all alone and in so much pain,
thoughts in my head and going insane.

I fight to stop thinking these thoughts of you,
wondering if I'm going to make it through.
You're out there and not thinking about me,
but in my mind, you're all I see.

I have to get these thoughts out of my head,
Or, I know, I'm going to end up dead.
I can't control what you say or do,
but I know I am forgiving you.

I was watching TV one night at eleven o'clock and it was Thanksgiving Day 2004. I saw my wife have another man's baby on the news. It was a devastating blow to my heart. It was televised because the little boy was born on Thanksgiving Day. At this time in my life I was at my lowest. There was nowhere to go but up. I remember thinking that my life was over. I wanted it to be over. From that night on I didn't care if I lived or died. It was right after seeing the news that I wrote this next poem. I was in Solitary Confinement at the time. Solitary confinement is hard enough to get through when you're feeling good let alone when you are so depressed you want to die. I contemplated suicide then but I could never do.

Whispers are not allowed!

There are no whispers in this hell,
Not even in the stillness of the night.
Because whispers are soft and gentle,
And soft and gentle is not allowed here.
Bated breath and lowered voices, sure,
As long as they're discussing criminal schemes.
You hear what sounds like a whisper,
Yet you know that this cannot be,
Nothing soft and gentle exists in this dark, prison.
One evening while lying there with my eyes closed,
Reminiscing and dreaming as always......
A large hand clamps over my mouth a knee on my chest,
I can't breathe or see who it is.
The perp leans forward and I smell his bad breath,
He quietly tells me what he's going to do......
Wait!! He was whispering, wasn't he?
No!! He can't be, it's not allowed in this place.
My eyes grow even wider as I feel the cold steel enter,
It goes between my ribs and it pierces my heart.
I start to get warm as I feel the live draining out of me,
I smile because all the pain is gone now.

It's funny how I can remember the day and time of every poem I wrote while I was in prison. I can remember how I was feeling at the time of each poem. I can't even tell you how many times I wish the heartache and loneliness would subside.

There were times when I wish it would all end and I didn't care how it ended. It could end just like this as far as I was concerned. This is a different kind of poem for me. I didn't even know it was considered a poem. I don't know anything about poetry. I just write from my heart and do it in a way that makes me think. I had to keep my mind busy. Time went by too damn slowly when I wasn't doing anything. I thought really bad thoughts when I wasn't keeping my mind occupied.

You don't care

I feel lost and don't know where I'm going,
Without the love that you were showing.
I keep remembering where I've been,
And I want your love all over again.
I should have known you'd walk away,
I wonder now if I'll be okay.
You don't know how bad you broke my heart,
But you didn't care right from the start.
I should have known I'd get burned,
Another hard lesson I have learned.
I don't know who you're with today,
I didn't want it to end this way.
It's going to hurt bad to let you go,
And getting over you will be slow.
But you're not mine and it's plain to see,
I don't even know why you were with me.
It's been awhile but I finally know,
How your love can come and go.
I know that you don't care about anyone,
All you care about is having fun.
I'm not the man you were looking for,
I wish you would have told me before.
I know I'm in prison and can't be there,
But you said that you'd always care.
You dumped me the minute I got here,
And I'm not going to shed another tear.
Your love has caused me too much pain,
Burned too many times by its flame.
I know I haven't done anything wrong,
And I've hung on for way too long.
Never again am I going to cry,
If you don't care neither do I.

Good-bye

Make things right

Even though my life revolves around lock and key,
I pray to God that He'll save me.
I'm in a world filled with evil minded men,
In Pennsylvania, in a federal pen.

I was supporting my family and doing it alone,
And I was working myself to the bone.
All I was doing was going the wrong way,
And now I have change on me today.

I wake up sweating and soaked in tears,
And now I'm wasting a whole lot of years.
I wish every day that this ordeal wasn't real,
Being in bondage you never want to feel.

Living in a cold, small, dirty cell,
Eating rotted food and not feeling very well.
Never getting a full night's sleep,
Finding myself beginning to weep.

Living day after day with a broken heart,
Praying one day for a brand-new start.
Lord, help me through this horrible plight,
So, I can go home and make things right.

Cell Restriction

I'm writing again from my solitary cell,
My power is off and I'm not doing well.
I'm definitely a lone wolf tonight,
And being alone never feels right.

This prison is turning me into a hermit,
And in here I don't really give a shit.
Being on this cell restriction,
Is worse than any addiction.

To keep me from going out of my tree,
I write these poems to save me.
I feel like I'll die in this slammer,
My heart was hit with a hammer.

Blood splatter all over my shirt,
You can't imagine how bad it hurt.
Excruciating pain inside my head,
At times I wish I was dead.

I feel abandoned and rejected,
My sanity has to be protected.
I need a woman to make it better,
So she can write me a letter.

Rage

It's hard for me to control my rage,
After all, I'm living in a cage.
Nobody really seems to care,
I'm not going to make it out there.
I feel the violence coming out in me,
It will give the guards job security.
With some of these inmates I can't deal,
Anger surfaces and it's very real.
Now, revenge is my core belief,
I'll pay them back and feel relief.
I dream of the ways I can kill you,
I hope it's something I'll never do.
You are the one that really hurt me,
Rage sets in until I can't see.
If I let it go, I'd feel really bad,
Hurting you would make me glad.
I've learned to listen to my "self-talk",
Make the choice to take a walk.
There are consequences to my reaction,
So, I think before I take action.

....

I had to take anger management because of the many fights I got into. It was a requirement to get out of solitary confinement. I wrote this poem for that class. It was my way of writing a paper. Everyone had to read something in class about anger. Over fifteen years in prison, I was forced to take Anger Management twice. That's not bad for me. Most of my stay in prison I was angry.

Divorce

Look what you've done to my head,
When you went to another man's bed.
Why didn't you tell me you didn't want me?
You let me dream of how I thought it should be.

Do you love him as much as I love you?
Or is he someone you just want to do?
I know you thought I was never going to find out,
But you've been seen with him out and about.

I'm not some loser that you can treat this way,
I was the one who took care of you every day.
I bought you everything that you ever want,
All the things you loved to flaunt.

I bought you the most beautiful diamond ring,
And now to you, I don't mean a thing.
I'm lost now in the feeling I had for you,
Locked in this prison with nothing to do.

You are in his bed now and you don't care,
Who sees you with him or where.
You've managed to tear my heart out with force,
Now I want you to give me a divorce.

....

I wrote to my wife and asked her to send me papers for a divorce. Even though she hasn't had anything to do with me for a long time, she said she didn't want a divorce. All the time she was out there sleeping around. She slept with the confidential informant in my case until he died of a drug overdose. After that she got pregnant and I saw her have the baby. I didn't have any way of getting a hold of her but I knew her aunt worked at the Indian Island court house. I wrote her aunt a letter and told her to tell my wife that she can file for a divorce with the grounds of Irreconcilable Differences or I was going to file them for Adultery. It wasn't long before I got the divorce papers in the mail.

"Hard Times"

I've realized that people are as happy as they make their minds up to be. I also know first-hand that some days are hard no matter what you do. For me, in prison, holidays are the worst. Thanksgiving and Christmas are by far the hardest but birthdays, anniversaries and even Valentine's Day can be a bummer. It is so hard and painful to be away from the ones I love. I feel heartache when there's a cookout or a celebration in the family and I'm left out. Sometimes I feel a little forgotten or overlooked. My birthday has come and gone in here and nobody even knew. I'm missing blowing out the candles and laughing. Christmas is without a nicely decorated and lit up tree with presents underneath. Thanksgivings are hard to feel thankful for, dinner is served cold on a cafeteria tray and the food is grade D. Nothing tastes good in prison.

My first Thanksgiving in prison, I didn't even walk up to the chow hall. My first birthday I spent in my cell alone and feeling hurt and sorry for myself more than I've ever felt before. On Christmas I wouldn't even get out of bed. I just stayed under the covers to hide the tears I cried all day. I know now why holidays were the worst for me. Because they were the times my whole family got together and openly showed our love for one another. There is no love in prison, only hate and discontent. Since being incarcerated I have learned to show my love for my family in different ways. It's been mostly through my writing but I show them I love them even without a holiday. I'm constantly writing.

Holidays were also elaborate excuses for me to take a look at my life, my successes and my failures. I've learned that in here or out there, I can still be proud, make plans, dream dreams, and look closely at my life and see what I like and what I don't like. I'm the only one that has the power to change what falls short of my ideal self-image.

Still, not being able to spend quality time with the ones I love is very rough. I have an inner peace knowing that the ones I love are always with me, in my heart and in my mind, and as they are with me, I am with them in spirit. The days that I can't be with them physically, I still take time to remember them and send them cards or letters. Prisoners can't make me happy. Special places and special people help my mood, but the feeling of love comes from within. It's easy to use a holiday as an excuse in here to be sad, edgy and depressed. I've been there! But with the love my family shows me, and the love of a few special people that have stayed by my side, I've found that life is a precious gift, whether in prison or not.

More hard times are when visitors come. I want to always look my best so I take a shower and put on my cleanest prison blues. When I'm in the visiting room, I try to put on my happy mask. I know my visitors have to travel hours, one way, just to see me. Then when they get here, they have to go through a metal detector and they are told what to do, what they can and can't wear and where to sit. One of my very first visits I saw the hurt on my family's face. It was then I realized I hurt the people who care about me the most. I used to think that I never hurt anyone even though I did commit a crime. But when I saw their faces, it hit me. I have hurt someone. I have stained their good name.

I also have a hard time dealing with the thought that people who don't know me are going to put me in a category. They think that all convicts are evil low-life's who deserve what they get. I've learned to never judge people, don't type them too quickly. In a pinch never first assume that a man is bad, first assume that he is good and that at worst he is in the gray area between bad and good. Before I was sentenced to prison, I believed in tough treatment - feed them only bread and water. Forget about the education opportunities, heat, medical care, and definitely no TV or air conditioning, but what a difference time makes. What a difference it makes when you are one behind bars.

Now that I'm one of them, I have a different view. I've learned that the traditional view of inmates is that we're all career criminals who "feed on the public." We're heartless, irresponsible, uncaring, lower-income people from broken homes whose family and friends also have criminal records.

What the public doesn't see is that there are many well-educated inmates that are here because they made a mistake. All inmates have jobs in here and some get paid. The pay is never much but it's an incentive to keep your nose clean and stay out of the hole. Most inmates are grateful to have jobs and take pride in their work. It helps build self- worth in a place where it's easy to feel worthless. Like me, many have never been to prison before and never want to return.

Prison is a cold, cruel place and its true people don't go to prison for being good. Most of us did something to deserve our time, but it doesn't mean that we're all bad. Looking for the good in everyone helps set us all free. I hope people see the good in me and get past labeling me as just a convict. I don't have a closed heart; my feelings are as strong as the next guys.

I've learned to recognize my anger and deal with it positively. I know that "an eye for an eye" is not justice, it's revenge. Justice is when you're able to change people from heir wrong ways through love and understanding. But anger is a god and powerful source of energy. Without some anger, we wouldn't be motivated to do anything.

Sometimes we misuse that energy for negative purposes. To direct my anger positively, I've learned to write, some things I write rhyme. I feel like this is a harmless and creative way to express my anger. And it also challenges me to write. I have also learned that knowing right from wrong and the meaning of violence has helped me to have inner peace. I know that passive or non-physical violence, such as hate, prejudice, intolerance and discrimination fuels physical violence because it generates anger.

Our minds must be like a room with many open windows. Let the breezes blow in from all directions, but refuse to be blown away by any of them. Imagine a room that is airtight. There will soon be no oxygen and the room will be unlivable. This is what happens to a mind that is closed. Open your minds! The hard times will be easier to bear.

I would like to give this message to my Dad. He drives the two and a half hours, one way, every week to come see me. "I am doing very well in here Dad, and my success is because of you! The way you always show up, week after week, and the way you always greet me with a smile and a big hug. The way you believe in me even when I couldn't believe in myself. Maybe these couple of hours every week isn't such a big deal to you, but to me, they are everything. Dad, I've learned that life is a process of making mistakes, learning from them and making wise choices. No one is perfect, but we can become better with each new day when we are ready to learn. I know I've had to learn the hard way most of my life and I've hurt people along the way. Thank you very much for being there for me and not giving up on me. I love you with all my heart and always will".

Good people are sometimes capable of doing bad things and allow stupidity to overcome rational thought. I blindly followed the wrong crowd. I'll live with that for the rest of my life, but I'm still a decent human being with ambitions, feelings and a vision for my future. Right now, I don't know what the future is going to hold for me. I haven't been to court yet. I'm still fighting my case from prison. No matter what happens to me, I will never give up. I'm going to do my best to get my story out there for everyone to see. I hope my story will help others live their lives in a more positive and meaningful way, instead of allowing poor judgment to make them endure Hard Times. I hope my story will help people to understand that life is short and you shouldn't take anything for granted. The United States Justice system took me from the streets without a court hearing at all and put me in the Maine State Prison with prisoners that are never getting out. I haven't even been convicted of a crime yet or even had my day in court. I am 47 years old and

I never thought the government of the United States could take away my freedom so easily. I have learned that they can and will do anything that they want to do. Laws are not for them. They are only for us. So now when I hear the national anthem saying "Land of the free" I laugh. You are not free in America. The American Dream is just that, A Dream! You are taxed to death in this country. The taxes are so the rich can get richer. You will <u>never</u> own a house and land in America. The town or city that the house is in, owns it. If you don't believe me, stop paying your property taxes. You will have what you paid for all those years taken away from you.

May 18, 2005
Maine State Prison

As you can see, after two years in the custody of our government without stepping foot in a courtroom, I've gotten pretty bitter. A person can easily get that way when they don't have a clue what their future holds.

****

I'm sitting here thinking how in the hell can I write this book and have it be interesting to all of you. I'm laid off for the winter and I've got ninety days to write two books. I've been working seven days a week, many hours a day. I get up in the night because I can't sleep. I have too much on my mind, so I get up and work on this book. I have thousands of poems but I don't know which ones to put in this book. I hope I pick some that everyone will like. I know that everyone has different tastes and that's okay. I just hope that this book isn't too boring for some of you. Right now, It's one a.m. and I'm reading a lot of poems in one of the books that I wrote when I first got to the feds. At the time, I didn't think that I was going to live long enough to get out of prison. I hadn't sent any to Christine or Tianna to put on Facebook. I wasn't planning on letting anyone read these poems. They were meant for me to pass the time and get the feelings off my chest. My mind is always moving at a real steady pace. Thoughts roll around in my head and I can't sleep. It was a lot worse when I was in prison, but it's still kinda rocky now. I don't sleep all night yet. I'm usually up a couple of times every night. When I lay there for more than fifteen or twenty minutes, I get up and work on my book. I just can't lay there and do nothing and let things roll around in my head. It drives me crazy. I would rather be doing something constructive with my time. I'm getting better all the time. I know that when I get my books written, there will be a weight off my chest. I'm not planning on making money from these books. A lot of people might not like them. I am writing these for my friends and family. I also hope that some other people will read them and they will help someone. I know that if this book is in prison libraries, the ones there will be able to relate to a lot of my poems. I think that this book can help others in prison learn how to do time and feel better.

Thanksgiving Day

Today is November twenty fifth, two thousand and four,
I'm not celebrating today, I'm locked behind this steel door.
You knew today was thanksgiving, as soon as you read the date.
I'd give anything to be with you, so that we could celebrate.

I'm alone now with my thoughts and i feel so confused,
Today is a day of happiness, but all my happiness is used.
I'm digging deep to find the strength, just to go on living.
I'm so tired, lost, and lonely I don't know if i can go on giving.

I wonder if I'll ever be free, so i can be thankful till the end,
I pray to God every day, to help me find a friend.
I dream of this beautiful woman, that someday I will get,
I know I'll find my true love, I wonder if I've met her yet.

Is it because today is Thanksgiving that I'm so lonely and blue?
This feeling has hit me twice as hard and there's nothing i can do.
I'm locked in this cold dark cell, and I'm feeling very depressed,
Today I don't even have the energy, to get myself dressed.

I'm wondering if it's worth it to go on living this way,
A man should never have to live like this, especially on
Thanksgiving Day.

Thanksgiving Day was written before I watched the channel 5 news at eleven pm. That night on the news I saw my wife have another man's baby. It was televised because it was Thanksgiving and in Bangor, Maine that's news. I can't even begin to tell you how that made me feel. I had my suspicions that my wife was with someone else but it still hurts to see something like that when you are alone in a cell. You can't prepare yourself for something like that, that's for sure. I wrote another poem after that. I'm not going to put it in this book because it's not a good poem. It's full of hate and it's hurtful to my ex-wife. I'm not trying to hurt her in any way. I wish her nothing but the best. But twelve years later on Thanksgiving I wrote this poem. In prison you can't move on. There is nothing to move on to. You have to wait until you get out to get a life.

Thanksgiving Day 2016

I do have something to be thankful for,
But its overshadowed by this day in two thousand, four.
When my wife had another man's baby on TV,
Every Thanksgiving since it has haunted me.

I'd give anything not to be able to remember,
What I saw on this day in that November.
Every time I remember it gives me heartache,
It's a curse that I can't seem to break.

She's at home with a duel celebration today,
While I'm still in prison and feeling this way.
Today her little boy is twelve years old,
While I sit in this prison lonely and cold.

But I do have something to be thankful for,
The day I won't be in prison anymore.
I'll find me a good woman and have a life,
And she will help me forget my ex-wife.

Then I will feel like a normal person out there,
Celebrating holidays with the ones that care.
I'll be the happiest man you've ever seen,
To get by Thanksgiving Day 2016.

....

I have so many poems that are along this same line. It was a memory that I couldn't forget. These poems were in the earlier years of my incarceration. All accept for the last one. That was years later. But every Thanksgiving the memory of watching the news came back to me just like it was yesterday. So many of my worst fears came true while I was in prison. My mom and dad both died. My one remaining uncle died. Four of my aunts died. Three cousins died, and one had a stroke that left her a vegetable and to this day she is in a nursing home. It seemed like every time I turned around a tragedy came my way. I couldn't show emotions in prison. I would look weak. So, I wrote about everything and got it all out of my mind. I just couldn't hold everything inside and survive. I thank God every day that I was taught to read and write.

Chapter Two

In this chapter I am going to show you some poems I wrote about prison and life in prison. I write about everything from the flowers on the grounds to the food and everything in between. I stayed to myself a lot and did everything I could alone. I wasn't into clicks or gangs. I didn't care what anyone did in there as long as they left me alone. Every time the feds moved me from one prison to another, it was a couple of months before the other inmates knew that I wanted to be left alone. I didn't hang with a very big crowd in the facilities that I went to. But in every one of them I did make a few friends that I am still in touch with today. Not everyone in prison are gangsters. Prison is a world of its own. You don't see society or keep up with the technology. After fifteen years I have so much to learn. I've never had a computer or a smart phone. I had a bag phone first and then a phone that had caller ID and call waiting and that was the top of the line back then. Gas was $1.29 when I got locked up. A 2003 was a brand-new vehicle back then and it didn't have a telephone or computer in it. You were lucky if it had air conditioning and cruise control. A basic car didn't have a lot in it. At least not like it does today.

After a while, I was hurting so bad in prison with all the heartaches, that I turned to God for help. I was so alone and very depressed. I've lost everything I had worked my whole life for and now I'm losing people I love. So, I wrote this.

"Stop Searching"

Most of my life I have gone from one heartache to the next, drugs and alcohol to a broken home. Lately I've had many tears to reflect the hollow man I feel like I am in prison. It seems like I searched so hard to find myself in the eyes of people who didn't even know themselves. It's no wonder my life ended up the way it did. Most people spend a lifetime searching for something to belong to or be a part of. I've tried it all, I joined the Elks Club, Allii's motorcycle club, Saracen's motorcycle club and finally the Hells Angels motorcycle club. I've always wanted to be a part of something. I wanted to belong! I moved from group to group and I still don't feel like I belong. As a result, I started messing with drugs, running with the wrong crowd but I felt like it was where I belonged. Of course, it was the drugs talking. But this crowd got me almost everything I thought I wanted and it came easy. But this all came with a huge price! It cost me my kids, my self-respect, my freedom and everything that meant something to me, including my wife. Instead of finding what I was looking for, it's caused me to feel powerless. I'm Sure I'm not alone in all of this but it sure feels that way in this tiny cell.

I'm sure there are many men and women in prison who are dying like me. Yes, I said I'm dying. I'm dying from the lifestyle, the failed relationships, the hold that drugs had on me, and the lack of communication with the ones I love the most. The lifestyle I lived stopped my spirit from being able to soar. I have a spirit that has never been able to fly. I've felt ashamed of myself inside. I hid my feelings well, just like I'm doing in this prison every day.

I've always wanted to change but I didn't know how until I was locked in a tiny cell all alone and forced to evaluate myself. I talked to a priest one day cause I wanted to talk to someone, anyone. I hadn't talked to anyone in weeks. I told him about my life and that I wanted to change. He said, "Yeah, he hears that all the time but some people just want to talk." That really hit me hard because that's been me for a few years. I've wanted to talk to someone about getting better but I didn't want to let anyone know I had a problem. No.! Not me, the one everyone looked up to and turned to whenever they needed something. I had inspiration back then, but inspiration with no motivation is like a dream you can't remember. You're bound to fail because you don't know where to start. I feel hopeless, depressed, confused and misguided but nobody knew. I was getting weaker and weaker. The drug was killing me. I was being led by the wrong shepherd. I was following the way that I thought was easier, only to sink deeper in the lies of the way. I was broken! I know now that the path that looks easier is the biggest lie there is.

Once in my life I was blinded by darkness. I would help everyone in God's world but myself. If nobody knew I was sick and broken, I sure wasn't going to tell them even though I knew I was going to hell. After all, I was the one everyone looked up to and depended on. Or, that's what I thought anyway. When I got arrested in April 2003, I said, "I'm tired of all this crap now. I've got to be honest with myself." It's then I took a long look at my life. It was quite a while before I figured I've always wanted to change but I didn't know how until I was locked in a tiny cell all alone and forced to evaluate myself. I talked to a priest one day cause I wanted to talk to someone, anyone. I hadn't talked to anyone in weeks. I told him about my life and that I wanted to change. He said, "Yeah, he hears that all the time but some people just want to talk." That really hit me hard because that's been me for a few years. I've wanted to talk to someone about getting better but I didn't want to let anyone know I had a problem. No.! Not me, the one everyone looked up to and turned to whenever they needed something. I had inspiration back then, but inspiration with no motivation is like a dream you can't remember. You're bound to fail because you don't know where to start. I feel hopeless, depressed, confused and misguided but nobody knew. I was getting weaker and weaker. The drug was killing me. I was being led by the wrong shepherd. I was following the way that I thought was easier, only to sink deeper in the lies of the way. I was broken! I know now that the path that looks easier is the biggest lie there is. Once in my life I was blinded by darkness. I would help everyone in God's world but myself. If nobody knew I was sick and broken, I sure wasn't going to tell them even though I knew I was going to hell. After all, I was the one everyone looked up to and depended on. Or, that's what I thought anyway.

When I got arrested in April 2003, I said, "I'm tired of all this crap now. I've got to be honest with myself." It's then I took a long look at my life. It was quite a while before I figured out what was missing in my life. What was I searching all these years for? One day it hit me like a ton of bricks. Just after the feds moved me for the fifth time in as many months, after seeing so many criminals with no values or morals, I knew that's what I've been looking for in myself. I've been searching for the good in me.

I asked for a Bible and when I got it, I read it every day. When I was in solitary confinement, the bible was the only book I was allowed. It was seven months before I read the whole thing. I have been studying the Bible ever since. It's been almost two years since I first picked up a Bible and, in the meantime, I repented all my sins and accepted Jesus Christ as my Lord and Savior. In prison there are Muslims, Jews, and every other religion. Christians are repressed. I wasn't allowed to wear my cross around my neck unless it was hidden under my shirt. But it was okay for all the other religions to wear anything they wanted that was religious. Jews wore their little thing on their head, Muslims wore whatever they wanted on their heads but Christians were not allowed to wear anything that showed. I just couldn't believe the federal prisons in the United States could adopt rules like this. So, Christians are a minority in federal prisons in the United States. But that didn't stop me and it never will. It's too bad our country is giving away its values. I'm very proud to say that I am a born-again Christian who once used drugs and committed crimes. I lied to get what I wanted and did what I wanted. It landed me in prison causing me more pain and heartbreak than I ever thought I could live through. Now I'm doing my best to walk with Jesus and I no longer desire to use drugs or commit crimes. Now instead of living a life of paranoia and fear, I live a sober life putting the talents God gave me to use, and loving every minute of it.

It's too bad it took corning to prison to make me realize what I was looking for. It wasn't a group, it wasn't money or power. In the lowest moment of my life I found what I was searching for, "The Family of God". You see there is no hope for us by our own standards. I mean just look how many of us are broken. No matter what anyone says, it's not what we can do to fix ourselves. It's what Jesus did for us on the cross. Jesus died so we can be healed from all things. Remember, inspiration is not enough. So, humble yourself and stop searching, the answer is Jesus!

The thief, the enemy comes to steal, kill and destroy. Jesus carne to save us. Is what looks easier, really easier? Take it from me, it's not!

Billy Leland
Maine State Prison

At this time of my life in prison I have come to accept it might be a long time before the government sets me free. I accepted that my wife has moved on and I can't do a damned thing about it. Even though it hurts like hell, I've accepted that I will lose people while I'm locked up and can't do anything about that either. The hardest part for me to accept is that I'm completely alone and there's nobody in prison that gives a shit about me. I'm just another inmate and just a number to the justice department. That number is 09650-036. Whenever I go to laundry, to the infirmary for a medical issue, to the commissary or anywhere else, they don't ask me what my name is. They as for my ID number. I've accepted that this is going to be the way it is until I'm back with the people that love me. So, in this chapter you will see that I wrote poems about people in prison or prison life itself. I didn't complain to anyone about anything. I just wrote things down to get them off my mind. It is how I survived 15 years by myself. The first poem in this next chapter is one that I wrote to try to help others stay out of jails and prisons. I worry about our young people today. They don't seem to want to do physical labor anymore. If it doesn't involve the internet and electronic devices, they don't have any interest in it.

Everywhere I go today I see signs asking for help or hiring for all shifts. The company I work for needs drivers and we can't find people. I saw so many young people come into prison that has never had a real job. Some of them told me they were a professional gamer. I didn't even know what that meant. I've never seen a game on the internet because at that time, I've never been on the internet. They didn't seem to take life seriously at all. It was all games to them. They talked about winning all kinds of money on the internet. I was also amazed at how many of the young people that came into prison couldn't read or write very well.

I write in cursive and many of them couldn't read my writing. It was really crazy to me that the world had changed so much since I went to prison. When I got out of prison, I couldn't believe the changes and in my opinion, a lot of them are not good changes. You can't find anyone's phone number in a phone book anymore. The pay phones are almost extinct. People walk down the streets staring at their phones and don't look where they are going. People are texting while driving and they are even on their phones in restaurants while eating a meal with their family, spouse or anyone else. It was really hard for me to see this nonsense.

Take it seriously!

I'm a federal prisoner just writing a story,
I'll never be a man bound for glory.
But I'll write you a poem that will last for ages,
You'll feel my love on those pages.
My words will be here long after I'm gone,
They'll stay with you as time moves on.
As long as you read these poems. I'll be alive,
Talking to you to help you survive.
I've got nobody to blame but me right now,
I wouldn't blame anyone anyhow.
I want you know that I made the mistakes,
Stay out of trouble no matter what it takes.
If I'm not around any longer to help you,
Anyone who loves you will do.
I didn't listen to the ones who love me,
If I did, I still would be free.
Instead, I'm living behind a locked steel door,
And praying to God on a cold prison floor.
You don't want to live this life like me,
So, please take what I'm telling you seriously.

·······

I've always tried to help people in one way or another. In this prison, I will help people but a very select few. I would rather be left alone to do this time on my own. I have a million thoughts running through my head. If I didn't write these thoughts down and get them out of my head, I feel like I would explode someday. I don't know if it works for everyone but writing things down as I think about them, really helps me to move on and not feel like I'm going to lose my mind one day. Solitary confinement has a way of making a person crazy. I wouldn't have thought that until I spent so much time alone in a five foot by nine-foot cell all along for months. I feel bad for the ones who can't read or write. I wonder how they get through. There are a lot of guys that yell back and forth from cell to cell and talk all day and sometimes all night. I think these are the ones that can't read and write and live in their own head. They need the interaction to survive. Guys like me get really irritated with guys like that, but I understand why they do it. It is their way of coping in a dire situation. It doesn't make it easy to get sleep or concentrate for me but I learned that I can do anything I put my mind to do.

This next poem is about the monotony of living in prison. Every day is the same as the last. There's nothing to look forward to at all. I find myself getting really depressed when I think about the future. I know that I can't show my feelings or complain about the living arrangements or the rules or let the other inmates know that I'm hurting inside. I would be considered weak. I would be prey for the strong. I will never let that happen. There are many people in prison that pay for protection and other things. If the gangs think that you have money, you are prey to them. They send a couple of people over to you to threaten you and do their best to intimidate you. If you get scared, they will turn the heat up. Then a couple of the bigger gang members will come over and tell the others to leave you alone. It's a pretty good act. Then, the bigger ones will tell you that they will make sure no one bothers you if you give them money every month. You'd be surprised how many people fall for that. I am not one of them. I would rather fight and get my ass kicked than pay these stupid fools anything. That is just one more reason why I stayed to myself mostly and kept writing.

I look back and read the poems I wrote and I don't like the memories it brings back. It's funny, but I can remember the exact day and time I wrote these poems when I read them over. I didn't think anyone would want to read them. I didn't write them for people to read.

I'll Hide

I'll still be a prisoner when the sun comes up tomorrow,
I'll still have heartaches, regrets and sorrow.
I'm sick and tired of counting all the day,
I'm beat down in so many ways.
Tonight, I hear the rain and it's filling up my mind,
And I feel myself slowly unwind.
Listening to the rain always helps me sleep,
As I pray the Lord my soul to keep.
Finally, my tears have stopped falling like the rain,
But every night I still feel the heartache and pain.
When the lights go out and I know I'm on my own,
It hits me that tomorrow I'll still be alone.
Every day when I open my eyes in here,
I still fight to hold back a tear.
I know that tomorrow will be the same as today,
And I'll have to get through it the same way.
I'll be sitting here writing for certain,
And I know I'm going to still be hurting.
Medication will kill the pain on the outside,
The heartache, regret and sorrow I'll hide.

......

I'm a master now at hiding what I feel. I wonder if I'll ever be able to how my feelings again. I'm so used to showing anger and talking mean and filthy that I hope I can control my language when I get out of prison.

Contraband

Please don't believe everything you read,
The newspapers don't care if it's the truth we need,
These newspaper companies are owned by the rich,
So, distinguishing the truth from the lies can be a bitch.
I get to read the Bangor Daily News every day,
I don't believe some of the things they say.
Especially when it comes to these prisons and jails,
Most of the staff here do their job like snails.
An article about visitation made me real mad today,
There will be no physical contact in any way.
They want to have you visit them on Skype,
But it's 25 cents a minute for that type.
A company from Texas sets it up for Maine,
If you go along with that you are insane.
The staff in these places blame it on contraband,
But most of it comes it at their own hand.
I've seen it many times in all these years,
Prison officials playing on society's fears.
Let me ask you a question that might sound rash,
How does an inmate fit a carton of cigs in his ass?
Most contraband comes in by a crooked guard,
Then it gets distributed all across the yard.

Too Much Strife

My whole prison sentence I'll be a recluse,
For most of these guys I have no use.
I've done my best to avoid them all,
You are better off talking to a wall.
I'm really tired of all the crazy bullshit,
As every day and every night here, I sit.
In a hard, plastic chair next to this small bed,
While living this life inside my head.
I get so lonely as I sit here and wait,
In a room full of people, I've learned to hate.
To survive, I have to look the other way,
But doing that is hard to do today.
I can't stop thinking of you sitting home alone,
I know it's hard for you on your own.
I hope you know how much I really care,
It will be easier once I am there.
When I was taken away it broke my heart,
Its broken so bad now, I need a jumpstart.
I'll get out and start a new and good life,
One with no heartache and strife.

......

When I wrote this poem, I was thinking about my young daughter that lived with me before I went to prison and now, she's out there without a dad. I think about her every day. That will never change.

Feel Alive

I'm so lonely every hour of every day,
It is really hard to live this way.
A million bad thoughts running through my head,
While I sit here writing on this old bed.
Some inmates here think I'm obsessed,
But for me to survive, this is the best.
I have carpal tunnel in my right hand,
It's a pain that you wouldn't understand.
I got it by writing all damned night,
It's making it awful hard for me to write.
I have a lot of other ailments too,
You'd never know by the things I do.
These prison years have been rough on me,
But that's how prison is meant to be.
I've seen prison kill many a strong man,
I have to get out while I still can.
On the outside I'm going to feel lost,
And I'm paying a heavy cost.
I'll do everything in my power to thrive,
To find happiness and feel alive.

......

I know I've told you this before but at first, I didn't think that I was going to make it out of prison alive. At the time, I didn't really care. But I've come too far now to give up.

I would gladly spit!

I'm sitting here staring at the second hand on the clock,
I'm lonely depressed and I'm feeling distraught.
I suffer from boredom and anxiety every day,
It's a struggle to pass all this time away.
Hour after hour I sit in this damn chair,
Wishing like hell I was out there.
Today, the time seems to pass extra slow,
It's depressing that I have nowhere to go.
I just sit here writing with freedom on my mind,
Praying for the day I leave all this behind.
You can't imagine what I hear and see,
I really hate the word diversity.
But this proves that life really isn't fair,
It's worse in here than it is out there.
In federal prisons the inmates are really diverse,
And from other countries they are worse.
I listen to what they all have to say,
And they really hate the American way.
I sit here and pretend I don't give a shit,
But on their graves, I would gladly spit.

......

If you haven't been around a lot of people from other countries in America, you probably think you should treat everyone with the love and respect you expect to be treated with. Well, I hate to inform you, they don't feel the same way! The truth comes out in prisons.

When this nightmare ends

I've learned to accept my broken dreams,
There's been too many changes it seems.
I've been gone so long, even my dreams are outdated,
Everyone has moved on, nobody has waited.
I don't know what to dream about anymore,
The world as I knew it is gone for sure.
I'm a little afraid to come home now, I can't lie,
But I'm coming home with my head held high.
You'll see how much I've changed on my arrival,
And the new scars I have for my survival.
You'll also see how much I have aged,
As a result of years of being caged.
The prison life hasn't been easy on me,
You'll see as soon as they set me free.
I think about it and it seems so surreal,
I'm anxious to see how freedom will feel.
Everything out there will be unknown,
I can't wait so I won't be alone.
I still have a great family and real friends,
They'll be there for me when this nightmare ends.

......

I never stopped thinking about how life was going to be for me when they finally let me out of prison. As the years went by and I lost more and more family members and friends.

I'm going to need a friend

I set out on an endless road a long, long time ago,
There were so many things I didn't know.
I joined the Army when I was just seventeen,
I needed to see things I've never seen.
I was sent to Germany for a couple of years,
I was alone and had to get over my fears.
Thousands of miles away from family and friends,
I couldn't wait till that deployment ends.
I got out of the Army and chose another long road,
A house, a wife, kids, a very heavy load.
I wanted to be a good dad and a good man,
I tried and tried as hard as I can.
Then the road I was on got extremely rough,
Making everyone happy was very tough.
I took a different road then and I got lost,
Broke the law and paid a heavy cost.
I ended up losing everything I ever had,
My house, my wife, my mom and my dad.
Someday this nightmare for me will end,
And that's when I'm going to need a friend.

••••••

Over the years, seemed like every other month actually, that I was getting news of friends of mine dying.
It felt like my world was being destroyed while I was in prison.

I really don't care

I'm out of time, I have no more to give,
What's left of my life, I want to live.
I'm sick of listening to all the lies,
And tired of all the fake alibis.
I can't go on living in here this way,
I feel like I'm full of hate today.
I'm fed up with all the noise in this place,
And I can't stand this small crowded space.
The smells are getting to me really bad,
The sights I see are really sad.
Razor wires on top of a 30-foot wall,
And I'm stuck living with it all.
All I do is sleep, read and write,
And I'm lonely as hell every night.
I've been living this life for so long,
Nothing is right, it's all wrong.
Now that I will no longer have a home,
If I get out, I'll be on my own.
The future for me is up in the air,
At this point, I really don't care.

......

I felt like giving up a lot, but I never did. I don't know how I make it through on some days though. There's nothing to look forward to but hatred and fights.

It's going to last

I look at this room as a man-made cave,
It's more modern stone but just as grave.
This cave was not made for humans to hide,
It was made by humans to lock others inside.
This prison is nothing but a human zoo,
They act like animals there's nothing I can do.
You've never seen anything like this place,
There's only six and half feet on living space.
I sit in this space writing many hours a day,
Wish like hell that I didn't have to stay.
Day after day, night after night I sit here alone,
And I know I have to live like this on my own.
Nobody else here does the things that I do,
They do their own thing that gets them through.
I've never wanted to blend in like the rest,
Doing what I'm doing, for me, is the best.
I'm not is a gang and I don't fit in a click,
I have a routine and to it I'll stick.
This routine has worked well for me so far,
I hope it lasts until I get back to where you are.

....

Every day is the same as the last in prison. People do time differently. I've seen people in prison do their time obeying what others say like a damn slave. They are weak and do that for the protection. I do my time on my own. I don't owe anyone anything. They don't owe me anything. Leave me alone and I'll leave you alone is my motto. I'll get through this on my own. My routine is going to last. I'll write and read until I can't anymore.

Misery

Misery loves company that's for sure,
But they can't make me miserable anymore.
Those fools will always be the same,
They're too stupid to grow up and leave the game.
They're still doing drugs and they lie and steal,
They think killing brain cells is a good deal.
They'll steal from their mother to get their next hit,
They'll tell on everyone and not give a shit.
They'll act like your friend as they sweet talk you,
But never trust them whatever you do.
When they get caught it will never fail,
They'll blame you and you'll go to jail.
There's a hell of a lot of them out there in misery,
I've learned my lesson, so they don't bother me.
I hope you'll listen to me, so they don't get you,
Because they want you to be miserable too.
They are the ones that think getting high is cool,
But in reality, they will always be the fool.
If these fools think they can do anything to me,
They're not just high, they're as stupid as can be.

....

There are as many, if not more drugs in prison as there are on the street. They are easier to get in Prison. The dealers come to you when it's obvious that you have a little money by the size of your commissary order every week. You can't hide anything in prison when it comes to how well off you are. It is a status symbol in prison when you have a new pair of sneakers. It's crazy but that's just the way it is on the inside. It's a world inside a world.

A normal day

When the dreadful bugle awakens me, the reality of prison pops into my head,

I feel the buzzards eating at my belly and I don't want to get out of bed.

Just once I'd like to have a good breakfast cause that's the meal I savor most,

It's a long walk to the chowhall and all I get is cereal and cold toast.

It's a normal start to a normal day and the future doesn't look very bright,

I go to the gym and try to get into shape, but I can't even do that right.

The bugle goes off just before eleven and they lock us in our cell.

They walk around and do their count and they are loud as hell.

Early in the morning I hear the steel doors unlock and the guards yell "Chow!",

And I slowly drag my ass out of bed and know I'll make it somehow.

In the afternoons I am the plumber and I sit and just wait for a call,

When I'm called, it's a stuffed toilet and I don't like it at all.

These are the jobs I'm called for all day every day until I do to dinner,

About once a week the food tastes good and the cook cooked a winner.

At six o'clock we're locked back down, and they make sure no prisoner broke out.

We wait around for them to count and it takes so long we all shout,

We have a couple of hours free in the pods and some have games they play,

They call "RECALL" again for the night at nine, and this is our normal day.

....

I wrote this poem when I was a detainee at the Maine State Prison in Warren, Maine. I was there just after the prison was built and it wasn't full. It wasn't long before the prison was full. I was there for two years and they had already put two bunks in every cell in the medium security section of the prison. They were trying to put the bunks in at the Maximum-Security section but were running into some problems with the prisoners that are in prison for life. They were not having a roommate. They told the guards that they would kill anyone that was put into their cell and they meant it. After all, what did they have to lose? They were never getting out of prison anyway. Some of them had multiple life sentences.

New Prison

I was one of the first men sent to the low security prison in Danbury, Connecticut when they turned it from a women's prison to a man's prison. The government does some pretty low handed things. They control what comes out in the media about the justice system. As a matter of fact, they control what comes out in the media about all aspects of the government. They don't want society to know what really goes on. When it comes to the justice system and jails and prisons, they are really clever. The crime rate in America hasn't gone up in almost ten years but there have been many jails and prisons built. America has twenty five percent of the world's prison population, yet, it has only five percent of the population of people.

The Department of Corrections in Maine wanted a brand-new prison. So, for almost a year, articles came out in the Bangor Daily News about fights and other problems in the old prison. For over a hundred years the 425-bed prison was sufficient enough for Maine. Yes, it new prison, such as electronic doors, and all the newest cameras and such. The guards actually had to walk to all the prison cells and physically lock and unlock all the doors. That became a chore that they became to hate as they saw the newer prisons were a lot easier to work in. They wanted a newer and easier prison and they knew how to get it. They fed the news to the media outlets enough so that society became nervous about the safety of the guards as well as the people in society. Although nobody has escaped from the Maine State Prison no guard has been killed or seriously hurt, society has been brainwashed into thinking that the prison has become more dangerous than ever.

When it became time to vote for the referendum to build a new prison, society was already to vote for the prison no matter what it costs. The Department of Corrections hired an architect to do a drawing of the prison and what the <u>individual cells</u> would look like and a big write up in the paper about the new school and all the new programs that the prison would have. It was very impressive. In the newspaper, it said that there would be seventy-five more beds than the old prison. Although the crime rate hasn't gone up, the Department of Corrections wanted seventy-five more beds for some reason. But, what they didn't tell society, in the plans for the new prison, they built the walls in every cell so that they could bolt another metal bed above the bed they already attached to the wall. They knew that they were going to put two beds in every cell as soon as they had full control over the prison. It wasn't long after the prison was built that the beds were installed. Now, Maine has a prison that holds over a thousand prisoners at an astronomical cost to taxpayers. It costs thirty-nine thousand dollars a year to house these prisoners. The crime rate still didn't go up, but the prison was filled up. An empty bed does not make the prison any money. They knew they would be filling the prison full. They kept giving the media stories about guards in danger even though they had an updated prison. They wanted more guards and with the media, they got what they wanted. There are men in prison because they couldn't afford to pay a speeding ticket. Prisons were originally built to keep society safe and house only the violent people in America. Now, they will put anyone in prison just to fill the bed and collect that money from the taxpayer. Prisons and jails or America's largest business now. It used to be our auto industry and then the clothing industry but that went overseas. America had thriving businesses when I was growing up but now, we went all to hell. America was a nation that was powerful, respected and feared. We were considered the greatest nation in the world at one time. I'm sorry to say, those times are gone. Now, America is the most hated country in the world and our allies don't even want to stand with us most of the time. I used to be proud to be an American. I joined the Army when I was seventeen years old. I joined six months before I graduated high school on the delayed entry program. I joined to go to Viet Nam to fight for our country. Over the years, I've learned that only the top one percent of the American people actually benefit for the ordinary man's efforts. This country is run by that top one percent. Laws don't apply to them. Their children never join the service. They certainly don't get sent to wars. Wars America shouldn't even be in. I have been charged crimes by "The United States of America". When you are charged federally, that's what it says on the paperwork. You can't imagine how that feels when you read that and know that you are going to fight those charges. You certainly feel overwhelmed. You feel like the underdog for sure and wonder how a simple man is going to fight the whole United States of America. Now, that I know the United States justice system and how it works, I know now why there are so many federal inmates. Locking people up is their biggest business. An awful lot of money is made through prisoners in every state in America. The goods at the commissary, the phone calls, minutes on a computer to email all cost ten times more than it would cost a free person. I say "free" very lightly, nobody in America is free. You pay to live here. Stop paying and see how fast your freedom is taken away. You are taxed on everything the government can think to tax. But you can bet your life on it that someone in the government right now is trying to think about what they can tax us on now that they don't already get. You are charged double and triple to use the highways in America. Excise tax was supposed to be our payment to drive our vehicles on the roads. Then they came up with tolls. Now, we have cameras positioned over the roads where there are no toll booths and when you drive under them your picture is taken and then you get a bill in the mail. You're not even told about the Un-manned toll booths. That's just one of many ways the states and federal government charge the citizens of America to live here "FREE". Land of the free, home of the brave, my ass.

You're more than a number

You're more than a number,
You're a human being too.
You can bet God knows your name,
And He will help you through.
Don't let anyone tell you different,
You're a person of worth.
Your life has purpose and meaning,
It has right from your birth,
You were made in the image of God,
Even though sin came along.
We'll have trials and tribulations,
And sometimes we do wrong.
Turn to God and confess your sins,
And with your heart, believe.
You can have a brand-new start,
And blessing you'll receive.
Though your sins be scarlet,
He'll make them white as snow.
You're much more than a number,
You're someone special to know.

....

Once again, when you go to prison, they give you a prison number. My state prison number is 57171. My federal prison number is 09650-036. I got so sick of being called by a number. I'm more than just a number. I'm a human being. To the United States government, we are all just a number, whether or not we're in prison. If you're not in prison, you are your social security number. They know how much money they can take from you. They know if you contribute to them or not. If you don't, you are dispensable to them.

Miranda Rights

As a United States citizen, I used to think I had rights. But I got myself into some trouble and met up with the Justice System. We do have a legal system set up here

in the United States, but I've found out that it doesn't apply to the people that work for it. It starts with the very first people that you come into contact with that works for the Justice Dept. The police! When arrested they read you your Miranda Rights. The ones they read you are far different from the ones they actually go by. Here are what they should read to you because these are the ones they go by.

1. You have the right to remain silent, no matter how severely we beat you tonight.

2. Any information we do beat out of you can and will be used against you in a court of law.

3. There will be a rubber hose present during questioning and if you don't tell us what we want to know, we will say you did anyway, then show you what the hose is used for. "In New York substitute toilet brush for hose"

4. You have a right to a lawyer, after we question you, if you cannot afford one, a rookie will be provided for you.

If you do not understand these rights please indicate at this so I can beat you senseless.

···········

Obviously, this is a joke. I put it in to get a chuckle out of you. But cops do get away with a lot of shit. When I first got arrested, the cops lied through their teeth at the bail hearing so I wouldn't get bail. This was my first offense, not victims and no violence. Yet, because of what the police said, I was denied bail. There are thousands of cases where people got bail that were very violent and were repeat offenders. I didn't get bail for the simple reason I was a Hells Angel and the judge wanted to make an example out of me.

No More!

S.M.U. in cell B one sixteen,
Dirtiest place you've ever seen.
Graffiti written all over the walls,
Racial slurs mostly but that's not all.
Walking bare footed on cold cement floors,
And constant slamming of cold steel doors.
The bed is made of cement and stone,
It makes me ache all the way to the bone.
I'm lonely and bored as hell,
If you could see me, you could tell.
This is driving me out of my mind,
It's living in hell of its worst kind.
This is more like torture to me,
And nobody really cares to see.
Treatment in these places are so wrong,
This is going on for way too long.
Now I lay me down to sleep,
I pray the Lord my soul to keep.
Hopefully, I'll die before I wake,
I have no more that they can take.

. . . .

I wrote this after I was put into Solitary Confinement after I got hit from behind with a lock in a sock. I had a broken nose, fractured skull in two places, two black eyes and one eye swollen shut, A hole completely through my nose and lacerations on my head. My father, sister and my brother came to see me and they could hardly recognize me. They never let me see a doctor or get any kind of medical help. They kept me in the hole until I healed. They don't want others to see you that way, especially since I was a detainee and not a sentenced prisoner.

Living in Hell

I'm all alone and forgotten,
Brokenhearted and in so much pain.
Locked away in a dirty, tiny cell,
Unwanted, like a biker would want rain.
I'm feeling awful sorry for myself,
And I'm hoping someone will care.
My life is just rotting away,
And all I love is out there.
God is the only one that knows,
Just how bad I feel.
To most free people,
Prisoners aren't even real.
We are locked away and forgotten,
In this warehouse full of hate.
I'm praying to be set free,
Before it's too late.
I'm thinking my life is over,
I'm going to die in this cell.
Right now, I don't think it matters,
Cause living like this is hell.
I pray to God I don't wake up,
In the morning in this place.
I'm tired of living like this,
Let me die, Lord show me grace.

Freedom

OH, sweet and precious freedom,
When will I see you again?
You're not only my first love,
But my very best friend.
The day that I was born,
You came into my life.
You stayed through it all,
And saw me through some strife.
But I took you for granted,
And now these words I sing.
God bless America,
And let sweet freedom ring.
Now, you are always on my mind,
Just as I've lost my wife.
I've also lost you, sweet freedom,
Is it the end of my life?
Here I sit in this lonely cell,
My dreams beginning to die.
Thinking of you sweet freedom,
Will we be together, you and I?

....

Not a day went by that I didn't think about life on the streets. I wondered what my family and friends were doing. I often wondered if I'd ever see freedom again. I know we're not really free in this country but it sure beats the jails and prisons that I was living in for almost fifteen years.

Giving Up!

Your love is keeping me alive inside,
I have feelings that I have to hide.
Prison is a place you can't be weak,
Emotions play hide and seek.
I'm not sure if I want to live or die,
And I am not a man to cry.
But this lonely cell I'm inside,
Makes my tears easy to hide.
Being a prisoner is not a good life,
It cuts your heart like a knife.
Segregation is a hell of a lot worse,
Loneliness sets in like a curse.
Loved ones tell me to be strong,
I can only be strong for so long.
Only so much beating I can take,
I just want to die before I wake.
I've had it with all of this shit.
I can't keep living my life this way,
I'm going to give up someday.

....

I've never been a man to give up on anything. This poem was written when I was a federal detainee at the Maine State Prison. At that time, I wasn't sure what was going to happen with my life. I was preparing to go to court. I was all for fighting my case. But in the end, I ended up being coerced into pleading guilty or they were going to charge my son with a crime. Of course, I would do anything to keep my son out of trouble. They got my plea that day. They said I would get ten years but they lied, the judge gave me twenty-one.

She left me!

She left me in silence and tears,
This broken heart will be broken for years.
She left me cold without a kiss,
And I've never felt deep sorrow like this,
I woke up with tears on my brow,
I knew how I'd feel all day now.
She broke our vows like a game,
And now, I don't like hearing her name.
Anything about her now I don't want to hear,
And I don't care if she'll ever be near.
It's obvious that I didn't know her well,
But what she did to me, no one could tell.
She'll never know about all the tears.
She'll remember me down life's stream,
Shame will come to her like a dream.
Now, my lips are mute and my eyes are dry,
And all the pain has passed me by.

....

This was written long after my wife left. I wrote poems like this every once in a while, when memories of her popped into my head. I did my best to forget about her but they say you can't forget until you find someone else. It's awful hard to find someone else when you're locked behind bars. You can't move on because there's nothing to move on to. Whatever the memories you have at the time of your incarceration, are the things you will always think about until you can make new memories. I'm looking forward to new memories. Fifteen years thinking about the same things over and over can really get to a person. I sat at my bed writing more days than I can remember. But I made it through without being too crazy.

Prison did it to me!

It's one in the morning and I'm still awake,
I don't know how much more stupidity I can take.
It's just a small gang that's loud as hell,
These other guys seem to be taking it well.
I still hear a lot of farting and snoring too,
Loud noise they can sleep right through.
I wish I could sleep just like they are,
I haven't been able to get to sleep so far.
I just lay there with so much on my mind,
It's hard to sleep with idiots of this kind.
I know this life is not for me,
I'm so tired of the stupidity I see.
I don't know what these guys would be good for,
I hope I never see them anymore.
I've had enough of them to last me a lifetime,
They make me want to commit another crime.
It's not legal to do the things I'd like to do,
It would make it a better place to live too.
Fourteen years in prison did this to me,
It's not how I wanted my life to be.

....

I've done my best over the years to keep myself alive and sane. Prison life has changed me. I hope that when I'm free I can be happy and have a good attitude. As it is now, I don't trust people at all now. I haven't had a woman to think about in so many years, I'm nervous just to try to have a relationship again. Change is hard and once you do, it's harder to change again. You get used to living one way and then you are thrust back into a whole new world. I'm a little nervous, I can't lie. Once again, the future is a mystery to me.

Because of a fight

Some days I feel like I'm at the end of my rope,
I have all I can do to hold on to hope.
It's so depressing to live with such ignorant guys,
And hearing all their bullshit and lies.
I do the best I can to stay out of the way,
Of the same bullshit twenty-four hours a day.
I get depressed, discusted and then I get mad,
I yell at the assholes and sometimes it turns bad.
I'm struggling with myself just to be good,
I want to knock someone out and I know I could.
Right now, this dumb ass is nowhere near me,
But he's running his mouth as loud as can be.
I can hear that dumb ass all the way over here,
And I'm wearing an earplug in each ear.
You can hear this guy a friggin mile away,
And I'm getting sick of his shit every day.
So, instead of knocking the dumb ass out this time,
I'm occupying my mind by writing this rhyme.
If I wasn't sitting here writing this tonight,
I'd be sitting in the hole because of a fight.

....

I spent a lot of time in Solitary Confinement for fighting. I spent a lot of the first year in prison in "The Hole". They call it the hole for a good reason. You feel so far down that it feels like you're in a hole. It's dark and dreary in solitary confinement. It's the most depressing place that I've ever been. You don't know loneliness until you've been in a place like that. Fighting isn't always worth it. You can't change anyone but yourself so no use trying.

When I leave!

If there's one thing I've done since I've been caged,
It's very evident how much I've aged.
I look in the mirror and I see a catastrophy,
A wasted life stares back at me.
I'm suffering from arthritis in a lot of my joints,
I've been pushed past my breaking points.
I need a knee replacement to proceed,
The doctor saw the MRI and he agreed.
It won't be the first time I go under the blade,
All these scars show you the mess I made.
I've broken way too many bones for sure,
I'll try not to get into fights anymore.
I'll give that decision an awful lot of dedication,
So, I can avoid a needless operation.
But I will always have a certain vulnerability,
It's not in my nature to let people mess with me.
This year though, comes a wonderful breakthrough,
It's the year I'll be coming home to you.
In my heart, is where I truly believe,
This animosity will stay behind when I leave.

....

I'm hoping that my attitude will change when I get out of prison. Right now, I fight at the drop of a hat now. I don't have much respect for people anymore. I'm not the man I used to be. I hope my heart isn't as cold as it is now. I feel very cold and indifferent to people now. I don't know if I have any sympathy left to give anyone. I pray to God that I'll feel different when I get around people that I love and care about. I hope I can get my sense of humor back. I used to love to laugh and make people laugh.

The next time

I'm writing this to you just in case I die,
I'm not writing this to make you cry.
We all die, it's just a matter of time,
And I'm pretty far past my prime.
Dying is the inevitable cycle of life,
It can be caused by stress and strife.
We shouldn't grieve and we should celebrate,
And remember the ones we loved were great.
Don't grieve when I'm no longer there,
Be glad about the love we had to share.
The ones I love know who they are,
I've let them know from afar.
It's okay to miss someone after their gone,
But still be happy and move on.
I don't want the ones I love to grieve,
So, celebrate my life when I leave.
Our time is relatively short here on earth,
Give your life to Jesus for your re-birth.
Then have faith one day that we'll be together,
And the next time it will be forever.

....

I've had to deal with a lot of deaths since I've been in prison. I lost my mom, dad, my remaining uncle, three cousins and another cousin that had a stroke and is in the nursing home. I also lost three aunts. I'm the second oldest in the Leland family now. It seems strange to me that all the adults I loved and grew up with are all gone now and I'm close to the age of their deaths now.

Diversity

I'm biding my time because only time will tell,
When they're gonna release me from this hell.
I know that I can find out any day now,
I made it through this madness somehow.
I'm getting nervous and more anxious to be released,
Or to find out the exact date at least.
I get my hopes up that every day will be the day,
Then get disappointed in the worst way.
It's depressing to have to put up with guys at night,
And so hard to stay out of a fight.
Night after night I swallow my pride,
Some nights I can't no matter how hard I tried.
Today seems to be one of those damn days,
To hold my temper, I've tried different ways.
Nothing has helped me except writing these rhymes,
That's why I've done it so many times.
In these poems I tell you about these awful places,
And all about the different looking faces.
I've spent many long years hating what I see,
And now I really hate the word diversity.

••••••••••••

Diversity is fine as long as everyone can be with the ones they want to be with. But, when you're forced to live with people that hate you, it really sucks. I don't care who likes and doesn't like what I say about this subject. Because of my race, I was hated by some other races in prison and since there are more of them than there were of me, I got into some good fights. If you think for a minute that the other races in America will treat you equally, you're wrong.

I apologize

I wish I could go back to when I was forty-four,
I would change my future for sure.
It's too bad that I can't turn back the time,
And I can't un-commit the crime.
If I could, you know I would, just for you,
But it's too late to do what you wanted me to do.
I want to say I'm sorry to you today,
I hope you can forgive me in your own way.
You were the best and did everything you could,
You probably hate me and you should.
I don't really know what the hell I was thinking,
Always partying, doing drugs and drinking.
You're not to blame, you were a really good wife,
I'm the asshole that screwed up our life.
I've had fourteen years to think about it,
Knowing that I was a selfish piece of shit.
I haven't seen or spoken to you in so long,
I realize now I did a lot of things wrong.
If you want to know who this apology is for,
You'd have to know who I was with at forty-four.

....

After so many years in prison, I feel like I have to apologize to some people in my past. I'm not going to contact them though. I'm going to leave the past in the past. If I ever see her, I will apologize. I hope she's found someone to make her happy and treat her right. I am so sorry.

The Game

You can't find love in a prison setting,
Through the mail you don't know what you're getting.
After years in prison you're filled with hate,
And to find love again, you can't wait.
Romance through the mail brings a little fun,
But you soon learned you jumped the gun.
You convince yourself she wouldn't lie,
Then you find they're with some other guy.
You think back at what a fool you've been,
Another woman writes and it starts again.
After so many times it's just a game to you too,
If they can play it, so can you.
Now, you don't believe a thing they say,
So, you play the game the exact same way.
You begin to think all women are the same.
And you believe they all play the game.
But then an honest woman comes along,
And you interpret everything she says wrong.
Now she thinks that it's a damn shame,
She likes you but she doesn't like your game.

....

I've learned that no matter how many times you get screwed over, you can't think that everyone is the same. They might be few and far between now but there are still some good people in this world. I know by experience that it's very hard to trust when your heart has been broken so many times.

Leave me be

A woman wants a man that has something to give,
Not one that needs help just to live.
They don't need one that lives behind bars and stone,
They'd be better off on their own.
At least out there they can find a man to touch,
A prisoner can't be touched much.
But I can be good for a laugh or two,
If you're bored and lonely with nothing to do.
You never have to worry about where we are,
Behind bars we are not going very far.
You can use us to take up some of your time,
Talking to us is not a crime.
It won't hurt anything to talk to me,
Let me give you and call and you will see.
But, if you're happy in someone else's bed,
Leave me alone instead, it messes up my head.
You're not happy when someone does it to you,
You bitch to me when they do.
You found a man that can give you more than me,
So, when I'm free just leave me be.

....

I've had women write to me in prison when they were lonely and didn't have anything better to do. They'd tell me all kinds of things to make me think I was really special and they were going to wait for me. All of a sudden, the letters stop and they don't accept my phone calls. It messes with my head. I get my hopes up. It breaks my heart. I got so tired of it over the years that I didn't write back when I got a letter from someone new.

It's not fair!

I've been telling you that life's not fair,
There are some that would argue that out there.
They're the ones brought up in the land of milk and honey,
They've never had to worry about money.
They're the ones born with a silver spoon,
Given everything under the moon.
They think they are better than the rest,
Everything they have is nothing but the best.
Mommy and daddy paid for them to go to school,
Got them out of trouble when they broke a rule.
All their lives they've been spoiled rotten,
Never had to struggle for what they've gotten.
They've never learned the value of a dime,
And they piss away money all the time.
They are usually the most popular ones in town,
And they put the less fortunate ones down.
As long as they live like that, they say life's fair,
And never expect any of them to share.
On the rare occasion on of them goes to jail,
It's not fair they bitch, cry and wail!

....

You can definitely tell the rich, spoiled ones from the rest in prison. They are the weakest ones. They complain the most and are always saying that it's not fair that they are in prison and being treated like this. It's poetic justice to see that when it happens. They are the ones that usually pay for protection. They are not so ignorant and high and mighty in prison. It's actually comical. I'm watching a guy pay someone else right now to make him something to eat. If you have money, you can pay others to do just about anything for you in prison.

A stubborn man

It doesn't bother me to say no anymore,
It doesn't matter what they ask for.
I used to help everyone that I could,
But they don't do what they should.
When I'm doing for them, I'm a great guy,
When it's done, they just walk on by.
They want everything done for them free,
But if I want something, they charge me.
A lot of these idiots can't read or write,
They see me doing it all day and night.
I'm always asked to write something in a card,
It's easy for me, but to them it's too hard.
I used to feel sorry for them in a way,
But I know them all too well today.
I'm a nice guy but I'm not going to be used,
They ask for something now, they're refused.
They still try to get from me whatever they can,
But they've found out that I'm a stubborn man.
When I decide I don't want anything to do with you,
There is not a damn thing you can do.

....

It happens everywhere, not just in prison. There are many people in this world that use others. As long as they can get what they want from you, you are a great person. But, when they can't get what they want, you don't mean shit to them. I always treat people the way I want to be treated. If they don't treat me the same way, I treat them the way they treat me or I don't have anything to do with them at all. Either way, they don't mean shit to me.

Get up and fight

I know that it's not going to be much longer,
And every day is making me much stronger.
There are some days that's harder, that's for sure,
Some of the stupid shit that goes on I can't ignore.
A lot of these idiots act like it's party time,
And can't wait to get out to commit another crime.
When they come to prison and have so much fun,
They talk about getting themselves a new gun.
I really hate the things I hear and see,
This isn't fun for me, I think it's misery.
The next time these dumbasses will kill someone,
Because to them, prison is a lot of fun.
My heart aches and I'm always lonely and sad,
This is the hardest time I've ever had.
But these guys seem like they're as happy as can be,
The next sentence for them will be life, you'll see.
I'm forced to sit here and listen to all this shit,
Knowing these guys are too stupid to get it.
So, In just sit here and put up with it every night,
It's either that or get up and fight.

....

I learned a long time ago that the only one that I can change is me. It doesn't matter what I say to them, they won't change if they don't want to. I have also learned that I can't beat the stupid out of someone. I've tried to help a lot of people in prison. I've taught reading and writing in the education department to the ones that are forced to go to get their GED. I didn't last long as a teacher. If an inmate is forced to learn, he's not going to learn a thing. I wanted to kick the shit out of them in class. All they do is run their mouths.

Paying the price

Lately all I've been doing is beating myself up,
For constantly drinking from the devil's cup.
He was always standing on my shoulder,
Trying to prevent me from getting older.
Of course, he was telling me I was doing well,
I was on the right path straight to hell.
He had me believing everything was good,
And I was doing everything I should.
Deep down I knew I wasn't doing anything right,
But I continued to party almost every night.
I lost control of myself after a while,
Until I finally took it to the last mile.
I never really gave a shit about the law,
That mistake was the last straw.
I was a fool to not have any fears,
Because it cost me twenty-one years.
Everyone in my life has finally moved on,
Everything I ever had now is gone.
Day after day I keep paying the price,
And my veins keep filling with ice.

....

It doesn't take a person twenty-one years to learn a lesson. Of course, prison time is appropriate in a lot of cases but long prison sentences for non-violent people is a waste. It's a waste of taxpayer's money, but most importantly, it's a waste of human life. Politician's children, the children of police, judges, lawyers and such very rarely are sent to prison. When they are, they are not sent there for very long. Justice is only for the people who are not related to someone or know someone who has some authority in this country.

Dave the Rat

I'm not prejudice, but I made a decision,
The Jews hide behind what they call they're religion.
There's this big, fat sloppy Jew where I'm at,
His name is Dave and he's a piece of shit rat.
He's got very ugly features that he can't hide,
He's got tits that wiggle down by his side,
He's way better than everyone else, he thinks,
I walk over near him and boy, that man stinks!
Other inmates do everything for him for a price,
They even go get him some ice.
One guy even cleans up all his trash,
He pays in stamps but in here it's like cash.
He's got guys that will make his bed,
But I'd like to punch him in the head.
I see other guys over there sweeping his floor,
But for that, he has to pay them more.
He runs his mouth like he's a damn king,
He's so friggin lazy, he doesn't do a thing.
I've got to be honest, I can't lie,
I'd like to watch that fat bastard die.
If he sees anything wrong that you do,
He runs right to the guards to tell on you.
He watches everything from where he's at,
And I can't stand the fat, lazy rat.

Tough Shit

Sometimes I say things that are not politically correct,
But you don't know these guys you want to protect.
I live in the same room as these child molesting, gays,
They force children to have sex on many days.
They have pictures of thousands of children being abused,
Then they lie like hell when they're accused.
You should hear some of the sick shit they say,
Don't get me wrong, I don't hate the gay.
But these sick bastards have sex with little boys,
And they're in here making little boy's toys.
They are not required to go through any rehabilitation,
They play games with each other like they're on vacation.
Dungeons and Dragons is the game they all play,
They have sex with each other almost every day.
I wish they'd put all these assholes in one big dorm,
Then they could all feel giddy and warm.
That would make them all just as happy as could be,
You should thank God you don't see the sick shit I see.
So, if I call them a faggot or something like it,
They can kiss my ass because I don't give a shit!

....

I told you at the beginning of this book that I write about just about every aspect of prison life. I really want to go over and beat all these child molesters to death but unfortunately, I can't do that. But you should know that they are protected by the prison staff. We are not allowed to say anything to them or touch them. If we do, we are the ones sent to the hole. They know this and act high and mighty. They all need a beating in my opinion.

I'm telling it straight

Living in these prisons you strip away the façade,
You find out how these people are made.
Chicken shit, child molesters are bedwetters,
Some of these dumbasses think they're trendsetters.
The ones that think they're cool walk with a stupid gait,
They're the ones filled with the most hate.
Some of them walk around in a medicated trance,
They aren't smart enough to pull up their pants.
There's a group of them that cause a lot of confusion,
They think they're cool but it's just and illusion.
They act like they're superior but it's just a bluff,
When it comes to brains they don't have enough.
After all these years I see this with brutal clarity,
These guys are the real danger to society.
I wish I had the power to send them to the abyss,
You'd agree too if you could see and hear this.
Setting some of these guys free you'd see a backlash,
They'd still molest children and steal your cash.
I'm not exaggerating anything, I'm tell it straight,
They shouldn't be let past the prison gate.

....

What makes me really mad is that I have a 21 sentence and these violent, child molesters didn't get anywhere near the time I got. Would you rather have me live next door to you protecting you, your children and your property or would you rather have one of these worthless assholes living there that would rob you in a heartbeat if they had the chance?

The Rest

I know that I can only write so much,
And not all hearts I'll be able to touch.
But everyday I sit here and I keep trying,
I want to help someone, I'm not lying.
I'm telling you these stories in my own way,
Hoping that they'll help you one day.
If you can learn from what I have done wrong,
To just say "No" and then stand strong.
Live a good life and be smarter than me,
You don't want to see the things I see.
You don't want to smell the things I smell,
You don't want to live in this hell.
Even if you think you know how to fight,
A gang of guys will be on you one night.
Please take it to heart the things I say,
So, you never have to find out this way.
Don't put yourself through what I've been through,
Listen to the ones that you know love you.
They are the ones that care and only want the best,
Nothing good ever comes from the rest.

....

One of the things I regret the most in my life is not listening to my family and the few real friends that I had. I listened to the wrong people. I listened to the people that did drugs and partied with me all the time. Those people didn't really give a shit about me. All they wanted was what I could do for them. Like a fool, I was the one who paid for the drinks and all the party favors. As long as I was doing that, I was an awesome guy. Once I was in prison, I found out that most of them ratted on me to stay out of prison themselves.

Living Well

Man, for a couple of days I lost my head,
Over something stupid that someone said.
Now I'm sitting here and I'm back on track,
I reminded myself to stop looking back.
Now, I'm concentrating on what lies ahead,
Thinking about the ones I love instead.
Looking back feels like I'm being cut with a knife,
I still have the scar but it was another life.
I know that someday soon that scar will heal,
It will disappear with a love that's real.
I also know now who my real friends are,
And they will also help heal that scar.
Years in prison have stopped me from moving on,
I couldn't until some memories were gone.
To forget old memories, I have to make some new,
And I want those memories to be with you.
I'm letting the old memories go as my time ends,
The only ones that count are family and friends.
When I come home, I'm going to be Living Well,
Whoever doesn't like it can go to hell.

··········

When I first went to prison, I had to wait a few months before I got my discovery. I didn't even know what they had against me. When I got my discovery and found out how many "friends" ratted on me, I was hurt really bad. Then when I found out my wife did it too, I was devastated. I wanted to kill people. Since then I've learned that the best revenge is Living Well. They are the ones that have to live with themselves. Karma has a way of finding them. Not only that, revenge is not mine, it's Gods. I'll leave it in His hands.

Leaving behind the Hate

I like writing the date now with two thousand, seventeen,
It's the prettiest number I've ever seen.
Getting to that number has made me strong,
And I've been waiting for it for so damn long.
Many nights I've laid awake under the sheets,
Wondering what's happening on the streets.
Everyone has moved on without me there,
And I have so much love I want to share.
I've been saving it all behind a prison gate,
In a world that's so full of hate.
Living in these prisons was the way it had to be,
But out there, haters better stay away from me.
If you don't like me, just leave me alone,
And I will let you live on your own.
You never thought about my release one day,
And you didn't care that date was so far away.
I'm going to be released and this year is the year,
But don't worry about it, you have nothing to fear.
I'm not going to do anything to retaliate,
When I walk out that gate, I'm leaving behind the hate.

....

As it got closer and closer to my release date, I often wondered how I'd feel if I saw the people that ratted on me. For years I hated them. But I learned to forget about them. I know that when they saw me happy and living well it would really bother them. They are not worth one more minute of my time. They aren't even worth thinking about. I know I will be happier than they ever could be. They know that they are cowards to tell on someone else and give them prison time just because they are so afraid to do their own time.

You can't tell

Every day I sit here waiting for my out-date,
It's so hard for me to wait.
My nerves are shot and I get anxiety,
Lately that's how it's been for me.
I look forward to hearing them say,
Pack your shit you are out of here today,
You have to be off the compound by four,
You can't be here for count anymore.
I see so many inmates come and go,
I can't wait until they let me know.
I got a lot more time that these fools,
They followed the prosecutor's rules.
I'm mad but nothing that I can do,
I did my time and it's almost through.
The ones that got caught doing the crime,
Rat on everyone and they do less time.
I haven't met very many stand up guys,
But I've met thousands who tell lies.
I don't trust anyone I meet anymore,
You can't tell if they're good anymore.

....

In prison you can be anyone you want to be until someone comes in off the streets that knows you. I've seen this happen more times than I can count. They will lie like hell to make themselves sound like they are stand up guys that can be trusted. Most of the time someone knows them eventually and you find out the truth. It's easy to get paperwork on them if you go to the Law Library. So, it's easier for me to not trust anyone until they prove you can.

This old prison

This prison is seventy-seven years old,
It's hard to heat, so it's unusually cold.
The plumbing leaks and never works right,
There's no one here to fix it on site,
We have stuffed up sinks that overflow,
Toilets that won't flush when you go.
Dumbasses pour food down in the sinks,
With that and the toilets, it really stinks.
You have to be careful brushing your teeth,
It leaks on your feet from underneath.
Tomorrow the old boiler is down for repair,
And it's cold as hell out there.
Many guys will stay covered up in bed,
We all will have hats on our head.
We are dressed warm from our heads to toes,
When we'll get heat again, only God knows.
I had to take a shower that was cold as ice,
It's not just the plumbing that doesn't surface.
This old prison needs an awful lot of repair,
If the doors are locked, that's all they care.

....

The sad part about this prison is that it's the prison that holds the most prisoners in the United States and Its smack dab in the middle of the Fort Dix Army base in New Jersey. You would think that the government would keep it in good shape since there are five thousand inmates there. The Army built new barracks and the government made the old barracks into a federal prison. It's not a good place to be though. No prison in the United States or anywhere else is a good place to be. Take it from me. Stay out of trouble.

Times like that

The windows are barred, the doors are locked,
The guard's guns are locked and cocked.
They yell at everyone to hit the ground,
There's a lot of noise and confusion around.
As I lay there, spread eagle and face in the dirt,
A shot rings out and someone is hurt,
I hear the most blood curdling screams,
I'll hear those in my dreams.
Another shot rings out and I see him fall,
I turn my head and see the blood on the wall.
A guard screams- "Hands behind your back!",
Just as I hear another rifle crack.
This one had to be just a warning shot,
Inmates were all face down in the lot.
This happens sometimes when you're in a pen,
You never forget those times back then.
Face in the dirt, soaked in sweat from the heat,
Guards yelling telling you to spread your feet.
You know if you move a muscle you'll get shot too,
Times like that you don't think you'll come through.

....

A federal penitentiary is the highest security prison in America. They have thirty-foot stone walls with armed guard towers and cameras that can see everything. The tops of the walls are cover in razor wire in case you were spiderman and made it up the wall. You'd be shot just for trying. When was the last time you heard of someone breaking out of a federal Pen?

Whatever Happens

Day and night, I sit here and feel the same,
I'm just a number in here, not a name.
I know there's more to life than this,
It has been so long, I don't know what I miss.
Some of the people I miss are dead and gone,
And the rest have all moved on.
My life fell apart so many years ago,
This prison life now is all I know.
My tattoo says, "Only God Knows Why",
I thought I'd live this life until I die.
But now, I have my sights on the road ahead,
I've got many years before I'll be dead.
I feel like I've been tied to a whipping post,
But on the inside, I hurt the most.
I can handle all of the physical pain,
The heartache is what drives me insane.
I've drowned myself in sorrow for what I've done,
And from the shame, I can't run.
Inside me now, is an empty space,
Whatever happens here, I'm ready to face.

....

I never got over the sorrow and shame of me being in prison and putting a stain on my family name. I'm the only Leland that has ever been in prison. I'm sorry to all the ones that I hurt. I'm sorry for taking things for granted. I didn't think about others when I was doing drugs. I only thought about myself and how I felt. I thought by paying for things and making sure everyone I loved was taken care of was what I had to do to justify me being gone all the time.

Stress is getting to me

For an hour I had to stand in the rain at commissary today,
But I bought my new watch and everything is okay.
It is a long cold walk back when you're wet,
It's been two hours and I'm not warmed up yet.
I'm mad at myself for letting down my guard,
Walking away from the asshole was really hard.
It wasn't the first time that I had to swallow my pride,
And hold back all the feelings I had inside.
After so many years of being locked in a cage,
I've learned it only hurts me to show my rage.
It's not an easy thing but I can usually control it,
And I can pretend like I don't give a shit.
Then I come sit here and write these poems to you,
To get shit off my mind it's the best I can do.
For many years this method has worked for me,
I'll keep writing them as long as you want to see.
I look at my new watch and picture my old one,
How I let someone pick it up and run.
It's stressful to always have to be on your toes,
The stress is getting to me, and it shows.

....

You have to bring your plastic chair in the shower room with you to lay your clothes on and hang your towel from. You leave the chair right outside the shower and do your best to keep an eye on it. When you close the shower curtain, you can't see the chair but you can see under the curtain. Someone came into the shower room and stole my watch off the chair without me seeing them. I think I knew who it was but I couldn't prove it. I did good by holding my temper and showed the asshole that I could go get a new one the next day.

Beware!

Some people don't like these poems at all,
They make other take the fall.
They've never been alone in a cold dirty cell,
They don't go to jail because they tell.
They've never had to fight a gang of guys,
And they're good at spreading lies.
They've never had to strip and spread their cheeks,
They will do anything to stay on the streets.
They will pretend to be your best friend,
And in a crowd the try to blend.
As long as they have something to tell a detective,
Staying out of jail for them, is very effective.
They will never be the biggest fish to fry,
They'll always be the peon no matter how they try.
They just like to get high on other people's dime,
If there's drugs, they'll be there all the time.
These people don't have any loyalty to anyone,
But they'll be there if you pay for their fun.
You don't have to believe this thing I write,
But, beware, they are out there tonight.

....

I've encountered many of these people on the streets but there are just as many in prison. As long as you have something they want and you are giving it to them, they act like your best friend. But, when the goodies stop coming, they don't like you one bit and if they can get you into trouble, they don't hesitate. Keep your circle small and don't trust as easily as I did. I'm paying for my mistakes and I'm certainly learning from them. I don't make the same mistake twice, that's for sure.

Clear my name

I'm not writing my poems to make anyone mad,
I just write about all the experiences I've had.
A lot of them are about the feelings I have inside,
In prison, these feelings I have to hide.
I've heard there were some people mad at me,
They didn't like the truth in the world I see.
I can prove everything I write in my rhyme,
I'm happy to show you the proof anytime.
In some of my poems I do name names,
Those people run their mouths and play games.
They are out there living their lives just fine,
And I'm the one in here doing their time.
They helped give me 21 years way back when,
They never thought I'd get out back then.
They're worried now because my release date is near,
And the truth, they don't want anyone to hear.
I've heard all their rumors and all their lies,
And now I'm going to destroy their alibis.
To me, the past 14 years was not a game,
From their lies, I'm going to clear my name.

··········

I got into many fights in prison because people came from Maine and spread the rumors about me that the real rats told on the streets. That's just what the rats do. They have to put eyes on others to get eyes off them. They do the same thing in prison. I started writing a book in prison and I'm not only clearing my name, I'm letting everyone know who said what in my case.

They don't have a clue!

It's almost midnight and it's a damn shame,
It's even louder since the new guys came.
The two new guys and they're from the hood,
They'd take this place over if they could.
The lights have been out for over two hours,
And now they are yelling from the showers.
That's where the assholes go to smoke,
And to them, everything here is a joke.
The dumbasses here are breaking them in right,
But they are just ignorant and not too bright.
They're over there rapping now for all their worth,
Their mother threw away the baby and kept the afterbirth.
They're nothing but a waste of a human being,
You'd agree if you were seeing what I'm seeing.
If just for one night you could hear what I hear,
When that generation runs the country, have fear.
They're do dumb their asses are hanging out,
They don't have a clue what life's all about.

....

As you can tell by this poem, I was not very happy tonight. This happens when new gang members come in off the streets and meet up with their friends. It's a big party to those guys. They don't give a shit that the other eighty people in that room are trying to sleep. Living with guys like these twenty-four hours a day is extremely hard. You have to hold your temper or fight. I've fought so much that I am tired of fighting now. I'll try to avoid fights if I can now.

A different way

I write a lot about pain, sorrow and heartbreak,
Because every day I live with the heartache.
For some of the things I've done, I live with sorrow,
And those memories will haunt me tomorrow.
Someday, I'm sure these memories will be history,
As for when that will be, it's a mystery.
I'm very anxious to see what the future will hold,
Because living in hell has gotten old.
I want my poems to make people shine,
Not about all this heartache of mine.
I want to share in the love and laughter,
Like a fairy tale, live happily ever after.
Right now, they are just my hopes and dreams,
And it is a fairy tale to me it seems.
For so many years nothing has gone right,
But I will never give up the fight.
So, I sit her day after day trying to kill time,
Writing my feelings down making them rhyme.
When I find happiness someday,
I'll write her poems in a different way.

....

I try to write upbeat poems that have nothing to do with prison but its hard. I've all but forgotten what life on the streets feels like. I haven't been in a romantic relationship for so long I've forgotten what that's like too. I live inside my own head here and I've done it for so many years that I don't write about anything except prison life and what I'm feeling.

A FIGHT TONIGHT

Somethings happening, I can feel it in the air,
it's tension I feel when I'm out there.
When the yard was full, I felt this feeling before,
a big fight is going to break out for sure.
I don't want any part of it so I'm staying inside,
if I was near it, I'd be dragged into it and I'd abide.
But I've had more than my fair share of fights,
and tossed in the hole for way too many nights.
I can feel it in the air really bad right now,
but I'll do all I can to avoid this somehow.
I was hurt really bad in the last fight I was in,
a broken nose, two broken ribs and a fractured chin.
Two younger guys made weapons out of socks,
in the socks, they had their padlocks.
After that I decided I'm too old to fight,
so, I'm going to stay out of this one tonight.
I don't mind fighting if the fight is fair,
there's no such thing as a fair fight out there.
There'll be shanks made from whatever they can get,
and vicious injuries you'll never forget.
I've seen a guy get his eye cut with a shank,
And now, his expression is always blank.
That was only one of the bad injuries I've seen,
When a fight breaks out it gets real mean.

....

SOLITARY CONFINEMENT

Fighting is against the rules and it doesn't matter why.
I'm walking around trying to hide this black eye.
If I get caught, I've got a story I've rehearsed,
and I'll be in the hole if worse comes to worse.
I'm walking around with sunglasses on my face,
I look like the rest of the weirdos in this place.
I got this black eye by accident late last night.
I went to the bathroom and got into a fight.
I was half asleep when I went to take a pee,
some asshole on K2 swung wild and hit me.
He was in there smoking that shit with another guy,
he just flipped out and hit me in the eye.
The next thing I know he's on his knees on the floor,
and he's banging his head on the stall door.
I had to get out of there and away from those fools,
before I forget fighting is against the rules.
He hit me hard and my eye turned black,
when I see a guard, I have to turn my back.
If they see me and put me in solitary confinement,
when I get out, he's getting a facial realignment.

··········

Note: This is a true story. Luckily, I didn't go to the hole that time. Most people in society don't have a clue what happens in prison nor do they care. I know I didn't when I was out there. It took coming to the jails and prisons in America for me to see for myself just how messed up they are. There are no corrections going on. The guards are nothing but babysitters. Many people in prison party as if they were at a nightclub. Drugs are easy to acquire in prison.

Chapter Three

Just Killing Time Writing Poems

These poems in this chapter are poems about what was on my mind at the time. You'll be able to tell what I was thinking all the time. If you've never had time to kill, and I mean a lot of time, you can't imagine how time goes by so slowly. I didn't have anything to do a lot of time. We are locked in our units most of the time. In one unit, there are anywhere between seventy-five and a hundred inmates at any given time. The inmates, range in age from eighteen to in their eighties. They are from many different countries and have many different religions. Racism is very prevalent. No matter what the other races try to portray, whites are the least racist of all the races. Whites use the word the least. The other races are always crying racist because it gets them what they want. Religion is a big one to also. People in prison don't really abide by their religion but certain religions get special meals and have special events in prison, such as Ramadan, for example. The Muslims are treated better in prison than Jesus Christ was treated on the streets. The United States justice department caters to all the other religions. They even let the terrorists have special treatment. There are terrorists in federal prison that were treated better than I was. But I don't cry about it all the time. It wouldn't have done any good anyway. The Muslims think pigs are dirty and don't eat pork. They've cried and bitched about it so much, prisons stopped serving pork, and I love bacon. Do you think an American in a Muslim country would be treated the same way in their prison? That's a joke. You and I both know they would behead an American just for being in their country. They would film it and send it by way of the media to the United States. Yet, the United States caters to them! I get so sick of seeing what goes on and it doesn't make me very proud to be an American anymore. I served this country in the Army during the Vietnam War. I'm treated worse than the Muslims are in this country. Something is wrong there.

These next poems are random poems that I wrote. There's no theme to them at all. I have thousands of poems and I really don't know what ones you would like and which ones you wouldn't. As I read these poems over and put them in this book, each and every one of them are bringing back the memory of the day I wrote them. I do have a couple of special people that I love reading some of them and picking them out for me to let you read. To tell you the truth, as I read them over again, I don't like them very much. But I've had a lot of people as me to publish a book of poems, so this is what I've come up with. I hope in some way that it helps someone. Maybe someone in the same situation I was in will find something to inspire them. Maybe it will give them some ideas on how to kill time. Time can eat at your brain if you let it.

I'LL KNOW

You say you want to spread your wings and fly,
chase your dreams, it's never too late to try.
Don't be afraid to venture into the unknown,
but the world can be hard when you're alone.

When you are out there trying to find your way,
you'll have someone here praying for you every day.
You have always had more than a friend in me,
I'll always be with you wherever you may be.

I wouldn't stop you from leaving even if I could,
if you want to leave then by all means you should.
I will pray to God you find what you're looking for,
and you are happy and won't need anything more.

I will always have the fondest memories of you,
and you can always call me if you want to.
I'd love to hear how you are doing out there,
I'll always be here and I'll always care.

You can talk to me, especially if you are sad,
I'll be the best friend you ever had.
If you're in the area stop by to say hello,
I won't wonder how you are, then I'll know.

A FEW

What I will know when I get there with you,
Is that everything out there is brand new?
I've been in prison since two thousand three,
all things out there will be foreign to me.

The closer I get to going out the door,
I worry and get stressed out about it more.
I don't know what I'm going to do when I'm free,
but I won't let anyone else support me.

I have to hold on to a little pride,
because it makes me feel better inside.
A few people supported me when I was down,
but that's over when I get back to town.

I appreciate everything they did for me,
I'll pay them back when I'm free.
But of the thousands of people I knew,
I only received support from a few.

When I get home to everything that is gone,
those are the few I know I can depend on.
They'll show me the things that I have to know,
and show me what direction to go.

A LIFETIME TO FIND

I don't need a doctor now that's for sure,
I know he doesn't have a cure.
It wouldn't help if I had a private nurse,
I think it might make it worse.

I don't need a prescription for this pain,
Drugs would only drive me insane.
I don't need diamonds, or a pot of gold,
I'd still be sad, lonely and cold.

I don't want to argue and I don't want to fight,
and I don't want to be alone at night.
I don't need a psyche telling me what to do,
there's only one cure for me and that's YOU!

I have been infected with a case of "love",
and you're the one who fits me like a glove.
I told you before and I'll tell you once more,
I'm coming home soon so open up your door.

Now believe me when I say all I want is you,
no other woman on earth will do.
You have taken me a lifetime to find,
and I'll never get you off my mind.

A LOVE BETTER THAN THIS

I don't care anything about the world outside,
as you lay next to me with nothing to hide.
You've had my heart since our very first kiss,
I've never felt a love better than this.

You've got me in the mood that's just right,
for me to make love to you every night.
All my life I've had really nice fantasies,
but compared to you they were just a tease.

I love the way your body feels next to mine,
anything you want to do will be fine.
When we're this close I can hear your heart beat,
and I love you from your head to your feet.

Your skin looks so beautiful in the moonlight,
and right now, everything feels so right.
I just want to touch you all night long,
a love like this can't never be wrong.

It's getting late but I don't want to close my eyes,
I'm so in love with you I'm hypnotized.
If I went to sleep look what I would miss,
I couldn't dream of a love better than this.

A Brand-New Start

If there's just one thing I never want to do,
it would be that I never want to disappoint you.
So, I really hope you're not seeing too much in me,
and you don't expect too much from me when I'm free.

It might be because I've been in prison so long,
I feel to promise anyone anything would be wrong.
I've had some women promise me they would wait,
I put my heart in it and thought it was great.

They had me feeling the way I wanted to feel,
and convinced me that their love was real.
I was a lonely man and they had my heart on fire,
and they woke up in me a deep desire.

I would write a lot of things for them to read,
and they would give me the love that I need.
But after a while, and it still hurts me to say,
They all end up just walking away.

And now I wonder who they're with every night,
and what it is that I didn't do right.
They know they broke my heart and disappeared,
I have to live with it as long as I'm here.

And once again I'm getting used to being alone,
I'm doing good dealing with the pain on my own.
At night, I listen to the beating of a broken heart,
and thanking God I'm close to a new start.

So, no promises just yet so they don't turn into lies,
you'll know if it's love, when you look into my eyes.
We can't just jump into this relationship fast,
it's my last chance and I want it to last.

....

Some women started writing to me a few years before I was being released. I haven't been with a woman for so long that I was starving for love. I would answer any letter I got from women. I have learned that with this new technology anyone can be anything they want to be and can look any way they want to look with photoshop. I've had to find this out the hard way. I've found out that people are not who they portray themselves to be now. Not all people are that way but a lot of them are. Since I've been in prison, society and technology has changed so much. A lot of this change hasn't been for the better either. I was surprised that it was so hard to meet women now a days. The ones I do meet, I had to meet through texting or on Facebook. I have been sent some pictures of women that were beautiful. When I actually met them, they didn't look anything like the pictures they sent me. Then they say that I shouldn't be mad, love shouldn't be the way someone looks. I say, love shouldn't start off with a big lie like that. What do you say? I don't know about you, but I have to be physically attracted to someone before I fall in love with them. I'm sorry if that's wrong and you think that I'm a chauvinist pig. That's just the way that I am.

A SMALL TOWN

Someone told me that you're married now,
they said all your dreams came true somehow.
He must give you the things I didn't give you,
the things I didn't do, he must do.

I've always had something inside wrong with me,
it stopped me from being the man I wanted to be.
Don't worry, I won't interfere with your life,
I know you want to be a good wife.

You could always be the best at what you do,
and I want nothing but the best for you.
When I get out of prison I'll stay out of your space,
I'll go the other way if I see your face.

But it's not because I hate you or I'm mad,
with you I had some of the best times I ever had.
I'm staying far away because I still care about you,
and causing you problems is something I'll never do.

But if you see me in passing please smile at me,
I'll smile too remembering the way it used to be.
It will be more pleasant when we see each other around,
which is bound to happen in a small town.

AFTER I'M GONE

I've been looking for you,
even though you are taboo.
I want love at my age,
but I'm locked in a cage.

But I want to send you a letter,
it would make me feel better
Because I want some things said,
before I am dead.

Just so you will know,
how much I love you so.
You've always had my heart,
even though we were apart.

I know you're living your life,
and you're someone's wife.
While I've been locked away,
thinking of you every day.

Your happiness is good to see,
even if it's not with me.
But never forget our song,
sing it after I am gone.

A Woman

I found a woman, one I truly love,
she is everything I've been dreaming of.
All I know about her is what I can see,
and I want this woman just for me.

I just can't wait to make this woman mine,
because I've never had a woman so fine.
She's got a beautiful smile when she shows it,
and she's the one for me and she knows it.

I melt, like butter, when I look into her eyes,
I can't think straight, I'm mesmerized.
I'll be the proudest man walking around our city,
holding her hand because she's so damn pretty.

I'm not a good-looking man but I'll love her more,
than anyone can and that's for sure.
And no other man will ever cause her to hurt,
or he'll be under six feet of dirt.

This woman can make all my dreams come true,
by waiting for me until this sentence is through.
If she does, I will gladly give this woman my life,
One day maybe she'll agree to be my wife.

ANALOG MAN

The world has changed dramatically since I've been there,
everyone puts on an air.
In the digital world, nothing is private anymore,
you can find everything in cyberspace, that's for sure.

I thought it was great when I got cable for my tv,
I mention it now and they think I'm out of my tree.
Since coming out with emails, I can't get a letter,
everyone thinks computers are better.

Now they have smart phones and even a smart tv,
do you know how dumb that makes me?
If I get me one of those things, I won't have a clue,
my granddaughter can teach me what to do.

I don't know anything about digital, I'm in a fog,
before I came to prison all I knew was analog.
I just learned how to hook up a stereo with no fires,
and now I'm told they don't have wires.

They say you don't even have to use a remote control now,
your computer recognizes your voice somehow.
There must be a lot of digital smart asses out there,
but it's made them the laziest people anywhere.

I'm so old that I have to stay as active as I can,
and I'm just happy being an analog man.
Now please get off your lazy ass and write me a letter,
you would make me feel a hell of a lot better.

I know you don't mind putting your whole life on a Facebook,
but you know I'm in prison and can't take a look.
You put a bunch of pictures on there for the world to see,
do you really care about everyone but me?

....

The first couple of years I was in prison I got a lot of letters. It wasn't long before the internet came out and the world changed. It was so easy for everyone to email and text each other that everyone got lazy. My letters stopped. Nobody wanted to pick up a pen and write anymore. It was crazy to me because I didn't even know what the internet or Facebook was. I wasn't in the real world. I was in an isolated world inside a world that was changing so fast without me. I can learn anything if given the chance but I didn't have access to information on the outside. All I could do was watch TV and see all the new technology coming out. Even vehicles changed dramatically. In my opinion, not for the better either. They are made mostly of plastic now and run by computers and sensors. They have a computer screen in the dashboards now. If looking at a computer screen while driving isn't a distraction, nothing is. The car companies and the lawmakers are always saying their goal is to try to make America a safer place. Yet, a computer screen is put in the dashboards of vehicles. That's just crazy! The computers in cars can do so many things. A person can look at that screen and not the road very easily and crash and kill someone or themselves. There are twenty-five times more gadgets in cars now than there used to be when I was growing up. The more the car companies put in vehicles, the more it gives the driver a chance to look away from the road. The lawmakers even came up with a distracted driving law, yet, they didn't make a law telling the car companies to stop putting so much in the vehicles. It doesn't make any sense to me to have a vehicle with so many gadgets and a law saying if you take your eyes off the road and your hands off the wheel to mess with those gadgets, you are breaking the law. If a cop sees you looking up and down, he will stop you. You tell him, "I'm sorry officer, I was watching my GPS. I really don't know where I'm going. Is that illegal? After all, it's a feature of my car and on a TV screen in my dashboard". How can you be ticketed for that?

ANGEL IN DISGUISE

I'm going to find me a woman that says I'm the one,
she won't condemn me for what I've done.
She'll be my Angel, my lover and my best friend,
and I'll never have a broken heart again.
I know she'll be loyal, loving, sexy but tough,
and what I can give her will always be enough.
She'll show me that her love for me is real,
by how she treats me and how she makes me feel.
In my eyes, she's the sweetest woman that could be,
she says her world revolves around me.
I'll thank God for this woman's love every day,
it would have to be Him that sent her my way.
He knows I've spent all these lonely years in prayer,
and I know there's a woman for me out there.
I know this woman sounds too good to be true,
but do you think this woman could be you?
Could you love a man like me and be loyal?
If you could you're the one I'm looking to spoil.
Not with diamonds and gold or even a fancy ride,
but with love and affection that I'll never hide.
Every day I'll kiss you and look you in your eyes,
and I would believe you're my Angel in disguise.
You're the closest thing to Heaven that I'll ever see,
and I thank God that you believe in me.

ANYTHING GOES

Common sense? These guys don't have a shred,
Or even a half a brain in their head.
They walk around acting like tough guys,
talking bullshit and spreading lies.

Most of them never graduated from high school,
and never obeyed any kind of rule.
They act like prison is just a game,
when they're free they'll do the same.

Every chance they get in here they smoke,
and treat everything as if it's a joke.
When it comes to getting into a fight,
they get all their friends to unite.

I haven't gotten into one fight that was fair,
a fair fight in prison is very rare.
Most guys hang with their own crew,
and their crew will beat the shit out of you.

All of my life I've fought a fair fight,
two or more on one isn't right.
When you're in prison though anything goes,
it's a fact that everyone knows.

Cadillac

I'm living in this world all alone,
And I feel like I'm on my own.
Growing up when I was a child,
my mom always said that I was wild.
She would gently take my hand,
and try to make me understand.
A few times when I got into a fight,
she'd tell me that it's not right.
But Mom and Dad made me strong,
enough to admit when I am wrong.
I should have listened and learned,
And not get busted and burned.
Now I feel the power of God's plan,
to make me a better man.
So, I won't see a downright disgrace,
looking in the mirror at my face.
Sure, I've lost everything I ever had,
and for years I was very sad.
There's nothing left from my old life now,
but I don't want it back anyhow.
I'll keep my eye on the road ahead,
and I'll find happiness instead.
Life is short and I'm not coming back,
I want love and a Cadillac.

BACK WHERE I BELONG

Am I a foolish man in love trying to hang on,
or is her love for me really gone?
From this prison cell, it's impossible to see,
I'm sure she has a man and it's not me.

She only contacts me now when she wants to,
it used to be an everyday thing she'd do.
I'll stop being foolish and see how that feels,
I'll come home and hit the road on two wheels.

It will help my heart by hitting the road,
and all my troubles It will unload.
Going fast with the wind in my face soothes me,
and right now, that's where I want to be.

I think about that often just to take my mind away,
then I know everything will be okay.
Some things about me were never wrong,
on the Harley is back where I belong.

Riding my bike is the very best feeling,
especially with a heart that's healing.
When you see me, you'll know I'm in the right place,
I'll be washing the bugs off my face.

BE YOURSELF

We are not perfect and we don't try to pretend,
and my love for you will never end.
Since you were born I've loved you unconditionally,
that will never change between you and me.

But I've got to say, and daddy doesn't tell you lies,
you are so perfect in my eyes.
You don't have to be like others or follow anyone,
just be yourself and have some fun.

You don't have to be a popular kid in school,
you don't have to go around acting cool.
Those kids might think they have a lot of friends,
but they are on their own when the good time ends.

Go through life and be proud of who you are,
you'll end up being a lot happier by far.
People will see the goodness and honesty in you,
be loving and caring in everything you do.

Don't try to be like anyone else out there,
be yourself and you'll attract people that care.
Stay away from the ones that think they're better than you,
they'll never be better than you no matter what they do.

I love you

DO IT OVER AGAIN

I'll find a woman who knows what love means,
she'll be the one in all my dreams.
We'll spend time in the RV seeing the sights,
and making love on moonlit nights.

She'll trust me as we travel the United States,
keeping her safe from the things she hates.
She can act young, wild and crazy with me,
I'll love her no matter how she wants to be.

I'll give her all the things money can't buy,
and I'll never do anything to make her cry.
Unless they're happy tears coming out of her eyes,
then I'll hold her and kiss her as she cries.

It's love and affection I'll always send her,
in her heart, she knows I'm not a pretender.
We can stay in one place as long as she wants to,
being with her is the only thing I want to do.

We'll always make love till our strength is gone.
if we feel like it, we'll get up and move on.
But when the morning light comes streaming in,
I think we'll get up and do it over again.

BODYGUARD

You can take more than you think you can take,
when it comes to pain and heartache.
When it comes your way, you're never really ready.
all you can do is stand strong and be steady.

Heartache is a pain that everybody knows,
because it's just the way life goes.
You were in a relationship that was abusive,
I wish that you could have been more elusive.

You couldn't get away and he hurt you bad,
I couldn't protect you, but I wish I had.
You lived a life nobody should have to live through,
it will never happen again because I'll be with you.

I couldn't be there and I'm full of sorrow,
I wish I was coming home to you tomorrow.
Someday, I will be walking through that gate,
Everyday it gets harder to wait.

There will come a day you'll be in my arms,
and you will be happy and safe from harm.
For someone to hurt you again it will be hard,
because I'm going to be your bodyguard.

BULLIES

Do something for your dad every day at school,
make not being a bully your number one rule.
Don't get me wrong, I know you're not a bully now,
I just don't want you getting mixed up in it somehow.

You're like me, you don't want to see anyone get hurt,
or being picked on and knocked in the dirt.
I know you'll do your best to never hurt anyone,
it's just something I want to remind you about son.

Sometimes we don't think when we say things,
and what we say sometimes stings.
You may not even know that kid was abused,
and every day he lives with feeling used.

So just be careful and aware of things you say,
try to say nothing but nice things every day.
Because hurting someone's feelings is no fun,
and I know you wouldn't like it if you did son.

If you ever see someone being bullied in school,
don't be afraid to stop that fool.
Bullies will only pick on someone they can beat,
and with you I do know they'll beat feet.
Love, Dad

BURNED

I went to bed last night angry,
and in a way, it scared me.
She told me she doesn't love me anymore,
I'm not the man she's looking for.

But I know I haven't done anything wrong,
And she told me she loves me for so long.
I know I'm in prison and I'm not there,
But she said she would always care.

She made me love her as much as I can,
and then she found another man.
Then dumped me in the blink of an eye,
but there's no more tears, I can't cry.

Because I've been hurt so many times before,
I don't think I can break down anymore.
I'm going to the shower and take off my shoes,
I'm going to jump in and wash away my blues.

I'm still looking to be loved for real,
I need a woman again to make me feel.
Love shouldn't have caused me so much pain,
I've been burned too many times by its flame.

COME BACK TO ME

I woke up this morning and realized what I've done,
I made her mad enough to run.
If you see the most beautiful girl you've ever seen,
please tell her the things I said, I didn't mean.

Tell her I'm a damned fool and I lost my head,
and I hate myself for the stupid things I said.
Tell her that I love her and I'm sorry she's crying,
but without her in my life I am dying.

I'm praying she comes back to me and comes back fast,
because I don't know how much longer I can last.
I was so blind yesterday that I couldn't see,
and I let my whole world slip away from me.

I can't function at all now, I'm not lying,
I can't get out of this bed because I can't stop crying.
I can't let anyone see me so I can't work like this,
I need to be in your arms for your tender kiss.

Please forgive me and I'll make it all up to you,
I love you and I'll do whatever I have to do.
And baby, I will never again talk to you that way,
just please come back to me today?

DADDY'S LITTLE GIRL

You are so beautiful just the way you are,
you are brighter than the northern star.
You don't have to look like a model on the runway,
or be the most popular girl of the day.

You don't have to be the one with the most friends,
the ones that are covered in make-up and pretends.
You don't have to have the most expensive clothes,
or be the girl that everyone knows.

You don't have to worry about what they think of you,
just be who you are and do what you want to do.
You are kind, loving, caring and you have a big heart,
you don't have to follow anyone because you are smart.

I'm sorry I'm not out there now with you,
but I'll always be there when this sentence is through.
Right now, I'm paying for the mistake I made in the past,
I learned a hard lesson but I learned it fast.

Every day I've been away you've been on my mind,
you are the best daughter, you are one of a kind.
No matter how old you are or where you are in the world,
you will always be your daddy's little girl.
I love you, Dad

DIVORCE

Look what you've done to my head,
when you went to another man's bed.
Why didn't you tell me you didn't want me?
It would have hurt, but I'd let you be.

Do you love him as much as I love you?
Or is he just someone you wanted to do?
I know you thought I would never find out,
I've been told you've been out and about.

I'm not some loser that you can treat this way,
I gave you everything day after day.
I was the one who bought you everything you want,
all those things that you loved to flaunt.

I bought you the most beautiful diamond ring,
you're acting like it don't mean a thing.
While I'm in prison and still loving you,
you're doing whoever you want to do.

You hurt me and I want to call you a name,
what you turned into is a shame.
You managed to tear my heart out with force,
now please just give me a divorce?

EVERY NIGHT

At one time, I didn't think I'd leave this cell alive,
at that time, I didn't have any drive.
I lost everything that I had to live for,
everyone else walked out, you walked in my door.

You won't have to worry about me making you hurt,
you'll never smell another woman on my shirt.
You'll never have to worry about what I'd do,
no woman in the world comes close to you.

I know a hundred ways I can make you smile,
let me touch you anyplace I want for a while.
I would drive you out of your head with the things I said,
as we made love in our big beautiful bed.

I love the way you move when you're under me,
I never want to stop, this is the way it's meant to be.
Then you lay next to me and everything feels so right,
the clock ticks away as we do it all night.

You look so damned good laying there satisfied,
you couldn't get rid of me now if you tried.
As the sun slowly shines in through the window,
and you tell me that's how every night will go.

EXPERIENCES I'VE HAD

Have you ever had days where you were so beat,
that it was hard to drag your ass to your feet?
You feel like nothing is going your way,
and there's nothing to get out of bed for today.

I opened my eyes this morning and I hate what I see,
loud and ignorant assholes staring back at me.
In this one big room, we are packed liked sardines,
they should have respect but they don't know what it means.

They lock us up and give us nothing to do,
how do they expect us to make it through?
I know from experience that by keeping a man still,
he'll fill up with hatred and rage against his will.

We are not wild animals that you keep locked down,
all of a sudden set us free to go back to town.
Why lock us up if we're not a threat to society,
and treat us like an animal like they did me?

The only thing they taught me was how to hate,
they give you plenty of reasons behind this gate.
If you can leave prison without feeling mad,
then you haven't had the experiences I had.

FAITH IN YOU

Don't get too frustrated and just quit,
your very next try you just might hit.
You can do anything you put your mind to,
and I have a ton of faith in you.

Never quit anything after you start,
put everything into it, even your heart.
You'll have days where nothing will go right,
just stop there and sleep on it one night.

Everything will look different the next day,
you won't believe how easy you found the way.
Some things will feel like an uphill climb,
but you can do it if you give it time.

Nothing comes easy and you might make mistakes,
but keep with it no matter what it takes.
As you get older and your life goes on,
you'll find most of your frustrations gone.

I've watched you and I've seen how hard you tried,
you're doing good and filled your dad with pride.
Nothing can stop you from doing whatever you want to,
you have the brains and my faith is in you.
I Love You, Dad

FAMILY

I was the happiest guy in the world when I became a dad,
when I was taken away, I was incredibly sad.
For fourteen years now, I've left my children out there alone,
two of them now have children of their own.

It hurts like hell because my grandkids don't know me,
if I was there, I know they would love grampy.
When I finally meet them, I've got a lot to make up for.
I want to take them camping, four wheeling and much more.

Also, I hope it's not too late for me to be a good dad,
my kids are all grown up now, but that's not bad.
As a family, we can go horseback riding and go on hikes,
and I want to teach my grandkids to ride bikes.

Yes, motorcycles are what I'm talking about now,
I think I can talk their parents into it somehow.
I think my own kids knew how this was going to be,
having a motorcycle man for a dad like me.

I also think it might be one of their worst fears,
I know how I worried about them for years.
I just want to be a family in so many ways,
and be together for the rest of my days.

FORGET ABOUT YOU

Just so I can get over you,
there's no telling what I might do.
With you, love had a hold on me,
but that was the way it used to be.

I watched your back go out the door,
and I knew there's no holding you anymore.
Everything I did I did just for you,
now I'll do anything I want to do.

I might go out and close down the bars,
or go out and buy some nice cars.
That Harley you didn't want me to buy,
is now mine in the blink of an eye.

That good-looking brunette that I like,
will feel good on the back of my bike.
And if she's the girl I want her to be,
I'm going to take her home with me.

I'm gone and I'll never look back your way,
or listen to anything you have to say.
I'm living this life just for me now,
I'm going to forget about you somehow.

FORGET ABOUT YOU (2)

She's beautiful but she was crying when I met her today,
I found out she was abused in a bad way.
She was faithful and loved you for so many years,
you're the one that's caused all her tears.

She's been walked on, pushed around and lied to,
and that's not all you put her through.
I can't get through to her but I've got to consider,
all the things you put her through that made her bitter.

I understand why she put up her walls today,
I can't condemn her, you turned her that way.
But if I stopped loving her, it would be a crime,
I'm going to give her my love and give her time.

I don't blame her for not giving me her heart now,
I love her so much, I'm going to win it somehow.
I'll prove to her that her heart is safe with me,
and show her how the rest of her life will be.

I will be the man she trusts enough to give her heart to,
I will never let her get hurt again or even feel blue.
Her eyes will shine and she will look brand new,
She will laugh and love again and forget about you.

FRIENDS OR ENEMIES?

I've never looked for trouble but I never ran,
I'll stand up to any kind of man.
Just like them, I'm made of flesh, blood and bone,
and all I want is to be left alone.

I'm afraid I've lost a lot of my compassion,
I don't put up with bullshit now in any fashion.
These past fourteen years have been hard on me,
but I've paid for my mistakes as you can see.

Now I want to live the life of a simple man,
and people better leave me alone so I can.
I used to fight when I was forced to before,
mess with me now and it will be so much more.

I'll treat you the way I want you to treat me,
I'll never say a word to you disrespectfully.
But if all you want with me is to start trouble,
I'm going to return it to you double.

You'll see how prison has made me a different man,
one who deals with problems any way he can.
Don't bring trouble to me when I get out there,
or you're going to see how much I don't care.

I don't want to be around anymore negativity,
I just want to live in peace and harmony.
If you want to be part of my life as friends,
we'll be friends until my life ends.

If for some reason, you think I'm your enemy
I'll stay away from you, you stay away from me.
There's been too much shit in my life already,
I'm going take things slow and steady.

I think about what my life will be like out of prison. For so many years, nobody on the outside has contacted me. I don't want a bunch of people contacting me when I've free. If I'm not worthy enough to them when I'm in prison, I don't want them to mess with me when I'm out of prison. I've been through enough! I just want to be a simple man. I want to live my life with peace and happiness. I want to find one woman to be with and travel with. There are so many beautiful sights to see in America. I want to buy an RV and travel as much as I can. I'll haul a trailer behind it with my Harley in it. That's all I need in my life today. No more drama or strife. Life is very short. I've wasted enough years.

•••••••••••

As I sit alone writing this book and reliving these incidences and memories, my life is going the way I planned. I bought a small but nice RV. I have a good job but I'm laid off for the winter so I can write this book. I have a nice Harley and a Cadillac and a beautiful truck. I'm living in my camper so life is very simple for me. I'm do much happier now than I have been for all those lonely depressing years I spent in prison. I'll never go back. I'd rather die than go back to that life. I'm tired of living with the types of people I had to live with. If you think for one minute that all the races in America get along, think again.

FROM THE START

Time waits for no one and it goes by fast.
Enjoy your youth because it won't last.
Don't take anyone for granted if you can.
Be a kind, caring, honest and loving man.

Show your love no matter what it takes.
It hurts you in the end to make mistakes.
You have to live with sorrow, shame and regret
and sometimes it's as bad as it can get.

You have to live with the hearts you've broken.
You'll regret the harsh words that you've spoken.
You'll feel sorry for the loved ones you've hurt.
You're alone now and feeling like dirt.

For the lies you've told, you live in shame
and you have only yourself to blame.
While you're young, live your life doing right,
don't be put behind bars for even one night.

I hope you listen and I've got you sold.
You don't want to be in prison growing old.
While you're still young follow your heart
and be a good man right from the start.

GHOST

I live with more than just one ghost
but one of them haunts me the most.
This one will never leave my memory.
I wish I did things differently.

I know this ghost, I'll never outrun
because I can't undo the things I've done.
I'll never get used to her haunting me.
the things I've done wrong, she shows me.

I try to remember all the things I've done wrong.
My head aches because the list is so long.
I know she haunts me because I hurt her.
When she starts to cry, she disappears in a blur.

She says she's going to make me see the light.
She's going to haunt me until I get it right.
I see her in the shadows even in the day
but she's slowly making me find my way.

I think I'm making her understand, I hope
that I wouldn't have done it if I wasn't on dope.
If I wasn't on drugs right from the start,
I never would have broken her heart.

HE WILL SEE

I heard it through a friend that you're messing around,
and my heart fell to the ground.
I hope you know this is not how it has to be,
just tell me the truth and set me free.

I don't want you to tell me any of your lies,
while looking at him with your bedroom eyes.
You are always talking to me and acting nonchalant,
when all this time he's what you want.

Knowing what I do now, I don't want you to remain,
you've already caused enough heartache and pain.
No matter how much it hurts I'll let you go,
I hope he gives you what you want though.

He better might you away to the sunshine land,
and never let go of your hand.
He might listen to everything you have to say,
and never leave you alone for even a day.

Because I know what happens when you're left alone,
you quickly find a lover on your own.
Just like you couldn't be honest with me,
if he leaves you alone, he will see!

HIS LOVING HANDS

With these words, I can still talk to you,
long after my life is through.
Everyone on earth is born just to die,
and for me I don't want you to cry.
I'm here now with my mom and dad,
and other relatives I didn't know I had.
There's more to it than just life on earth.
it's what you do with it after your birth.
Try to do your best to follow God's way,
because He will watch over you every day.
You're not perfect, you'll always be a sinner,
but that don't mean you can't be a winner.
I'm a lawbreaker and a sinner, look at me,
God opened my eyes so I could see.
In a small, cold prison cell I was sent,
I read the Bible and learned to repent.
I felt His presence with me in there,
through His word, I learned He does care.
So, I left my life in His loving hands,
because I know He understands.

....

Reading the bible while I was in prison helped me a lot. IF you look at the people with Jesus in their lives and compare them to the people without Jesus you will see that the ones with Jesus are a lot happier and live better lives. I know a lot of people don't believe in God and they argue about things in the Bible. But, ninety nine percent of those people have never read the Bible. They know parts of it and they don't like it. The Bible was not written to fit their lifestyle. It was written to guide you and tell you what lifestyle is best to live.

HOLD MY HAND

I wasn't easy to love and harder to hold,
but things have changed since I've gotten old.
I'm looking for a love now that will last,
I'll take things real slow, nothing fast.
I've lived in the fast lane most of my life,
that's why I couldn't keep a wife.
Nobody could have loved me and been justified,
I couldn't be good no matter how hard I tried.
I was never there when they needed me,
I was being the biggest fool I could be.
I never took anything in life seriously before,
I've paid dearly for it all that's for sure.
After fourteen years alone in a cold prison cell,
I've learned my lesson very well.
Add on all the times I've gotten into fights,
and the countless long sleepless nights.
It's a recipe that can change any kind of man,
to take life as seriously as he can.
Now I'm an easy guy to love and understand,
you'll see if you love me and hold my hand.

....

I've had so many years by myself to look back at my life and think about it. I realize now that I was a hard man to love. I took off on my motorcycle for as long as I wanted at the drop of a hat. I wasn't thinking of others. I thought because I bought the one's I loved everything that they wanted, I was a good man, a good father and a good husband. I realize now that it isn't material things that show love, it's time. If you love someone you will spend as much time as you can with them.

HOME

I'm heading home but I've got a long way to go,
where I'm going to live, I don't know.
I don't have a home of my own anymore,
but I'm going to make one that's for sure.

I'm going to say a little prayer that I'll be okay,
and that God helps me find a way.
When I say home now, all I mean is Maine,
away from this heartache and pain.

They say home is where you hang your hat,
not for me, my home will be more than that.
In all kinds of weather my home will be warm,
Strong enough to stand up to any storm.

There will be a woman sharing the home with me,
I'm going to make her as happy as can be.
This home I have may very well be on wheels,
but inside she'll know how true love feels.

She'll be able to feel the love in the air,
it feels better than any mansion out there.
Because inside my home the love will be real,
and this is how a real home should feel.

I BELONG TO YOU

One time with you is not enough,
living without you is too tough.
My heart is beating just for you,
it knows what you can do.

The love that you have shown,
is the best I've ever known.
Your love is something new,
to make me feel the way you do.

You'll have me with your first kiss,
your lips are what I'll truly miss.
I open my eyes and I see your face,
and I feel your sensual grace.

You are so beautiful to me,
you are the one I want to see.
You're everything I prayed for,
and I will never want more.

Please believe me when I say,
I want you in every way.
God knows you belong with me too,
just like I belong to you.

I CAN SHOW YOU

Shut all the shades and lock the door.
Get into the bedroom and I'll show you what for.
The bad weather is here, let's stay in bed.
I'll show you what's going through my head.

Shut out the lights and turn off the phone.
We'll pretend that there's nobody home.
I love you baby and I'm going to give you proof.
We'll make love listening to the rain on the roof.

I'll show you why this is my favorite room
and you won't be leaving until it's after noon.
Over and over I'll see the smile on your face.
You love it when my face invades your space.

And I love it when you don't want me to let go,
so, after the first time I take it real slow.
I start at your toes and end up at your head
and we get so hot we rock the bed.

We smile at each other as we lay nose to nose.
This is the way I hope every day goes.
It's times like this that I want to get back to,
So, I can show you how much I love you.

I CAN'T GET YOU OUT OF MY HEAD

You can't help how you feel about me,
but it's not the way I wanted it to be.
I want you to love me so bad it hurt you,
So, you told me you found someone new.

I know you didn't want to hurt me that way,
but you weren't happy and couldn't stay.
When you look at him you have fire in your eyes,
I know you love him and I hope he tries.

Now, I have to find a way to live without you,
it most likely will be the last thing I ever do.
I know I shouldn't tell you, but I confess,
I'll probably never get over this emptiness.

Losing you hurt me deep down to my soul,
and inside my big chest is one hell of a hole.
With nothing there I feel like I'm rotting to the core,
and it's all because you don't love me anymore.

But I will always cherish the good time memories,
those are the ones that bring me to my knees.
I'll be thinking about you when I'm on my death bed,
because I can't get you out of my head.

I DON'T WANT YOU ANYMORE

I'm wondering if you're worth fighting for,
you don't even contact me anymore.
What! Are you just trying to test me?
You want to see if I let you go easily?

When you tell me you're going to move on,
I take it your love for me is gone.
I'm not the type of guy to beg you though,
so, I'll accept it and let you go.

I'm in prison so what else can I do?
I don't have anyone else to move on to.
Now that you're gone, I'm completely alone,
a1nd I'll have to finish this on my own.

I don't have anyone else depending on me,
and maybe this is how it's meant to be.
Now I don't have to worry about anyone out there,
you're with someone new and I don't care.

You know I am here and can't be with anyone,
I'm not coming back after you have your fun.
When I'm free I won't be knocking on your door,
because I sure as hell don't want you anymore!

I HOPE

I don't know what to think anymore,
there's been a lot of changes in the world, that's for sure.
It's a world I don't know too much about,
I've got so much to learn when I get out.

I've adapted to living behind a prison wall,
where I can't see the outside world at all.
I've become really good at prison living,
that's full of hate and unforgiving.

I don't expect compassion or loyalty,
and they don't get any from me.
Most of these prisoners are selfish pricks,
to get what they want they use tricks.

I'm accustomed to none of these guys caring,
keep to myself and not sharing.
I don't have a job or a lot of responsibility,
most decisions are made for me.

I've been living like this now for so many years,
learning the ways of the world is one of my fears.
There are so many changes I don't know if I can cope,
I'll find a good life for me, I hope!

I KNOW

It's hard when someone you love says goodbye,
You do your best not to cry.
I put on an air like I'm real tough,
I hold it inside and it's real rough.
I pretend I've got a heart of stone,
when it's killing me to be alone.
She says she loves me but she's moving on,
then I know her love for me is gone.
She's going to make herself happy somehow,
I know she wants someone else now.
When she said, "I've got to find me",
I know she just wants to be free.
She let me down as easily as she can,
I know it was for another man.
Or she'd feel like she was cheating on me,
I know a cheater she'd never be.
She's a good woman with a very big heart,
for too many years we've been apart.
And now some other guy has come along,
now she's decided I'm all wrong.

In this poem I'm not talking about the wife I had when I was arrested and went to prison. By now, you know what she did to me. I'm talking about another woman and if she ever reads this, she will know who she is. My head was all over the place in prison. I'm sure you see that now in my poems. You cannot imagine how hard it is to kill so much time without losing your mind. When the judge said "I'm sentencing you to the federal prison for two hundred and fifty-two months my heart sank to my knees. I honestly thought my life was over.

I LOVE YOU

I know you don't understand why daddy got taken away,
so, I'm going to try to explain it to you this way.
There are consequences from the choices that we make,
and daddy made a choice that was a mistake.

I hope you don't think it had something to do with you,
I would never hurt you intentionally by the things I do.
I wasn't thinking straight and I committed a crime,
and to pay for it I have to do this prison time.

Please believe this for all you're worth,
I have loved you with all my heart since your birth.
While locked away in prison I'm straightening out my life,
when I come home there will be happiness and no strife.

We'll always be together then and it will be so nice,
your daddy will not make the same mistake twice.
I want you to know I love you with all my heart,
and this will be the last time we are apart.

Nowhere in the world could there ever be,
anyone who loves you more than me.
You're the best gift I've ever had.
I'm so proud to be your dad.
I love you

I SHOULD HAVE KNOWN

Sometimes I don't know where I'm going,
without the love that you were showing.
But I sure know where I've been,
I wish you would do it again.

I should have known you'd walk away,
and I would never be okay.
I never knew how far I let myself go,
getting back up will be slow.

I should have known you'd break my heart,
for too long we've been apart.
I didn't want us to end this way,
but I saw you with him today.

I should have known I'd get burned,
I should have already learned.
I saw today what I didn't know,
how your love can come and go.

You're not mine and it's plain to see,
why were you even messing with me?
I should have known you don't care about anyone,
as long as you are having your fun.

....

I've gotten letters from women while I was in prison and because I was starving for love, I believed everything they told me. I was hoping and praying to get out to a woman that loved me. I wanted it so bad that I would have done anything and believed anything. I felt so lost and alone for so many years. It wasn't long before I realized that I was just someone to pass the time writing to until they found another man. I know it was foolish of me but I kept trying. I gave my heart too easily back then and nothing worked out. I look back on it now and feel so foolish.

Reading as many poems as I do right now all at once, I realize it makes me sound like a desperate fool. Keep in mind, these poems were not written back to back in a day. I would write about six a day on a good day. I also wrote books, worked in the craft room on copper plaques, painting, and on things made out of potato chip bags. I would do anything to stay busy. When I let myself be idle, I'd think about how much time I had and get really depressed. You have heard people say, "Take one day at a time". Well, that's exactly what I had to do because my future didn't look too bright. I didn't know if I would be alive to see the streets again.

I WILL PLAY

I want a woman to call my own,
one who doesn't want to be alone.
A woman who's sensual and has charms,
and wants to be held in my strong arms.

She will always have a hand to hold,
and we'll be together as we grow old.
Across the lake, we'll watch the sunset,
I'll light a fire but I'm not done yet.

I can tell how she looks as the fire lights,
that it's going to be one of those nights.
She whispers to me and tells me what to do,
I'll do anything she wants me to.

I'll tell her, "Make the call baby, I don't care,
I will do that to you anywhere.
Oh! Right underneath the Milky Way,
you watch the stars and I will play."

"Yes, baby I know I'm being bad,
but it will be the best time you ever had.
You know that was just what I wanted to do,
to show you how much I love you."

I'D STILL WISH YOU WELL

You told me it was over between you and I,
and we're friends so you didn't say good-bye.
You still emailed me every couple of days or so,
and I enjoyed that, just so you know.

You said you're going to move forward with your life,
being with me would cause you too much strife.
You said that you couldn't give me all your time,
not helping others to you would be a crime.

I sadly accepted everything that you have said,
but I can't get you out of my head.
I feel like there's something else you're not telling me,
I'm going find out if there is when I'm free.

Because everything always comes out in the end,
why wouldn't you tell me if I'm your friend?
I haven't heard a thing from you in over a week,
I called you one night just so we could speak.

You didn't answer your phone when you always did before,
maybe you don't stay home every night anymore?
It's none of my business and you can tell me to go to hell,
I'll understand completely and I'll still wish you well.

But if you have someone else, just say good-bye,
I hope he loves you and gives it an honest try.
I never want to see you deceived or hurt anymore,
you deserve happiness that's for sure.

. . . .

This is one of the poems I wrote because of one of the women that said she loved me and would wait for me. She all of a sudden, stopped all contact with me and never gave me an explanation. It wasn't the first time this has happened to me. I got pretty tired of it happening and I stopped letting women into my life. I told myself that I'd get one when I get out of prison. One I can talk to face to face. I didn't realize how it was in society today. Everyone meets on the internet. I was in for a rude awakening when I got out. I couldn't believe how people were interacting with each other in the world today. Snap chat, email, texting, Facebook and shit like that. Face to face meetings come much later. I've had women send me naked pictures before I even met them. The world is a crazy place now. It sure has changed. I'm old school and not happy with these changes. I'm not mad at the women that wrote to me. I'm sure they meant everything they said at the time. Someone else comes along that's not locked up and they are lonely. That guy can give them what I can't. They can be there with them to love and to hold while all I am is an email, a letter and at best, a phone call. I know how it feels to be lonely and I don't blame them for finding someone. I just wish they'd be honest and tell me. I know they probably didn't want to hurt me. I certainly can understand that. I don't want to hurt anyone either. If you're reading this book and I've hurt you, please know that I am sorry. It was not my intention. Nobody knows what the future will hold. You meet someone and the feeling is there but it doesn't work out. That's why we date. At least that's the way it is supposed to be. Nobody can make someone feel something that they don't. I can't make someone love me just because I love them. The only way I could get these feelings out in prison without anyone seeing how I was feeling was write poems about it. That's my way of coping and eventually moving on. I never forgot about anyone but the feelings I had weren't there anymore. I'll always remember and have regrets over some. I'll move on though until I find what I'm looking for and then I'll make sure she knows that she's the one. I won't take anything for granted anymore. I'll never make that same mistake again.

I'LL ALWAYS REMAIN

I know someday, somebody is going to see inside,
I'll have to fess up, I can't run and hide.
I could swear you off forever, for all I'm worth,
or I could give you every day I have left on earth.

I've been hiding all my feelings since my time began,
If you've been in prison, you understand.
With every beat of my heart I need you to be with me,
my heart knows this is how it's meant to be.

I could never stop loving you or leave you behind,
as long as I'm breathing you are on my mind.
If you have harder times than you can go through,
I will be by your side helping you.

If the weight on you is too much for you to bear,
put it on my shoulders, I'll always be there.
If there's a mountain too big for you to climb,
I'll be there giving you a boost every time.

I'll be there on the days the sun doesn't shine,
to hold you in these two strong arms of mine.
Nobody can steal me away, I'll always remain,
and I will gladly take all your pain.

Sunshine

Nothing ever goes right for me it seems,
all I have now, are broken dreams.
I'm waiting for the good Lord to take me away,
that's how bad things are for me today.

I'm trying hard not to lose my mind,
I'm ready to leave all this shit behind.
I might not make it through the night,
I'll be lucky to see morning light.

Beat up again and another broken bone,
once again in a tiny, cold cell alone.
I'm mad as hell and I'm not going to quit,
even though no one gives a shit.

I lay down on the hard, dirty bunk and pray,
and wonder how long they'll make me stay.
They catch me talking to someone they can't see,
that conversation was between God and me.

He doesn't want me to die this season,
he's keeping me around some more for a reason.
He told me He knows I'm a good man,
and He's keeping me around as long as he can.

I broke down and asked Him why,
he said I was going to make it if I try.
He filled me with the faith that I'll keep,
and then I drifted off to sleep.

When I woke I knew I would never be alone,
but I have to figure this out on my own.
I was in that hole for the next sixty days,
and in that time, I learned His ways.

I've spoken to God on many nights,
Alone in the hole because of fights.
He's my companion in that cold cell,
Without him, I wouldn't do very well.

Every morning the bugle rang at five,

Because of God, I was still alive.
I prayed sometimes to make it end,
But a message He would send.

He let me know it wasn't my turn,
and in a voice that was stern.
It was then that I knew I'll be fine,
And I was going to see the sunshine.

I'LL NEVER LIE TO YOU

Don't believe everything that you've heard,
I've lost everything except my word.
Ask me anything that you want to,
and I promise I'll never lie to you.

I've heard hundreds of rumors involving me,
I'm a prisoner, they should let it be.
I don't want any secrets from you,
I'll tell you everything if you want me to.

Baby, I just want to feel the wind on my hair,
I'll know where I'm going when I get there.
I'm going to come home to you on two wheels,
and show you how true love feels.

We'll hit the road with the sun in our eyes,
and we'll forget about all the damned lies.
When we get where we're going there will be no fears,
I'll love you for the rest of my years.

You'll have my heart in the palm of your hand,
and nothing about me you won't understand.
You'll be glad you picked me to be your man,
nobody can love you the way I can.

I'M CONFUSED

There is so many things I've had to endure,
it's okay, I think you're my cure.
I am torn apart and I have no control,
if you want to you can make me whole.

I am like an eagle with a broken wing,
and my heart is hanging by a string.
I was wondering what was left to live for,
I don't know if I want to anymore.

I'm at the end of my rope and feeling small,
and so sick and tired of it all.
I needed a reason to continue this fight,
then I had a dream of you last night.

I woke up praying that my dream was true,
because I'd love to live my life with you.
But you haven't told me you felt the same way,
I'm hoping that you will one day.

There was a time that I was sure I could have you,
but now I'm confused at what I should do.
Should I come home and try to get you into my bed,
or move on and get you out of my head?

I'M GONNA MISS YOU

It's a shame after waiting for so long,
to just give up and walk away.
I never thought it would go so wrong,
we were so close yet so far away.
There's something that I want you to know,
even if I never get to see you.
I love you so much I'll sadly let you go,
find happiness is what you need to do.
I always thought it could be with me,
but you want to do so much more.
That's you and the way you'll always be,
I'd want you all to myself for sure.
You are right to break it off now,
never change the person that you are.
You wouldn't be happy with me anyhow,
I wouldn't let you go too far.
I am definitely the jealous kind,
I'd always want you close to me.
Too far away and I'd go out of my mind,
but I love you so I'll let you be.
In my heart, I knew this day was near
and I'd be helpless to stop you.
There's nothing I could do from here,
so, my heart is breaking in two.

I'M NOT YOU!

I am in a federal prison but we still met,
through her kind words that I'll never forget.
But she's the woman that was in love with you,
and she was pushed around, cheated on and lied to.
She never treated her love for you as a game,
and it's too bad you didn't do the same.
She showed you she loved you with all her heart,
and all you did was tear it apart.
She had a lifetime of love to give you,
and look at all the shit you put her through.
She stayed and listened to every one of your alibis,
while you looked at her through lying eyes.
Now I'm trying once again to get her to live,
because I have a lifetime of love to give.
But she thinks she's seen and heard it all,
and she's built herself a strong wall.
And now I don't think she believes a word I say,
because of how you treated her that way.
I'm doing the best to get her to love me,
because you abused her, she won't let it be.
I don't know if I'm enough to restore her trust
but for her to love me it's a must.
She'd have a hard time loving me even if I can,
all I have to offer her is me as a man.

I'M OKAY

I write about sorrow, shame, pain and heartache,
and about the things I can't take.
I often mention all the loved ones dying,
and about all the times I was crying.

I write a lot of things about my prison life,
and all too often about losing my wife.
Things I think about when they turn out the lights,
and how much I hurt on sleepless nights.

I write about making too many mistakes,
making up for them no matter what it takes.
Being a man admitting when I'm wrong,
apologizing for being in prison so long.

I'm always writing things about growing old,
living in small cells that are dirty and cold.
And having to obey so many stupid rules,
living with so many ignorant fools.

But what I haven't written about is me physically,
because there are so many things wrong with me.
I don't want anyone to worry about me that way,
as long as I'm breathing, I'm okay.

I'M OUT OF MY HEAD

I really hate to let this moment go,
So, I hold you tight and kiss you slow.
I want to make love but make it last,
I have so much desire I want to go fast.

Because nobody has ever made me feel like this,
you had me from the very first kiss.
I love you and always want you to stay,
I want forever to feel this same way.

As we kiss, I run my fingers through your hair,
I have so much love I want to share.
My mind is racing but my body's in the lead,
as you are giving me everything I need.

I try to make it last but with you I can't wait,
I'm so turned on I can't see straight.
I'm on the edge now, you must have heard my plea,
just then you gave all your love to me.

At that moment, I felt the magic of your charms,
I never want to let you out of my arms.
You've made me feel so good I'm out of my head,
and then I wake up alone in this prison bed.

I'M SCARED AS HELL

It's been so long since I've used a real metal spoon,
or been outside under the stars and moon.
Of course, weapons can be made from a fork and knife,
but those aren't needed in prison to take a life.

Fourteen years of using a metal toilet with no seat,
I can never take a shower in my bare feet.
And for fourteen years I haven't been in a car,
I don't even know what most of them are.

It will feel like Heaven just to sit in a soft seat,
and have a good meal with real meat.
I know out there I'm in for a mind-blowing change,
it will all be different and probably very strange.

Right now, I don't like most of the people I meet,
will it be the same out there on the street?
I have been living this way for so long,
I'm afraid something out there is going to go wrong.

Everywhere I go I am going to have to beware,
because my future is up in the air.
There's a lot of things I've got to figure out,
and learn what the new world is all about.

It is making me nervous now, I won't deny,
for a while it's going to be hard just to get by.
I'll be leaving this life and everything that I know,
I'll have to find my way wherever I go.

It soothes my heart to know that I'm not alone,
and won't have to figure everything out on my own.
I know I have some good people that truly care,
and I can depend on them when I get there.

....

Watching TV once in a while in prison has shown me some of the new technology that has come along after fourteen years. The vehicles out there have been changes drastically. The phone systems have gone wild. I was really nervous about getting out of prison and not knowing about any of it. I knew I had a lot to learn and I had to learn it fast. I had to get a job and take care of myself because I was literally starting out with nothing. Starting all over again is really hard, especially when you spent so much time in prison and don't know anything about the world you are being thrust into. I'm a stubborn guy. I don't want to invade anyone's space or let anyone support me. I don't want to be a charity case. I want to be able to support myself and I will do anything to do it, short of breaking the law again. I'm not letting anything put me back into the hell holes I just came from. I set goals for myself and I'll work very hard to complete those goals. I don't expect anything from anyone. I know that if I was in dire need, I have some people that I can depend on. That is a good feeling. I was afraid when my out date got closer and closer. Not knowing what to expect at my age is a scary thing. I wondered who would hire an older felon. I knew that I would have to prove myself to an employer. I wouldn't give up though. I was going after what I wanted. Here I am now, getting my second book ready for publication. I've worked hard at my job and completed my other goals and I know I will finish writing this book as fast as I can. I hope you like it.

I'M STRUGGLING

If you ever loved me, have some mercy on me,
get as far away from me as you can be.
You were the one who swept me off my feet,
only you could make my life complete.

The memories I have of you are so cute,
I'll never be able to find a substitute.
Every time I think of you it takes my breath away,
it's killing me that I'm not with you today.

Every day I struggle just to make it through,
and it's all because I'm missing you.
In this prison, I have to masquerade,
trying not to cry from the mess I made.

I'm with others while they tell a joke or two,
I fake a laugh because inside I'm blue.
I know that my smile is out of place,
because I have to force it on my face.

A lot of these guys laugh loud and hardy,
acting like every day is a party.
I can't laugh like that knowing you're gone,
I'm struggling just trying to move on.

IT WOULDN'T BE FAIR

She's stolen my heart but she's out of my league,
it's too bad because she's what I need.
She used to love me but too much time has passed,
and now I don't know how much longer I'll last.

I'm in prison and I've had a very rough time,
while she's still beautiful and in her prime.
She's everything my dream woman would be,
she's as sweet as my favorite candy.

But people would talk and at the very least,
they would call us the beauty and the beast.
I've written to her and told her that before,
but she doesn't care what people say anymore.

I can't deny that she has a piece of my heart,
but for her sake we should stay apart.
Somewhere inside me there's still a wild man,
that would love her for as long as he can.

But before much longer he wouldn't be able to anymore,
and she needs love for a long time that's for sure.
It wouldn't be fair for her to watch me die,
and I couldn't leave this world watching her cry.

JUST ME AND YOU

When you need a friend, I'll be there for you,
this prison sentence is almost through.
I'm a different man now that's for sure,
I care about true friends so much more.

I took people for granted all those years ago,
I lived my life fast when it should have been slow.
I spent money like it was going out of style,
always trying to make the wrong people smile.

I spent a lot of time with the wrong ones,
when I should have been with family having fun.
This has been the hardest lesson I've learned,
but I've learned what bridges should be burned.

I've paid dearly for making a mistake,
many lonely nights I've laid here awake.
All those nights when you felt just right,
my heart was broken just like tonight.

Soon there will be a new sun rising,
I'll be with you and finally realizing;
That I can forget about the past and start new,
a life where it's just me and you.

JUST THE WAY YOU ARE

As long as you are happy, I am glad,
you don't deserve to be sad.
Look to the future and stay on track,
be happy and never look back.
Don't be sad over what's left behind,
get it right out of your mind.
You're starting a new chapter in your life,
so, forget about all the strife.
Sure, you made mistakes along the way,
but today is a new day.
You're a lot smarter and wiser now,
I know you can make it somehow.
Stop being insecure about yourself,
put those thoughts away on a shelf.
You're a lot stronger than you think you are,
and a much better person by far.
Never think you are not good enough,
be yourself and stand tough.
Don't change just to please someone,
trying to live a lie is no fun.
Besides, they wouldn't do the same for you,
they'll always do what they want to do.
You are perfect just the way you are,
so, get your ass back in my car.

LEARN FROM MY MISTAKES

It is definitely not easy to be a mom or dad,
but it's the most incredible experience I ever had.
My whole life changed right from their birth,
and I wouldn't give them up for anything on earth.

With unconditional love you take care of your child,
while praying to God they don't turn out wild.
But as a parent there is only so much you can do,
they get it in their heads and do what they want to.

I'm not just guessing at this, I know it first-hand,
I was a wild child that refused to understand.
I know now I caused my parents a lot of heartache,
when I got hurt, their heart would break.

No matter what I did they were always there for me,
a parent will always love their child unconditionally.
The only thing I can do now is learn from my mistakes,
and be a good dad no matter what it takes.

I'm afraid that it may be too late for me,
but you can learn from my mistakes you see.
Keep your family first and your priorities straight,
and stay away from this side of a prison gate.

LET YOU GO

I know that you know I never strayed,
I never had to with the love we made.
When I stood there and said for better or worse,
I knew I would never screw up first.

When we were together from the very start,
I fell in love with you with all my heart.
Until I met you, I've never had so much fun,
when we made love, I knew you were the one.

I was going through life thinking everything was fine,
the happiest man on earth because you were mine.
Then all of a sudden, a raging storm came on,
you never said a word, you were just gone.

I went screaming for you in the cold pouring rain,
being torn apart by the searing pain.
I fell to my knees, out of breath, wanting to die,
but all I could do in the pouring rain was cry.

Now my life isn't long enough for me to take the time,
to say what I want to say to you and make it rhyme.
I love you, but those words have been said,
So, I'm just going to let you go instead.

LOVE AND AFFECTION

I'm starving for love and affection,
please point me in the right direction.
All my attempts from prison so far,
have left me with an internal scar.

Out of the blue I'll get a letter,
from a woman that makes me feel better.
But now I know I'm going to get burned,
they're hard lessons that I've learned.

They write to me because they're lonely,
it's not because I'm their one and only.
As soon as another guy catches their eye,
quick as hell they say goodbye.

They know he's a better catch anyway,
he's not in a federal prison today.
He's all set up with a place for them to live,
he can give them more than I can give.

I guarantee though he's not a better man,
and he's also getting all he can.
And all I want is love and affection,
for us to go in the right direction.

LOVE LIKE MINE

Till all the rivers in the world run dry,
you will be the only one to catch my eye.
When you look into my eyes you will see,
just how much you mean to me.

Until all the life on this earth is through,
I'll be the one needing you.
There is nothing in the world I want more,
and for you my love, I would die for.

In my eyes, everything about you is so fine,
and you won't find another love like mine.
I think you have the most beautiful smile,
I'm going to see it a lot in a little while.

I'll put a smile on your face every day,
and wild horses couldn't drag me away.
I also love the way you wear your hair,
I'll run my fingers through it when I'm there.

Everything I do I'm going to do for you,
until my life on this earth is through.
There's one thing that you'll always know,
that I will die before I let you go.

LYING EYES

You didn't think I'd see through your disguise,
but I can tell you when you lie by your eyes.
You told me you were never gonna stray,
no matter how long it took you to stay.

You said you never wanted anyone but me,
who was that man last night you went to see?
I would think by now that you would realize,
my friends out there have eagle eyes.

I don't ask anyone to keep an eye on you,
I want you to do anything you want to do.
But if what you want is to be with other guys,
don't come visit me with your lying eyes.

If you feel like you want to cheat,
or meet someone who'll sweep you off your feet;
Come visit and don't tell me any lies,
you'll never be able to hide those lying eyes.

....

I wrote this poem because women have told me they loved me and would wait for me. The letters they write to me are full of lies. They date other people while they are writing to me and telling me that they are going to wait for me. My friends see them and I'm told about it.

MORE THAN I CAN GIVE

I've been known to make a mistake,
and cause a good woman's heart to break.
I've often thought I might have a disease,
No woman have I been able to please.

So, you should keep your distance from me,
I'm not the man you want to see.
I don't think I can be faithful to you,
and hurting you I don't want to do.

Leave now, you are stronger than you know,
forget about me and let me go.
You want much more than I can give,
go out and enjoy yourself and live.

You are sexy, smart and very strong,
a true love for you will come along.
I don't want to but no matter how hard I try,
chances are I'll end up making you cry.

I don't know if it's a disease inside of me,
I can't be the man anyone want me to be.
I can get a lot of woman to do what I say,
but I can't get one to stay.

MORE THAN MY FRIEND

She doesn't want anything but friendship from me,
and she's always where I asked her to be.
After school, she asks me what I want to do,
when I ask her, she says, it's up to you.
She is so cool when she's hanging out with me,
I know this is how a real friendship should be.
We have so much fun when we go to the mall,
we shop, we eat, we laugh and have a ball.
She tells me how mice I look in my new dress,
she always comforts me when I'm a mess.
I can tell her anything about what I want to do,
and she'll always keep it between us two.
I can talk to her about anything I fear,
and I know she'll always be here.
I feel happy and safe to know she's there,
and she always asks me to do my hair.
But I know everything can change in a blur,
so, I never miss a chance to tell her I love her.
I would never dream of swapping her for another,
because she's more than friend, she's my mother.

....

I wrote this poem for a little girl to put in a card and give to her mother for her birthday. Her mother was so happy with it that she cried.

MY FRIEND

He's my friend and very special to me,
he makes me feel alive and free.
When I'm lying around and feeling blue,
he's always there with something to do.

He's the one who stops me from feeling sad,
he's the best friend anyone's ever had.
He brought me fishing and taught me how to bait a hook,
and never got frustrated at how long it took.

We were at the lake and he taught me to swim,
I love going everywhere with him.
One day after we got back from a hike,
he taught me to drive a mini bike.

He would always do whatever I wanted him to do,
he didn't mind spending the whole day with me too.
He brought me camping on a lake that was crystal clear,
he showed me in the woods we had nothing to fear.

He's a whole lot more than just a friend to me,
when I'm older that's just how I want to be.
Besides showing me the best times I've ever had,
he's been the most fantastic dad.

MY HEART BELONGS TO YOU

I've worked hard but I didn't amount to much,
nothing becomes of anything that I touch.
All the plans I've made have come undone,
I've gambled on life but I never won.

Some guys have so much luck, they never lose,
but I prayed for some luck I could use.
And then I had one of my dreams come true,
I got a beautiful love letter from you.

I've been living with heartache and it's rough,
but now I have you and that's enough.
With you in my life I'm always winning,
I've loved you from the very beginning.

Now I'll never need anything more,
you are more than I could ever ask for.
We are together now and everything feels fine,
When you kiss me, chills run up and down my spine.

When you wrap your arms around me, I'm on fire,
and you fill my heart with desire.
I'm going to love you no matter what you do,
and my heart is always going to belong to you.

NATURALLY

I don't want to want you like this,
I don't want to think about your kiss.
Every time I think about you holding me,
the weaker I seem to be.

I haven't had anyone to move on to,
So, all I can think about is you.
You were the last one I loved out there,
I can't get you out of my hair.

I still love you but not because I want to,
I'm not stupid I know that we're through.
In prison I live off fantasies and memories,
and you have brought me to my knees.

You made me weak and I wanted to die,
you tore me apart and I don't know why.
I did everything you ever wanted me to,
and I loved nobody but you.

When they came and put me in prison that day,
you very quickly went your own way.
You hurt me but I find it hard to blame you,
it's probably the same thing I would do.

I got mad but if the truth be told,
I'd also need someone to hold.
But you did it so fast and naturally,
you couldn't have loved me.

And now it's time for me to close my eyes,
and in a prayer to say my good-byes.
You are always going to be a part of me,
you were so easy for me to love naturally.

....

Years and years later I still thought about how it was when they first put me in prison. Memories linger on when you don't have anything to move on to. In prison life is so monotonous that you only have past memories. Until you can get a life and start making new memories, you will hold onto the memories from the past no matter how much they hurt you. I was constantly haunted by my past memories. My memories were the subject of so many of my writings, whether they be poems or short stories or, whatever I felt like writing at the time. I thought that I would never be able to forget about the pain of the past. I thought it would haunt me until I die. I was told that I would stop hurting one day and everything would be fine when I moved on. I couldn't wait to move on. I didn't have anything to move on to for so long that I didn't think I'd ever find happiness. After all the letters that I've gotten from women in prison and the promises they made and then broke, I didn't even want to meet women anymore. On the other hand, I was starving for love and affection from a woman. I was nervous about pleasing a woman again. It has been so long. After so long, your mind plays tricks on you and you always think the worst. I thought I'd never be enough for any woman again.

NO JUSTICE

In a different life many, many moons ago,
I was with my family that I loved so.
I fit in by being a husband and a dad,
but I screwed that up really bad.

I was put in chains and taken far away,
I will never forget that horrible day.
Over the years, it's gone from bad to worse,
this corrupt system has been my curse.

I was supposed to get ten years but it was double,
and that was just the start of my trouble.
I studied the law and the more I learned,
the more I understood how I got burned.

There is selective justice in the United States,
prisoners are the ones that the government hates.
They never prosecute their relatives or friends,
they'll lie and cover them up till it all ends.

With reckless abandon, a lot of cops kill,
while they put you in the pen up on the hill.
Judges, Lawyers and cops all break the law,
more times than anyone I ever saw.

A cop can force a girl to get laid,
he might get suspended, but he still gets paid.
Anyone else gets fired and goes to jail,
and they sure as hell don't get bail.

Very rarely do you see one of them go to jail,
when they do, they all get bail.
A judge's son had fifty pounds of drugs in school,
he got a slap on the wrist for breaking a rule.

I read all about it in the paper today,
How easy a judge's son can get away.
I was sentenced to twenty-one years,
While his son had no fears.

He knew that his daddy would get him out

That's what the "Old Boy" system is about.
They help each other out all the time,
They can get away with any crime.

....

A Piscataquis County Judge's son was attending college in Rhode Island. He was caught coming out of his dorm with a hockey bag full of drugs and twelve thousand dollars in cash. He went to the county jail and his father went to Rhode Island to talk to the judge there. His son got out of the county jail after only five months. The judge said that five months in prison has had the desired rehabilitative affect on the kid. That's funny because a county jail certainly isn't prison and the kid didn't even have one hour of rehabilitative counseling. You never heard anything about that case again. Because he was the son of a judge it was covered up quickly.

Chapter Four

"Stop Searching"

Most of my life I have gone from one heartache to the next. Drugs and alcohol to a broken home. Lately I've had many tears to reflect the hollow man I feel like I am in prison. It seems like I searched so hard to find myself in the eyes of people who didn't even know themselves. no wonder my life ended up the way it did. Most people spend a lifetime searching for something to belong to or be a part of. I've tried it all! I joined the Elks Club, Allii's motorcycle club, Saracen's motorcycle club and finally the Hells Angels motorcycle club. I've always wanted to be a part of something. I wanted to belong! I moved from group to group and I still don't feel like I belong. As a result, I started messing with drugs and running with the wrong crowd. When I was a member of the Hells Angels, I felt like it was where I belonged. Of course, it wasn't the family or brotherhood I thought it was. But this got me almost everything I thought I wanted and it came easy. But this all came with a huge price! It cost me my kids, my self-respect, my freedom and everything that meant something to me, including my wife. Instead of finding what I was looking for, it put me in a position for the government to give me a twenty one year prison sentence and caused me to feel powerless. I'm sure I'm not alone in all of this but it sure feels that way in this tiny cell.

I'm sure there are many men and women in prison who are dying like me. Yes. I said I'm dying. I'm dying from the lifestyle, the failed relationships, the hold that drugs had on me, and the lack of communication with the ones I love the most. The lifestyle I lived stopped my spirit from being able to soar. I have a spirit that has never been able to fly. I always kept it going down the wrong road and now I'm locked in a tiny, cold prison cell all alone. I have no idea when I will be getting out.

I've felt ashamed of myself inside. I hid my feelings well, just like I'm doing in this prison. I've always wanted to change but I didn't know how until I was locked in a tiny cell all alone and forced to evaluate myself. I talked to a priest one day cause I wanted to talk to someone, anyone. I hadn't talked to anyone in weeks. I told him about my life and that I wanted to change. He said, "Yeah, he hears that all the time but some people just want to talk." That really hit me hard because that's been me for a few years. I've been in prison so long and I've wanted to talk to someone about getting better but I didn't want to let anyone know I had a problem. No.! Not me, the one everyone looked up to and turned to whenever they needed something. I had inspiration back then, but inspiration with no motivation is like a dream you can't remember. You're bound to fail because you don't know where to start. I feel hopeless, depressed, confused and misguided but nobody knew. I was getting weaker and weaker on the inside. When I was free, I knew the drug was killing me. I was being led by the wrong shepherd. I was following the way that I thought was easier, only to sink deeper in the lies of the way. I was broken! I know now that the path that looks easier is the biggest lie there is. Once in my life I was blinded by darkness. I would help everyone in God's world but myself. I knew I was going to hell. After all, I was the one everyone looked up to and depended on. Or, that's what I thought anyway.

When I got arrested in April 2003, I said, "I'm tired of all this crap now. I've got to be honest with myself". It's then I took a long look at my life. It was quite a while, before I figured out what was missing in my life. What was I searching all these years for? One day it hit me like a ton of bricks. Just after the feds moved me for the fifth time in as many months, after seeing so many criminals with no values or morals, I knew that's what I've been looking for in myself. I've been searching for the good in me. I knew I was a good man inside. I knew I had value.

I asked for a Bible and when I got it, I read it every day. It was seven months before I read the whole thing. I have been studying the Bible ever since. It's been almost two years since I first picked up a Bible, and in the meantime, I repented all my sins and accepted Jesus Christ as my Lord and Savior.

I am a born-again Christian who once used drugs and committed crimes. I lied to get what I wanted and did what I wanted. It landed me in prison causing me more pain and heartbreak than I ever thought I could live through. Now I'm doing my best to walk with Jesus and I no longer desire to use drugs or commit crimes. Now instead of living a life of paranoia and fear, I live a sober life putting the talents God gave me to use, and loving every minute of it.

It's too bad it took coming to prison to make me realize what I was looking for. It wasn't a group, it wasn't money or power. In the lowest moment of my life I found what I was searching for, "The Family of God".

You see there is no hope for us by our own standards. I mean just look how many of us are broken. No matter what anyone says, it's not what we can do to fix ourselves. It's what Jesus did for us on the cross. Jesus died so we can be healed from all things. Remember, inspiration is not enough. So, humble yourself and stop searching, the answer is Jesus!

The thief, the enemy comes to steal, kill and destroy. Jesus came to save us. Is what looks easier, really easier? Take it from me, it's not! It took me losing everything I worked my whole life for to realize that I've been living a lie. I was on the path to hell.

I'm on the right path now, but the feelings of loneliness, sorrow, heartache and despair are still there. I pray a lot now and feel confident that someday I will be free to start a better life. I still have to do time and the following poems are how I did a lot of that time. I just kept writing my feelings down this way. I get them out without anyone knowing.

NO LIFE LEFT

No one answers your phone when I call,
it's starting to make me feel small.
I check every hour to see if you emailed me,
and for days now there's nothing to see.

It has been a long time since you sent me a letter,
I should let you go so I can feel better.
It feels like I have a big weight on my shoulder,
and eventually I'll be crushed by that boulder.

I didn't want to lose you and do this time alone,
but I know I hurt you and left you on your own.
You're going to leave, it's just a matter of time,
or you will also have a mountain to climb.

I'm sorry I was selfish not thinking of you,
I did the crime but you're paying for it too.
Don't feel guilty or forget that you are free,
go live your life and try to forget about me.

That old judge gave me so much time to do,
there will be no life left for me and you.
I love you, but I know I have to let you go,
Theirs is no more me and you, I know.

NO PLANS YET

Since you left, I've been living day by day,
wondering how you could just walk away.
It really broke my heart to see you go,
I'm missing you so much, I've got to know.

Since you left me are you happier now,
did you find whatever you were looking for somehow?
I love you so much that I'm going to stay gone,
I'll respect your decision and I'll move on.

We were friends long before this started,
we'll stay friends even though we've parted.
I will never criticize who you date,
and the ones I date I hope you don't hate.

When you decided to go forward, you let me go,
so, I will date the women I get to know.
I can't control how anyone feels about me,
and now this is the way it has to be.

I won't wait around for anyone anymore,
especially if they've already walked out the door.
I have no plans now when I get out there,
but I'll find a woman that will care.

NOBODY IS BETTER THAN YOU

Your family might not have a lot of money today,
or have a fancy car in the driveway.
You might not have a thousand-dollar pair of sneakers,
or ten thousand dollars, worth of speakers.

You don't have a big house with a 10- inch TV,
or the best clothes that there could ever be.
You don't walk around in five hundred-dollar jeans,
Your dad doesn't have a car with four TV screens.

Your family can't afford a fifty thousand-dollar vacation,
to some far off and exotic destination.
And you don't own a fancy two hundred-foot yacht,
that's worth more than everything your family has got.

You are not always flying around the world on a plane,
don't you think to spend money like that's insane?
While the place you live in is smaller but it's neat,
and you are getting enough to eat.

You may not be rich but you are living okay,
and you are around people who love you every day.
They might have money but no matter what they do,
they could never be better than you.

ONE MORE TRY

If I could turn back time you know I would,
I would do things differently if I could.
There are so many things I've done wrong,
and I let it go on for way too long.

I've made mistakes, but I hope you know I've learned,
some of the ones I loved and their bridges I've burned.
I live with that sorrow for the hearts I've broken,
and for the hurtful things I've spoken.

For so many years now I've been paying dearly,
and the toll it's taken on me you can see clearly.
My cards are on the table now and they're showing hearts,
I'm laying it on the line, this is how it starts.

If I could reach your heart now you know I would,
I would give you my love the way I should.
I don't know what's going on in your beautiful mind,
you're gone now and you've left me behind.

If you take a chance and open up your heart to me,
I'll show you what true love should be.
Don't give up now and let your memories die,
please give our love just one more try.

NEW WORLD

I just can't get you off my mind,
you are so beautiful, loving and kind.
I've missed you more than you'll ever know,
and every day I've loved you so.

It is hard being locked up so far away,
this is a different life that I live today.
First of all, I live with all guys,
almost all of them will tell lies.

In prison, you can be what you want to be,
all you do is make up your story.
Unless someone knows you from the outside,
with your story the truth you can hide.

I don't love anyone who lives with me,
Every day I hate the things I see.
It's the life I've lived for so long,
and it has always felt so wrong.

We live in two separate worlds now,
I hope we can get connected somehow.
I'll need to learn the new world ways,
After being here for so many days.

So much has changed since I've been free,
I'll need someone who'll help me.
There are so many advancements in electronics,
I'm the guy still hooked on phonics.

Will someone teach me about new technology,
and about all the other changes I see?
You don't learn much behind a prison wall,
and no modern technology at all.

I'm looking for a woman who will share,
Her life with me when I get there.
It will be a whole new world to me,
And so many things for us to see.

It has been a year since you contacted me,

I know it is because I'm not free.
I know together we'll never get to see,
The new world isn't for you and me.

....

This is another one of the poems I wrote after a woman who has been writing to me just suddenly stopped writing with no explanation at all. She sent me some beautiful pictures of herself and I was looking forward to trying to make a life with her when I got out. It was just one more disappointment in a life on the inside that was full of disappointment. It seemed like every week or two I would get news that one of my relatives or friends died and as soon as I started to have hope for a future with a woman, that dream would get shattered too.

OVERDRIVE

I'm going to pack up my RV and I'm going away,
I no longer have a reason to stay.
When I'm heading down the road in overdrive,
I'll be looking for someone to make me feel alive.

I need to leave all the bad shit behind me,
there's a world out there for me to see.
Everything I had in my life is gone,
I have no choice but to move on.

At one time, I wanted to give up and die,
fourteen years in prison living a lie.
I honestly didn't think I'd make it through,
what did I have to live for if I do?

Now, that I'm very close to the end,
I'm going to be needing a friend.
I'll need some help when I get to the street,
at least till I get on my feet.

Even then I'd still want to hang out,
I've forgotten what friendship is all about.
In prison, everyone wanted something from me,
I know that's not how friendship should be.

So, I spent most of my time in prison alone,
I got along a lot better on my own.
Every time I thought I could believe some guy,
I find out everything he said was a lie.

I learned that I can't trust anyone anymore,
they take anything they can take you for.
Whatever they can't con you out of, they steal,
but I've got to forget about it all for real.

One thing I know that will make me feel alive,
Will be flying down the road in Overdrive.
Or on a Harley with the wind in my face,
I can't wait to get the hell out of this place.

....

I only rode in a vehicle four or five times in fourteen years. I'm a driver! I love to travel and I can drive anything. I am a person that was always on the go. I travelled to many different countries and I've driven to every state in the United States. I've driven millions of miles driving anything from an eighteen-wheeler, regular trucks, cars and motorcycles. It kills me to be locked in a tiny cell in one spot. I felt like a wild animal in a cage. I look back at these poems and think some of them are not very good and the reader will think some of them are boring or stupid. But, writing these poems are what got me through the hardest times I've ever had and I'm still fairly sane.

PHOTOGRAPHS

When I see old photographs, I see dreams that are gone,
because in every one of them we had a smile on.
I wonder how it all went wrong so fast,
those photos show love that should last.

When I got locked up and they threw away the key,
in a few short months, you gave up on me.
I still keep looking at the old photos of you,
I can't tell that smile on your face isn't true.

After all these years in prison I still wonder why,
you chose to believe every single lie.
It made it easier for you to do what you did to me,
if hurting me bad was how you wanted it to be.

I can go a long time now without thinking of any of it,
and I almost convinced myself, I don't give a shit.
Then I opened up my photo album again today,
I knew I should have thrown your pictures away.

I don't because I want to remember the good times we had,
forgetting the good times in life would be sad.
If all I remembered were the bad times in my life,
I'd be stuck in a world full of hate and strife.

PROTECTION

It's not too late to make something out of this mess,
maybe you can help me find happiness?
I'm going to leave this prison a better man,
and I'll make amends to everyone I can.

Thanks to all the faith you've restored in me,
I know I can win this battle when I'm free.
I'm ashamed of the way I used to feel,
you gave me something I know is real.

You helped me break the habit I've had for years,
that caused the ones I love countless tears.
Thanks to you, I have a reason to believe now,
when I got myself so lost somehow.

I played with fire and I got what I asked for,
but I don't want to get burnt anymore.
I admit I was wrong and now I've changed my mind,
I'm leaving all the pretenders far behind.

I've got to live everyday now like it was my last one,
and find a woman that wants to have some fun.
She'll know we are going in the perfect direction,
and with me, she has protection.

RDAP

The only one that can change you is you,
so, decide now what you want to do.
This is your perfect opportunity,
take advantage of it because it's free.
Make something good come from your crime,
change now, don't waste your time.
Being a prisoner is not a life,
just ask your children and wife.
You are not the only one alone,
they are also out there on their own.
Some do think this program is crap,
but you can get a lot out of RDAP.
You get out of it what you put in,
if you want to change, you'll feel it within.
You can fake your way through this class,
get a certificate proving you pass.
But the only one you cheated was you,
and you also hurt the ones you love too.
So, do the right thing while you're here,
and with the ones you love, you'll be near.

....

RDAP stands for Residential Drug Abuse Program. It's a prison inside a prison. It's a nine-month program for drug users in prison. You have to move into the dorm it is being taught in. In Danbury, Connecticut it held ninety-eight inmates. The program is stricter than prison rules. It has rules of its own. I took the class and it wasn't easy. But, it did help me.

SHE DOESN'T WANT MORE

This week someone I love made a decision,
she doesn't want me when I get out of prison.
I was never with her, so I've always been free,
I'm sure not going to beg her for mercy.

I'll leave her alone so she can get on with her life,
maybe she can take the place of his wife.
I don't know if she broke my heart or hurt my pride,
either way I'll hold those feelings inside.

I'll be getting out of prison as a single man,
I'll find a woman that loves me all she can.
She'll know the rest of my life is for living,
and the love I have inside is for giving.

She wants that love and she really wants me,
and I'll show her everything she wants to see.
I'll love her like there'll be no tomorrow,
and we'll never again feel sorrow.

She loves me and doesn't want me to change,
that kind of love to me is very strange.
The women in my life all tried to change me,
I wasn't the man they wanted me to be.

This awesome woman will never be hesitating,
to tell me she loves me and she'll waiting.
And she doesn't care how long it takes,
or about all my past mistakes.

She is never lost and she's not confused,
and she knows by me, she won't be used.
A heartbreak turned into a blessing for me,
I'll have real love when I'm free.

I know I'll find this woman when I get there,
And she'll get all the love I have to share.
With just a little help from the Lord above,
It won't take long to find this love.

Now, I know I'm headed in the right direction,

And that I'm starving for love and affection.
I never want to see this woman at my door,
Because my woman is going to be so much more.

....

This is just one of many poems I wrote because of a woman that stopped writing to me and found someone out there to be with. I can't blame them for finding someone that they could feel and touch for real. I know what it's like to have a relationship through letters, emails and phone calls. It doesn't work!!!!

SHE WAS THE ONE

I was buying groceries at the Shop and Save,
I saw my ex-wife but I had to behave.
She still looked good with that long dark hair,
she didn't see me so I acted like she wasn't there.
As I watched her, I thought about the good times we had,
but she probably remembers all the bad.
It's the first time I've seen her in fourteen years,
I got a lump in my throat and held back tears.
I wanted to walk over to her and say hello,
she'd probably get mad and tell me to go.
She looks happy now as someone else's wife,
and I will stay out of her life.
I went the other way and got out of there,
I felt like I was trying to breathe thin air.
When I saw her coming out all I could do was stare,
she noticed me but she acted like I wasn't there.
I started up the truck and got out of the parking lot,
and it was less than a mile I got.
Tears filled my eyes from a defeated broken heart,
She was the one that I didn't want to depart.

··········

I wrote this poem long before I was released from prison. In my head, this is how I envisioned seeing my ex-wife again. I didn't know how I'd react, especially after reading the Grand Jury testimony she did against me. I knew I'd get over her when I had a chance to find someone else. But, in prison, you only have the memories you've already made. It hurts to have a life that seems like it stands still. It feels like you are in Limbo, going nowhere. You can't wait to get out and start a new life and find some love and happiness.

SHE'D HAVE TO BE BLIND

Everything will be different when I get out,
I'll learn what this new world is all about.
But I've lost a lot of my family ties,
and as each one dies, a part of me dies.

I've got to stay focused on the road ahead,
and find love and happiness before I'm dead.
So, I'm looking for a woman with love to give,
a woman that wants to get out and live.

With her, I want to have a lot of fun,
if we disagree, she won't cut and run.
We'll be open and honest with each other every day,
we'll listen to what each other has to say.

We'll never let our relationship burn and crash,
or walk away and toss it in the trash.
And a day won't go by that she won't know,
just how much I love her so.

She'll know I loved her yesterday and the day before,
and every day, I'll love her so much more.
She'll know that she's the only woman on my mind,
because if she doesn't, she'd have to be blind.

SHOOTING STAR

This nightmare is almost at an end,
some relationships I'll have to mend.
I've survived and I'm coming home at last,
to some I'll always be an outcast.

They believed everything on the news,
and they are entitled to their views.
But I've done this ridiculously long sentence,
behind these vicious razor wire fences.

I'm the one who felt the sharp end of a shank,
and I know I have only myself to thank.
I've often been in shackles with my hands cuffed,
and spending time in the hole has been l rough.

Many more times I was forced to fight,
by some tough acting parasite.
But I thank the good Lord that I still live,
some of them had a very sharp shiv.

I've been doing this for way over a decade,
and I've laid in this bed that I alone made.
Remember that I have paid a heavy price,
and not one day of it has been nice.

I've asked the good Lord through prayer,
to help me repair my life out there.
Many times, He's already come to my rescue,
He's shown me every day what I had to do.

He's shown me what I've had to leave behind,
and to go forward with an open mind.
I've learned not to think of my life as a catastrophe,
to think of it as a new beginning for me.

I'm going to try to forget all the awful screams,
And start living all my dreams.
I wished one thing on a shooting star,
To come home to where you are.

....

Nobody has wished any harder than I have. Nobody has had more dreams of a happy life more than I have. I've been locked up for over four-thousand and fifty days. Not a night went by when I was laying in a small, cold cell that I didn't wish I was out there with people that cared about me. I did my best to think about good things and have good dreams. Unfortunately, I had more nightmares than dreams. But, when I did have a good dream, I was happy. To you it is just a dream, but to me, it was getting me out of the worst place in the world and into a happy place. No matter how I try, I could never explain to you how it feels to be in prison for so many years. You lose who you really are if you're not careful. You can get caught up in the ways and the life of prison and forget who you used to be. You can leave there and all the good you used to have inside you could be gone. You get used to talking trash and get used to having no respect or love for anyone. I fought to maintain myself and writing these poems and getting all this shit off my mind was my way of doing it. I'd like to think that I'm still the good man I used to be with more knowledge and more common sense. I look at my experience as a learning experience, one that I know I will never have to learn again. The government gave me 21 years to learn a lesson that I learned in one year. The rest of the time I spent there was just a waste of my life.

SICK AND ALONE

Two days ago, a bunch of guys in here got a flu shot,
and now the flu is just what they got.
I live in a crowded dorm that sleeps eighty-four,
and only a couple of them were coughing before.

Now, half the room is coughing and blowing snot,
last night I came down with what they got.
I'm coughing really bad and I've got a runny nose,
in this environment, this is how it goes.

I really hate getting sick in this God forsaken place,
you know nobody cares by the look on their face.
Today I was so weak and tired I couldn't even eat,
going to the bathroom was the only time on my feet.

I spent the whole day covered up in my bed,
coughing, blowing my nose and an ache in my head.
I have a dry cough making my throat really hurt,
and waking up with a sweat soaked shirt.

Sometimes I'm really hot but then I'm cold,
being sick and alone is getting really old.
I wish I had someone to take care of me,
this is not how life is supposed to be.

SICK AND ALONE DAY 2

I woke up this morning after a night of broken sleep,
it feels like this sickness has settled in me deep.
A fever, watery eyes, runny nose and congested chest,
it looks like I am sicker than the rest.

I laid back down but only slept off and on,
I was hoping to wake up and find the fever gone.
But of course, it wasn't, I don't have that kind of luck,
my body aches now, like I was hit by a truck.

I went to the bathroom and couldn't stop sneezing,
I lay back down trying to breathe, but wheezing.
I haven't eaten all day or slept very good,
I can't get the medication that I should.

And now here it is another Friday night,
I'm sick and alone and nothing feels right.
Not one person has stopped and asked if I'm okay,
I know I'm on my own at the end of the day.

I'm sick and tired, but I'm sitting up to write,
to tell you about this prison life tonight.
All along I've been telling you that no one here cares,
It's an attitude in prison that everyone shares.

SICK AND ALONE "The Diagnosis"

I've been sick for the past thirteen days,
I tried to get better using many ways.
Instead of getting better, I've gotten much worse,
I was afraid I might leave here in a hearse.

I made it to sick call this morning at six-thirty,
breathing hard, soaked in sweat and feeling dirty.
I had a temperature of one hundred and four,
and I didn't have any strength anymore.

I'd take a deep breath and my chest really hurt,
I had a cold sweat and it soaked my shirt.
My throat was sore and it was really dry,
I can't hold anything down when I try.

She listened to my lungs with her stethoscope,
and looked at me like there was no hope.
She said, "You've got pneumonia and it's bad,
you didn't come last week but I wish you had."

She gave me a shot and ten days of amoxicillin,
"You should get better now if God is willing."
It's just my luck to be so sick and alone,
when I'm so close to coming home.

SICK AND ALONE "recovering"

Last night I finally slept pretty good,
I put earplugs in like I should.
I only woke up twice to go pee,
but that's not unusual for me.

I woke up at seven, sweaty and dirty,
So, I went to lift weights till eight thirty.
For three day's I was in bed with no shower,
So, I stayed in the shower for half an hour.

In the gym, I was soaking wet in sweat,
I felt weak but I got all I could get.
I'm still coughing, but not nearly as much,
blowing my nose now it hurts to touch.

I am hungry now, I haven't eaten in days,
I don't have any food but there are ways.
I do have a powdered chocolate health shake,
it was the only thing I had to make.

For ten stamp's I bought a bag of cereal,
I used the shake as milk even though it's not real.
I ate it and it didn't taste all that bad,
just for something to eat today I was glad.

I have a cold chill right down to the bone,
It sucks so bad to be sick and alone.
At the gym I weighed myself today,
I lost seventeen pounds the hard way.

When you're sick in prison you don't get to eat,
When you're too sick to get up on your feet.
It is not like it is when you're out there,
In here, there's nobody to care.

Nobody here cares if you live or die,
They just look at you as they go by.
They don't care if you are sick and dying,
They laugh if you are crying.

No matter how sick they see me,

Crying is something they'll never see.
I just can't wait until I get home,
I won't ever have to be sick and alone.

....

I'm not kidding you one bit. If you are sick in prison, nobody really cares. You can't get the right medication unless you are dying and they send you to an outside hospital. When they do send you there, they send two armed guards with you and if you stay overnight, two armed guards are with you at all times. In a twenty-four-hour period, four of the guards are on overtime. All they do is sit there and watch TV. Some of them walk around flirting with the nurses. They don't realize how stupid they look guarding a person that is so sick he can't get out of bed. The inmate is still shackled to the bed. The guards both have guns. What a waste of taxpayer's money!!!! I know society doesn't have a clue about how much money is wasted in the Justice Department. They probably wouldn't care if they did. That's too bad.

SIXTY DAYS IN THE HOLE

I live with guys that think they're shrewd,
most of them are just stupid and rude.
Living with them has been a real nightmare,
meeting someone you can trust is very rare.

You wouldn't believe how hard I've tried,
to be good when these idiots pried.
They push me so far that I explode,
and I go into "I don't give a shit" mode.

I can't remember how many times I have fought,
and sat in a hole feeling distraught.
As the days go by, I get filled with rage,
for being locked up in a small, cold cage.

A month alone in the hole with nothing to do,
is their way of trying to break you.
Two months and it feels like you're going insane,
and you want to cause someone else pain.

It's not that I mind getting into a scrap,
because I really don't give a crap.
But sixty days in the hole is the worst,
So, I have to control my outburst.

SILENT TREATMENT

Do you know that you are acting like a kid,
over something someone else did?
It's okay if you no longer speak to me,
it's your prerogative you see.

But, be an adult and talk about it,
don't say that you don't give a shit.
You're lying and you know it too,
just as well as I do.

I know that you really care about me,
but you don't like the comments you see.
I'm not the one that said you had to look,
you're the one that wanted to see my Facebook.

Twenty-one women said they love me,
you're taking this one differently.
But if it will make you feel any better,
she still hasn't written me a letter.

If she hasn't taken the time to write,
over her we shouldn't fight.
Comments on Facebook that say "I love you"
is the best they'll ever do.

I require much more time than that,
especially in this place that I'm at.
So, for all the women that say they love me,
it's only for the social media to see.

I can't control what people say,
And I really don't care anyway.
If over Facebook comments you fight,
Something about you isn't right.

If you get mad and don't talk to me,
The silent treatment is how it will be.
I'm used to not talking to people anyway,
In this shithole where I have to stay.

The silent treatment used to bother me,

I got used to it because I'm not free.
But I'll be right here if you want to talk,
Right now, I'm going to take a walk.

··········

In prison I didn't even know what Facebook was. My friend started a Facebook page for me. I sent poems to her and when my daughter took over my Facebook page, she put poems on it almost every day. A lot of people commented on my poems. I was writing to a woman at the time. She saw some of the comments and she got mad at me. She was so mad that she wouldn't answer my phone calls and I didn't get another letter from her. She gave me the silent treatment. What she didn't realize was, I've been in the hole "solitary confinement", for a total of about nine months. The longest I was there was ninety days at once. But, I got used to not talking to anyone.

SMALL TOWN LIVING

I'm afraid I'm going home to a ghost town,
everything I knew has closed down.
I want to go back to the small-town living,
where people don't take, they're giving.

There's nothing like a small-town neighborhood,
it's safe and everyone feels good.
You never have to lock your door at night,
and very rarely was there a fight.

If you weren't home, they'd watch over your place,
and everybody in town knew your face.
I've been told that those times are no more,
now everybody has to lock their door.

Some old folks died, some good folks moved away,
I won't recognize many neighbors today.
They'll be no more small time living I'm used to,
and if I stay, I'll have to start over new.

It will never be the way it used to be,
but that's the kind of life I want for me.
It proves that change is not always for the best,
and I'll probably move like the rest.

SMILE

I could tell she was going through hell,
somebody didn't treat her very well.
I saw it in her eyes as she sat there and cried,
she couldn't hide the tears, but she tried.

I wanted to hold her and tell her she'd be okay,
but I don't know what she went through today.
She didn't look like she was going to be alright,
I wondered if she'd want a new friend tonight.

I felt so bad as I sat and watched her cry,
I couldn't leave as she was barely getting by.
I walked over to her and said my name is Bill,
and whoever did this to you I would kill.

Nobody should ever hurt you this way,
just for a while do you mind if I stay?
She patted the bench and I sat by her side,
the tears still fell that she tried to hide.

I told her she was beautiful when she cries,
but I'd rather see a smile reach your eyes.
I sat there and talked to her for a while,
and I finally got her to smile.

SOMEBODY NEW

We think so much alike, we're one and the same,
opposites attract, so for us that's a shame.
Are we too much alike for you to be with me,
or do you think it's just not meant to be?

For a while I thought you were going to be the one,
when we were together, we had so much fun.
You just left but it seems like a long time ago,
you want someone else now, this much I know.

I'm not going to be a fool and try to hang on,
I've let go and have accepted that you're gone.
As hard as it will be, I'm letting some memories die,
I can't get you back and I'm not going to try.

I put my heart into nothing but a fantasy,
that you wanted to make love to nobody but me.
I tried to show you I love you with the things I made,
I must have fell short and didn't make the grade.

It broke my heart that you would give up on me,
I never got out of prison to see what could be.
That might be the reason you found somebody new,
because he's there now to be with you.

STRONGER

It's not always easy even though I'm strong,
to say I'm sorry or admit that I was wrong.
But I've learned to swallow my pride,
and now I'm finally satisfied.

The mistakes I made started when I was a kid,
I never grew up like everyone else did.
I hardly ever took my life seriously,
everything was fun and games to me.

I acted like I was single my whole life,
when in fact I always had a wife.
I did drugs and a whole lot of drinking,
half the time I didn't know what I was thinking.

I hurt the people that really cared about me,
drugs and alcohol made it so I couldn't see.
I ended up losing everything I worked so hard for,
but I'm not that same man anymore.

I'll be released from prison soon and you will see,
how I've changed and you'll be proud of me.
I'm not doing any of that shit any longer,
I'm smarter now and a whole lot stronger.

STUCK IN MY MEMORY

They say when you get old you forget,
everybody forgets I bet.
Although I did forget something today,
So, I'm writing about it in my way.

I've forgotten some good times I've had,
but I sure remember the bad.
I wish sometime my memory would break,
So, I could forget the heartache.

Forgetting things drives me insane,
but I never forget the pain.
Sometimes I wish I could forget,
and then I'd be all set.

Thanksgiving Day is a day for joy,
and my wife had a baby boy.
The sad thing is, I won't lie,
the boy's dad is some other guy.

I wish I could forget that tidbit,
and say I don't give a shit.
But that is stuck in my memory,
right where I don't want it to be!

TAKE IT FROM ME

When you're in prison time passes so slow,
Tell me the truth, because I already know.
You don't have the time I need, but isn't that a cover,
you don't want to tell me you found a lover?

You thought you were letting me down with ease,
but don't think I'm that naive please?
If you ever talk to me again, here's what I'd say,
no matter who you are with, I hope you are okay.

Don't ever try to hide what you truly feel,
especially if the love you have for him is real.
And don't forget that I know who you truly are,
the trials and tribulations that got you this far.

From a small prison cell, I gave everything I had,
we were together through good times and bad.
But I wasn't enough for you and you needed change,
so, my future plans I have to rearrange.

I can't stop my feelings, they're like a runaway train,
but I would give anything to stop the pain.
I have love to give once I am free,
I'll find a woman who'll take it from me.

I CAN'T WALK TALL

I kept it inside for way too long,
I fight to hold it back when I hear our song.
I can feel how heavy it is on my heart,
it's there because we're so far apart.

It comes out when I think of you with another man,
to hide it, I do everything I can.
When I admit to myself there's nothing to hold on to,
that's when it really shines through.

I put my face in my hands and bow my head,
I tell the ones that see me that I'm sick instead.
I don't want anyone to see me this way,
but it's hard when I think of you every day.

You didn't say goodbye, you left a note, that's all,
and you didn't leave a number that I could call.
I've always thought that it was too good to be true,
I didn't think I'd find someone as good as you.

When you came to me, I didn't think you'd stay a year,
now it's a constant battle to hold back a tiny tear.
I'm strong but no match for something so small,
and when the tears fall, I can't walk tall.

TENDER KISS

This is not how I wanted my life to be,
I wanted somebody to believe in me.
I made some mistakes when I was out there,
people I trusted vanished in thin air.

Some of the I trusted way too much,
they took me away from your sweet touch.
Every night I'm alone now writing on my bed,
wishing I was there with you instead.

There's a lot of things that I really miss,
but nothing more than a tender kiss.
Someday I'll be walking through your door,
for that kiss and a whole lot more.

And then you'll see how hard I try,
with a love I know you can't deny.
It won't be long now before I'm free,
looking for a woman that's good for me.

Are you going to be the one that walks away,
when I so badly need you to stay?
Or are you going to bring out the bad in me,
to do things no one else will see?

You are the woman that can turn me around,
and I promise I'll never let you down.
In my dreams, your lips taste so good,
I woke up missing you like I knew I would.

I can't stop dreaming of a tender kiss,
That's all I have in a place like this.
I dream of getting out of this place,
To plant that kiss on your beautiful place.

I'm sorry I'm not out there with you now,
I sure wish I could be, somehow.
I know I will be in Heaven's bliss,
When I do get that tender kiss.

....

You miss a lot of things when you're in prison. You miss eating with a real fork, spoon and knife. You really miss good food. You miss riding in or driving a vehicle. For me, I missed riding my motorcycle. You miss being with the ones you love, especially on their birthdays or holidays. You miss your kid's graduation and their marriages. You miss your grandkids being born. You miss being with your loved ones during their last days on earth. I could go on and on, but I really missed intimacy and hugging, snuggling and kissing the woman I love. I never stopped thinking about finding a new love and live a life of happiness. I knew that all I wanted in life now was to live a simple life and have a good woman to share my life with. That's why you read a lot of poems about this subject. I hope I'm not boring you with these kinds of poems. That's what prisoners think about and that's what passed a lot of my time in prison.

I've been in a situation in prison where there was nothing at all to do except think. Thinking too much can put a person into depression so deep that he or she wants to kill themselves.

TENDER LOVE

All I ever think about is being close to you,
you've caught my eye, but that's what you do.
You are the beauty and I am the beast,
I hope that don't bother you in the least.

You could have anyone you want that's for sure,
but they could never love you more.
Thoughts of you are keeping my head turning,
and your love keeps my heart burning.

Every day it is you that I wake up missing,
every night it is you that I want to be kissing.
I'll come running for you, I'm right around the bend,
to bring you love you can't comprehend.

You have never been loved this way before,
and I'm praying that you'll always want more.
I'm sorry for the time that's been wasted,
and all the sweet kisses you could have tasted.

I won't be bringing a lot of riches your way,
but that can't make you feel like I can every day.
You are giving me the best reason to live,
and I have a lot of tender love to give.

THE CRYING BEGINS

She left me quietly with no explanation,
and made it clear there will be no reconciliation.
She took all of the pictures off the wall,
I'm not stupid, I know that says it all.

I go through a whole bottle of whiskey,
but that doesn't come close to fixing me.
So, I get up and stagger out the door,
it hurts so bad I can't take no more.

I jump in my truck and drive too fast,
I don't care how long I'll last.
And on the radio, comes our favorite song,
then in a flash everything goes wrong.

I fly off the shoulder and hit a big tree,
and now not even you can fix me.
As I slowly float up in the air going higher,
I look down at my truck that's on fire.

I see other vehicles stopping to see what's wrong,
I hear myself screaming but it doesn't last long.
And now I stay on the outside looking in,
at the pain I've caused as the crying begins.

THE DEVIL

The devil and I are the only ones up this late,
he is constantly badgering me to hate.
I try hard to mind my own business and write,
but he's on my shoulder trying to get me to fight.

He's always reminding me of my painful past,
he wants my hatred for some people to last.
I try not to think of revenge and forgive,
but he says some people shouldn't live.

I tell him that God says, "Thou Shalt Not Kill",
he's relentless though and keeps after me still.
He's sure that one day, he'll get me to give in,
but I know listening to him, I can't win.

With God on my side it's easy to walk away,
and not listen to what the devil has to say.
The only thing he wants from me is my soul,
he doesn't care if I ever feel whole.

Nobody is perfect and everyone is going to sin,
but with God on our side we're going to win.
The devil lies to you and makes everything look good,
and he'd bring you to hell if he could.

THE GOOD LORD MADE ME

I am not a wise man but I'm not a fool,
God knows I only have one rule.
You treat me the way I do you forever,
and there's no doubt we'll always be together.

You are the woman that I'll always need,
in the new life that I'm going to lead.
If you are going to love me, do it now,
we'll work everything else out somehow.

Love me the way I am, don't try to change me,
I'll feel trapped when I want to feel free.
So, try to be with me just the way I am,
I can't pretend to be another man.

If I had to be, I'd be better off on my own,
but I want you, I don't want to be alone.
I can promise you that I'll love you tomorrow,
and you'll never again have to live in sorrow.

I want you more than you'll ever understand,
and I will never let go of your hand.
But I am the way the good Lord made me,
and this is the way I'll always be.

THE GRASS IS GREENER

I thought I was giving her everything I had,
I didn't know she was so sad.
She said if we had a problem we could talk,
but the first sign of trouble she took a walk.

She left me before we even got started,
and she left me alone and brokenhearted.
I dreamt and fantasized about what could be,
but she decided that she didn't want me.

Maybe she got tired of waiting for so long,
or she's right and for her I'm all wrong.
I don't really know because I can't think straight,
I'm so hurt that she wouldn't wait.

It could be that someone else came along,
and her feelings for him were real strong.
She could have told me, she had nothing to hide,
and maybe the grass is greener on the other side.

It doesn't matter, whatever the case may be,
it's for certain she doesn't want me.
I'll have to look for a woman far and wide,
and see if the grass is greener on the other side.

THE REST OF MY LIFE

In my world that is being torn apart,
you've come into my life and touched my heart.
I've been alone in cold, dirty prison cells dying inside,
and because you love me you've changed the tide.

You woke up in me a long dead and forgotten desire,
and you filled my broken heart with fire.
You make my life worth living with a love that's real,
you gave me life again and made me feel.

I gave up and told myself that I'll always be on my own,
I got used to the fact that I was going to die alone.
I'm finding it hard to believe you want to be with me,
there are some who'd say loving me won't be easy.

They'll ask you what are you doing with this guy,
he's a cheater, he's a criminal and he'll lie.
But they'll be telling you about the man I was before,
I paid my dues now, I'm not that man anymore.

I was on drugs and didn't have my priorities straight,
and I turned into everything I hate.
I had my heart torn out when I was eighteen,
and that was the start of the man they've seen.

I was thousands of miles away in Germany,
I was in the Army where I wanted to be.
I was madly in love and she said she'd be my wife,
and without warning she disappeared from my life.

I had a very hard time living with the pain,
but I was a soldier and had to live with the strain.
But while I was in the Army, my heart couldn't heal,
I gave up trying to find a love that was real.

I thought I would live for the rest of my life,
Traveling around without a wife.
Even back then love came in a letter,
So far away and making me feel better.

In this prison, I get love through the mail,

That's just the way it is when you're in jail.
But I'm not going to be here for the rest of my life,
And someday I hope to find the right wife.

....

I was over three thousand miles away in the Army in Germany when I was just seventeen. I was in love with a woman that was still in Maine. Letters were the thing that kept me going back then too. Then when I was sent five states away in prison, I didn't get many visits and because of modern technology, nobody sits down to write letters anymore. The women that did write to me in prison, were just lonely and bored. Oh, I was their friend and I'm still their friend today. I don't blame anyone for moving on. I couldn't wait for a woman for years either. I was actually better off not having someone to worry about. So many men in prison drive themselves crazy wondering what their woman is doing on the streets.

THEY DISAPPEAR

As the days go slowly by,
and the nights I fight to get through.
I'm thinking you know that I don't lie,
but you don't believe that I love you.

I love you now as a close friend,
but soon we'll see if it's more.
Either way it will never end,
I'll always love you for sure.

I can't make a commitment to you,
or anyone else while I'm here.
Wait until this nightmare is through,
and we'll go from there my dear.

There'll be no promises from me today,
to give any one woman my heart.
I never know if they'll stay,
since we're so far apart.

No promises that I might break,
will be coming out of my mouth.
I've promised and it caused heartache,
when everything went south.

You wanted a commitment from me
but when I said "No can do!"
You were as mad as can be,
but I'm never going to lie to you.

I've been through this kind of love before,
and then they would always leave.
I am not going to do this anymore,
And then I won't have to grieve.

If I put my hopes and dreams in you,
And I never have any fear,
Like the others, we'd be through,
And you would just disappear.

I'll just stay single while I'm incarcerated,

And try to make through all this time.
Love through letters is over rated,
I'd rather write these rhymes.

I don't need someone to worry about,
And wonder where they are.
I'll wait patiently until I get out,
And then she won't disappear too far.

THIS BED

I sit here beside my bed for hours every day,
I don't talk much because I have nothing to say.
There is a big difference from me and these guys,
most of them laugh, are really loud and tell lies.
There are so many here that act like this is a game,
it seems like they're glad they came.
I get tired of their bullshit, especially at night,
they never shut up even when they turn out the light.
For the past couple of weeks, I've been sick in bed,
these guys won't let me sleep so I write instead.
My nose is running, I'm weak, cold then hot,
I'm coughing and my nose hurts from wiping snot.
I have pneumonia and you can see it in my face,
and it keeps all these guys out of my space.
I'm either laying on or sitting writing on this bed,
I write about the first thing that pops into my head.
So, I hope you don't get sick of the things I write,
this one is telling you about my life tonight.
I know most of my poems are about prison life,
how my heart has been cut out with a knife.
I write about pain, heartache, sorrow and shame,
trying to make it all rhyme sometimes is lame.
But it's my way to keep me from losing my head,
while being forced to live here with this bed.

'TIL MY LAST BREATH

I'm going to be coming back to Maine at last,
I've paid for the mistakes I made in the past.
I'll never go back to the fast life I had,
it won't be the same without my mom and dad.

I'm definitely not the same man as I used to be,
I'm the man in the mirror looking back at me.
I'm older now and I've cut off my long hair,
I'm different from when you knew me out there.

You'll see how much I've aged in fourteen hard years,
and the toll it took to shed a million tears.
Every day of every year my heart was torn in two,
there wasn't one night I wasn't sad and blue.

I'm always thinking back to where it went wrong,
I've accepted the blame and tried to stay strong.
I'm older now and time has not been my friend,
but this long hard road is almost at its end.

It was hard to struggle through day after day,
I figured out how to survive in my own way.
But now I don't want to be alone anymore,
I want true love when I walk out that door.

They say everybody needs a hand to hold on to,
I want that hand to belong to you.
Every night that I've laid here in this cold bed,
I've had your beautiful image in my head.

But I'm afraid for you, I won't be enough,
I'll always be there if the going gets rough.
I know you won't trust me easily,
I'll never hurt you, put your faith in me.

I'll hold your hand and stand by your side,
With you, my feelings I won't hide.
I'll go wherever you want to go,
With my last breath, my love for you will show.

....

For a long time in prison, I never had anyone write to me or visit me. I wrote so many poems for the woman in my mind. A woman I was praying to God to find. I had love still in me while living with nothing but hate every single day. Hate was an emotion everyone in prison understood. All other emotions were kept inside in fear of being considered weak. The weak are prey. The weak are the ones who have to live by the rule of others. I'm not good at following others. I'd rather fight and I don't care how many I fight. It's not whether I win or lose, it's showing others that I will not bow down to them. I would rather be dead. In prison, I found out that I can do things to others that I never thought I'd do. I found out that I could do anything that I had to do to survive by my own rules, not the rules of other inmates. I could obey the rules of the prison because that's what I had to do to get through and get released. I didn't want to spend any more time in those shitholes than I had to. I often avoided fights because I was close to the end of my bid and I didn't want to lose good time credits. The faster I could get out of there the better. If I had to swallow my pride, I would. I don't care what other idiot inmates think of me anyway.

TOO GOOD FOR ME

I saw her when I looked over my shoulder,
and right there I wished I could hold her.
I never believed in love at first sight,
until I saw her under the street light.

I couldn't say a thing as she walked by,
she stunned me when she caught my eye.
I wish I could have asked her to stay,
I should have never let her get away.

I ended up searching for her my whole life,
she's the one I wanted to be my wife.
I never saw her again, so I tried to move on,
I tried getting married, but now she's gone.

I've been in prison for over a decade,
I wouldn't want her to see the mess I made.
If I ever ran into her again, I'd hide,
I'd keep all my feelings deep down inside.

I'd be ashamed if she found out about my past,
so, I'm over looking over my shoulder at last.
I don't want her to see the man I turned out to be,
because she's definitely too good for me.

TRUST

I've been told I have to learn to trust,
if you love somebody it's a must.
But trust is definitely a two-way street,
and you can't trust everyone that you meet.

In my case, the hard way I have learned,
because by many, I have been burned.
In this place, I can't trust these guys,
they try to deceive you with their lies.

But, when I was out there roaming free,
I always gave my trust too easily.
It turned out most of the people I trusted,
betrayed me as soon as they got busted.

They used me to stay out of a prison cell,
I hope that none of them are doing well.
For many years, I've been doing their time,
they got away with doing their crime.

So, for me to trust now it has to be earned,
and just recently, still I got burned.
I'm finding it hard to trust anyone,
to keep being betrayed is no fun.

Nobody has a reason to lie to me
if you're going to lie, just leave me be.
Even if the truth hurts, I won't lie to you,
I wish you felt the same way that I do.

I can't love anyone without trust,
For me, trusting you is a must.
If I don't trust you, I'll leave you alone,
You don't trust, that you've shown.

....

How can I trust anyone when I've been burnt so many times? Maybe it is Karma that is coming back to bite me in the ass from my past life. I wasn't the guy I am today. I wasn't to be trusted in a relationship back then either.

TWO WHEELS AND CHROME

Honey, I saw you in a dream I had last night,
you were crying and something wasn't right.
I don't know what it was because I couldn't see,
there was a man in the dream that wasn't me.

I could see you so clearly, just like it was real,
and seeing him, I felt as bad as I could feel.
I'm sorry honey but I had to call my friend Lou,
I hated to but I asked him to check up on you.

When he got there, he saw you kissing another guy,
I know I'm in prison but you didn't have to lie.
You didn't tell me about him and that was cruel,
you've been playing me for a damn fool.

I prayed to God that my dream wasn't true,
it breaks my heart at the thought of losing you.
But now, when I'm free I can't come back to town,
everybody knows and I look like a clown.

My heart is broken now, but it doesn't belong to anyone,
I'm going to hit the road like I'm on the run.
Someday, maybe I'll stop and build me a home,
until then I'll be on two wheels and chrome.

WE CRY

We are locked in a tiny prison cell for years,
and we cry.
Our wives get lonely and they find someone else,
and we cry.
We can't be there when our children graduate,
and we cry.
We're in a prison cell on our children's wedding day,
and we cry.
As the years go by both of our parents die,
and we cry.
We get pictures from home and everyone has grown,
and we cry.
We look in the mirror and we see an old man,
and we cry.
They finally release, but we have no home to go to,
and we cry.
We're too old now and we know we'll always be alone,
and we cry.
We spend Thanksgiving alone, Christmas alone, New Years alone,
and we die!

F.C.I Danbury, Ct
2013

WHAT ARE YOU THINKING?

Baby, where are you going or do you even know,
or was it just an excuse to let me go?
Maybe it's just easier for you to be free,
So, you'll feel no obligation to me.

Or you just don't want to feel tied down,
you want to help everybody in town.
But I'm betting that you still think about me,
you wonder how it could be.

You don't know how much I think about you,
I do it a lot even when I don't want to.
I have to move on to get you off my mind,
in prison, there's no one to find.

It's easier for you to forget about me,
there's plenty of men out there you can see.
I know they don't take up all your time,
that's when I pop back into your mind.

Are you thinking you should make love to me?
Just to see how great it could be?
But you don't do casual sex with a friend,
and all you want to be is friends till the end?

MAD AT YOU

I think most of us have a jealous streak,
but it doesn't make us weak.
Some people say they're not the jealous kind,
but that would be a real rare find.
If I get jealous, I'll try to hold it inside,
that's something I try to hide.
Jealousy is an emotion I've always had,
I'll disguise it by acting mad.
I'll show the anger, but it's really heartache,
a heartache I'm forced to take.
While in prison, there's nothing I can do,
so, I don't even think of who's with who.
I know every woman needs someone,
don't be alone, go have some fun.
I won't ask if you went on a date,
I won't say anything if you're out late.
I'll never ask who you see or where you go,
because I really don't want to know.
I wouldn't ask you to wait for me,
I'll see what happens when I'm free.
What I don't know, don't hurt me,
and I'm not filled with jealousy.
I'll never tell you what you can and can't do,
Whatever you do I won't be mad at you.

WHEN SHE'S IN MY ARMS

In someone else's eyes, I can do no wrong,
and her faith in me is strong.
I am trying and I'm trying desperately,
to live up to the man she sees in me.

I don't cheat and I don't tell lies,
I'm a good man in her eyes.
Nobody has ever looked at me that way,
I love her and I want her to stay.

In her eyes, I'm the man she wants me to be,
but I'm afraid I'm not the man she can see.
I pray she doesn't, but I think she'll realize,
that I've caused a lot of tears in others eyes.

She doesn't know I was in prison for fifteen years,
I'll probably screw up and cause her tears.
She doesn't know I lied, cheated and did drugs a lot,
the man she sees, I'm definitely not.

But I'm going to tell her the truth, no more lies,
she'll see the real me with those beautiful eyes.
I pray to God she sees the change in me,
when she's in my arms I'm sure she'll see.

WHEN YOU'RE GONE

When I try to think back fourteen years,
I have to wait now till the cobweb clears.
My memory is as fuzzy as it can get,
how come the bad things I can never forget.

I can remember the most painful events,
and my stupid revengeful comments.
I should have kept my big mouth shut instead,
and I left a lot of things unsaid.

I've got a bad temper and I used to let it go,
and for all these years I've regretted it so.
It's my fault a lot of my heart was broken,
by words that I have left unspoken.

It's too late for some for me to say I'm sorry now,
but if I could only get to Heaven somehow.
They were good people so I know they went that way,
maybe I can meet up with them someday.

Because my time on earth is close to its end,
and I want to thank you for being my friend.
Tell everyone how much you love them so,
So, when you're gone, they will all know.

WITHOUT YOU

I'm a prisoner behind this thirty-foot wall,
and I can't be with you at all.
There is no way for me to show my love,
but it's only you I'm thinking of.

You are the woman in the poems I write,
and the last one I think of at night.
When I fell for you, I fell head over heels,
and I'm sure this is how love feels.

In my mind, we are lovers and friends,
and my love for you never ends.
I thought we would end up in the bridal suite,
because this love for you made me complete.

Why doesn't it matter to you what I say?
Is it because I can't be with you today?
You've always known how much I love you,
don't do what I think you're going to do.

You're going to do more than break my heart,
you are going to tear my whole world apart.
I'm sorry, but more than my hands are bound,
and without you, I'm better off in the ground.

YARD SALE

I was a lucky man because I wasn't there to see,
the yard sale with all the things that belonged to me.
I can imagine, for my family it must have been hard,
to empty out my house and clean out the yard.

I worked hard my whole life and everything was there,
it was all sold right down to the last chair.
I hate it that they got yard sale prices for it all,
while I lay in a cell staring at the wall.

I picture strangers on the lawn all sorting through,
all the things that I bought brand new.
It breaks my heart to know everything is gone now,
after all those years, I don't want it back anyhow.

I've grieved enough because all I owned is gone,
I've let it go now and moved on.
I hope I don't see any of it again when I'm free,
it has already caused too much heartache for me.

It's sad to know my life went for a yard sale price,
when I'm free, I will not let it happen twice.
I'll never forget when every time I see a yard sale,
I'll think about all those years I spent in jail.

YOU KNEW!

It was February 18th, 2004 but I wasn't there,
for the last breath that you had to share.
I am so sorry I wasn't there to hold your hand,
even though you told me you understand.

Twelve years later but on a different day,
dad took his last breath and passed away.
Here I am still locked away and crying too,
every time I think of you two.

I'm sorry I wasn't there for you or dad,
you were the best parents anyone ever had.
Not a day goes by that I don't live in sorrow,
and I'll live in sorrow every tomorrow.

So, I've listened to a lot of things people had to say,
they couldn't comfort me then and they can't today.
Because I wasn't there, I'll always hurt inside,
it will be something I'll always hide.

I'll always have that feeling of sorrow and shame,
and I only have myself to blame.
Today the only reason I can make it through,
is because you know how much I love you.

Dedicated to my Mom and Dad

YOU TURN YOUR BACK

Should I get up and put another log on the fire,
So, the chill doesn't kill your desire?
I can't stop this feeling, you don't want me anymore,
and that my love, is what I lit the fire for.

I would like to know what is going on in your head,
you're as cold as the sheets on our empty bed.
I'm not blind, I know there's something going on,
you're leading me to believe your love is gone.

There are some days that you take me by surprise,
and I can see the desire in your eyes.
But I don't think that desire is for me,
this is not the way we are supposed to be.

You haven't looked my way in so long,
you sure haven't told me anything is wrong.
I've done everything I can waiting for you,
but I've got to know if we are through.

You've spent a long time trying to change me,
to be the man you want me to be.
And just when I thought you were on the right track,
when I want to make love, you turn your back.

YOU

I thought I knew what love was, but I didn't have a clue,
when you kissed me, that was when I knew.
No one has ever kissed me the way that you do,
nobody has made me feel the way I do about you.

Don't ever think that I don't love you,
because you have me till my life is through.
My love will always feel like it's brand new,
no one will ever have my heart but you.

You are the woman that I can't live without,
and you should never have any doubt.
I want to travel every road in life with you,
I will always love you like you want me to.

Until life ends, it will be only you and me,
look into my eyes and love is all you'll see.
Yours is the perfect love for me, I've found,
and I don't need anyone else around.

The love I have for you is not easy to acquire,
but you are my one and only desire.
I am positive that you and only you,
can make all my dreams come true.

YOUR SMILE

People change and I have too,
I'm so glad that I have you.
All this time that I lost my way,
you were faithful enough to stay.

It seems like a long, long time ago,
you said you wouldn't let me go.
I'm a fool for drifting away from you,
and all the shit I put you through.

You told me we were meant to be,
and I was too blind to see.
You were faithful to the end,
you were my long, lost friend.

Friends are where we have to start,
before we give away our heart.
We don't have to fit like a glove,
for us to fall in love.

You can melt my heart of stone,
from a long time of being alone.
If you can put up with me awhile,
I can fall in love with your smile.

YOU'RE ALL I SEE

I know right now that I am far away,
but I'll be there with you someday.
I can't wait till the time is right,
So, I can be with you every night.

I'll give you everything that I can,
and I'll always be your man.
Some days I'll be a pain in the ass,
but my love for you will always last.

I don't have much more time to do,
and all I can think about is you.
Now and again right before your eyes,
I'll give you the best surprise.

I'm a spontaneous guy, I don't plan,
that's what you'll like about your man.
I'll buy you roses on no special day,
with you, I'm always ready to play.

I'll hold your hand everywhere we go,
I love you and I want everyone to know.
When I close my eyes, you're all I see,
we'll be together forever when I'm free.

Chapter Five

From the Inside Out

By

Billy Leland

For the first time in my life I was locked like an animal in a cage. No one came when I called begging to use the phone, when I asked for a book to read just to keep my mind busy, or when I needed a pencil and a piece of paper. I tried desperately to get a hold of someone who cared about me. My jailers tried putting me on drugs so I would sleep all day and night and leave them alone. Others here are on so many drugs they act like zombies or walking dead. Endless months have passed and I feel so alone. I'm beginning to feel that everything is hopeless and I'm irrevocably lost in the chaos that I can never hope to understand, much less solve.

But in the darkness of prison life I have acquired a sense of my own unique mission in the world. I know now that I must have been preserved for some reason. It must be something that only I can do, and it is vitally important that I do it. Because in the darkest moment of my life, when I lay abandoned as an animal in a cage, I called out to Him, He was there. In the solitary darkness of the "hole" where men had abandoned me, He was there! God was there!

He made me feel like I was still a "somebody", a loved human being. Not just a number that makes money for the prison. Something deep and unexplainable happened to me from there on. I found myself reliving my life. In the stillness of this small cell, I experienced a most unusual religious feeling which I never had before; I was able to pray with the utmost sincerity. I have surrendered the pain and sorrow to a Higher Power that doesn't need an explanation.

Today I am at complete peace with the world and myself. I have found the true meaning of my life, and time can only delay my fulfillment but not deter it. At forty-eight years old I have decided to reconstruct my life. I am sure I can accomplish my goal. I have also found a new great source of unexpected vitality. I am able now to laugh over my own miseries instead of wallowing in the pain of failure, and somehow there are hardly any great tragedies left to fret over.

Even though God walks with me every day in this prison I see things that are very disturbing to me. I'm writing this "not as a treatise on prison reform", but to "raise awareness and initiate a public discussion on the American Penal system." I want to shed further light on the need to prevent crime: to prevent the

218

mistakes and ignorance, the hostility and hopelessness, that can condemn the young and often not so young to a lifetime imprisoned.

America's overcrowded prisons has largely been credited to the rise in mandatory minimum sentencing and on the three strikes laws legislation that guarantees that, in some states, a 40-year old convicted drug dealer will almost certainly spend his next 30 years behind bars, before there is even the slightest possibility of release. We have a nation of grandfathers dying behind bars. The cost of housing America's prison population continues to skyrocket. America has only 5 percent of the world's population, but it has a quarter of the world's prisoners. A country that, because it has increased the length of sentences and virtually eliminated parole, has seen its prison population grow seven times larger than it was in 1970. The United States is a country that puts a larger percentage of its own citizens behind bars than any other country in the world. Maine is at the top of the list for incarcerations per-capita.

America's penal system is not only cruel and vindictive, but also a huge waste of money. Currently, "5.66 million adults in the country either are now or at one time have been in prison" and yet prison populations continue to grow even while crime rates have plummeted. Why? For one thing, America has huge prison guard unions and for-profit corporate prison operators. Prisons are making private corporations in the United States billions of dollars a year. Another reason our prison system continues to grow is the media. "Murder reports on network TV news rose 336 percent from 1990-1995 while the actual homicide rate fell by 13 percent. Violence raises ratings!

Did you know that almost 600,000 of America's 2.1 million prisoners are forced to have sex against their will? This results in an HIV infection rate that's 28 times as high in prisons than in the civilian U.S. population. Prosecutors know full well they are in effect imposing capital punishment-by-virus whenever they put a juvenile on trial as an adult. But failure to do so would mean losing their next election, so the gruesome practice of providing hardened convicts with underage sex toys continues.

Alongside all the fact illustrating the brutality, excessive cost, and ineffectiveness of prisons, there is a battery of statistics proving that the opposite is true of rehabilitation programs. They're cheap and they work. Yet, funding for any sort of betterment of inmates has continued to vanish while at the same time the number of inmates has exploded.

Inmates who completed a college degree program re-offended at less than half the rate of those who didn't go to school. But despite the success rate of education behind bars, the college degree programs behind bars have now been cut almost entirely.

In 1994, as part of it's get tough on crime mania, Congress abolished the practice of awarding Pell Grants (federal education loans that need not be repaid) to prisoners, this effectively ended chances for inmates to get a college education behind bars. Sen. Kay Baily Hutchinson, R-Texas, led the fight against college for the incarcerated. She said, "Pell Grants were sold (to Congress) to help low, and middle-income families send their kids to college. They were not sold for prison rehabilitation." Just like that, Pell Grant funding came to an immediate end, even though a number of studies concluded that education reduces repeat offenders. College programs demonstrated that when prisoners are engaged in self-understanding, skill development and knowledge acquisition, the result is life changing.

An effective penal system has two main concerns: security and rehabilitation. If a facility is secure, it will have a low record of trouble, violence and escapes. Effective rehabilitation will be reflected in a low recidivism rate. (Recidivism — prisoners getting out of prison only to return again.) When a prison system only does half its job, if it shirks its duty to rehabilitate its prisoners, then the prison population increases and prison expansions occur. The system ultimately requires more and more taxpayers' dollars. Does this scenario sound familiar? It is happening all over the United States but nowhere as fast as it is here in Maine.

Rehabilitation programs should be made readily available to every prisoner in the system. Such programs not only contribute to the orderly running of the facilities, but also ensure that the prisoner is able to return and function in society as a law-abiding member, no longer a threat or a financial burden to society. Most prisoners want to be rehabilitated so they can be better people. Goodness thrives within everyone, even those of us who have made some bad choices. That is why the prison college program was such a success when it existed, and why it produced low recidivism rates. How could anyone not see that taking away such a program was a blow to rehabilitation, and thus harmful to society.

Prisoners were not receiving a "free" education. We pay for it by "doing time". Time is all we have left but we want to rehabilitate ourselves, so that we will be useful members of society and we no longer cost taxpayers money. It costs in the ballpark of $39,000 a year to house an inmate in Maine.

I'm amazed that the taxpayers of Maine are not demanding that the college programs be returned to prisoners, and to make sure that the department of corrections starts to take its duty to rehabilitate more seriously that it does now. Then America can stop building prisons and start building people.

What you have just read are some of the issues I struggle with in prison. I pray to God all the time that our prison system will get a drastic change. But, one thing is for sure; I know that someday I'll be able to help others. If I can open the eyes of society on some of these issues, I'll be happy. I know most people in society today would like to see the spending of their tax dollars so foolishly come to an end. If the justice department both federal and state stop the foolish spending, our taxes wouldn't be half as much.

Christ is in Prison Too!

After I came down from the constant high I had on speed, and came out of the power Satan had on me, I thought I was at the end of my road. I thought that there was no more life left for me. I might as well just go ahead and die and give up.

I didn't think, after what I've been through and the things I've been associated with, that I could come back into a good life. A life that I could be genuinely happy, where I'd be loved, and people in the free world would care about me. I look for the day that I can be restored to freedom so I can live a good, affirmative, and worthwhile life. Right now, it's only a dream that a thing like that can happen.

Many people have the idea that prisoners aren't worth much. So just lock them up and forget about them. Get them out of sight and out of mind. That is what we hear all the time. The guards are constantly reminding us by saying, "remember where you are" every time they give us an order. It's a terrible thing when a prisoner accepts that evaluation just because we hear it so often. We begin to think: I'm no good, my life doesn't mean anything, and I'm unworthy. So, in prison you tend to act the way people think a convict should act. It's the tough who survive and the weak that are abused. You have to make a choice which one you're going to be. I know that in my past I was wild and I fell for Old Satan's tricks. Now I know what a fool I was. But I'm in prison, can a worthless criminal like me change and would it be worth it to try? Why would Jesus care about me for all my years of doing drugs, sex and sins?

While I was locked up in a small, cold cement cell with nothing in it but a steel sink, toilet and cement bed, I asked for a Bible. I was contemplating suicide and trying to figure out a foolproof way to do it. But after reading John 6:37 ". . . him that cometh to me I will in no wise cast out." I never knew God loved me the way he does. I read in the Bible that God sent His only Son to earth to die for me too. He didn't die just for those who told a lie or something, but he died for everyone. He died for murderers, drug dealers, and all sinners. Including me! That's amazing. All through the Bible there are stories about prisoners. It's as if God paid special attention to prisoners. That's when I really got hit by the Holy Spirit and gave my life to Jesus. I came to the conclusion God did create us and the entire world.

Now that I have accepted Christ as my Savior, I know that old things have passed away. I am a new creature in Jesus Christ. To follow Christ in prison it takes a lot of courage. I praise God every day for giving me that courage. I feel it takes a real man to be able to live for Jesus, stand up for Jesus, and to walk, as He would have us walk behind the walls of prison. I have found that through Jesus Christ, with his boundless love, comes into your heart that His love isn't limited to the circle of Christian brothers who share your interests, your faith, and your concern. I find myself really loving and caring for all the inmates in prison. It's a love for everyone that I've never been able to give before I came to know Christ. What gives Christians a bad name in prison? It's when people profess Christianity solely to win sympathy and privileges from prison authorities and possibly getting lighter sentences and even parole. I am well aware of the phenomenon known as "jailhouse religion". It's a cynical device characterized by an insincere conversion, used by some prisoners to curry favor with guards, wardens and the parole board. But the sad part is, it makes it hard on the true believers in Christ to spread the words of Christ. Other inmates see so much of the insincere that they don't listen to the sincere.

It is my prayer, that through me Jesus will touch many more men inside this prison so that they who are able to would seek Bible study classes and go to the church services. I also pray that they would seek fellowship with their fellow brothers and sisters inside and outside.

Jesus Christ is my dearest friend and he is serving time with me. I'm not sure why I'm writing this, but I'm assured He knows why and will rest assured that my small testimony will be a benefit and inspiration to you and others.

··········

I wrote this back when I was just a federal detainee in the Maine State Prison. I was in the hole, solitary confinement for a couple of months. It was the first time in my life that I have been locked up. I felt lost and like a wild animal in a cage. It was the lowest point in my life. After I was sent to the Federal System and found out that the United States caters to other religions, I found out why it is so hard to be a Christian in prison. You might not think so but there are forces at work in the United States to abolish Christians. President Obama did a lot of harm when he worked so hard to get so many Muslims into the United States. I don't care if they are Muslims or a person from any other religion. I want them to treat us with respect, the way we do them. But they don't!!! I'm still a Christian today. I'm also a sinner. But I don't sin as much as I used to and I will repent when I do sin. I try to walk the way of a Christian. I know I fall short but I am a work in progress. I know this is a poem book. I hope you don't mind me voicing my opinion on other subjects. I not only wrote poems to stay sane. I wrote a lot of other things that were on my mind and I had nobody to talk to about them.

Writing these things stopped me from getting into fights when the subjects were discussed. I saw and heard so many fights and arguments about religion that I got sick of it. I just wrote my opinions down and thought that maybe someday somebody would read them and know that I am not a bad guy. I still treat everyone the way I want to be treated. I still respect the opinions and views of others. I have an open mind. I've seen more than most people from Maine or any other state because I was in the Army in another country, I traveled the world as a Hells Angel and I've been through the Federal Prison Systems with men in prison from many different countries. I was educated on a lot of different cultures. I'm not an expert by far.

A Loser Turned Winner

By

Bill Leland

Often those who win in the courtroom because of their high-priced lawyers, who got them off on a technicality, lose at life. They get off and therefore never have to face the real problems of their lives. In fact, winning in court hurts them in the long run. They are not forced to stop and truly evaluate their lives. By winning, they lose.

I, on the other hand, was shaken so bad by one of life's wake up calls. Have you ever found yourself in the midst of a crisis that forced you to look at where your life was headed? On April 7, 2003, I was arrested at my home in front of my fifteen-year-old daughter. Tears were trickling down her cheeks as she watched her daddy being placed in handcuffs by policemen in swat gear with M-16's aimed at him. I was overcome with shock, shame and fear. What had I done to my family? Why had I allowed my life to take this direction? What am I going to do to make this up to the ones I love?

Prison need not be the end of the road, but the beginning of an interesting and productive life. I've learned in prison that wisdom comes more from living than studying. Prison can make or break a man, that's for sure. I hear prisoners talk about how they learned how to fight well with their hands. No one ever admits that they're just plain scared. Instead they hide behind huge muscles that they get from working out in the weight room every day. They think this proves they are real men. They think because they have muscles people are afraid of them. They try to intimidate others.

When you come to prison you have to prove yourself. Most of the time this is done ultimately in some type of battle. For me, prison has been an environment that necessitates a tremendous psychological preparedness, a place where your life is always at stake. A prisoner has to earn "jailhouse respect", by either being tough or being able to operate inside the system and get things done by a variety of ways, a gambling ring, drug distribution, food supply, smuggling, etc. Prison is a society unto itself, it has its own heroes and leaders. In here we must deal with the situation at hand, even if it's a violent one. It's easy to earn a reputation as a dangerous prisoner. All you have to do is show that you are ready and willing to use violence to the extreme when anyone crosses you. For instance, an inmate made a shank (knife), out of a broken chain link fence and stabbed another inmate in the chest, just because he wanted the reputation. It was about perceived respect. Their types of people have nothing else. He does not have a career, a house, a car, fancy clothes to distinguish himself. All he has in prison is his reputation. It remains a warped basis for this new way of life. This prison environment is one where the more powerful a person is, the more respect he receives, from both staff and inmates. Staff will use him to help keep order and give him some leeway in some other way. Those who can't earn status in any other way frequently become predators, aspiring to become known as a dangerous convict. If successful, he will be left alone.

The others are called "targets" or prey. Once marked as a target, an inmate's life is nearly worthless, as his possessions will be stolen, and he will be the victim of violence at every opportunity (unless he has money). Then he will have to pay for protection. The ones with no money and no one to turn to for real assistance, his weakness will overwhelm him and he eventually submits to the lowest realms of man's inhumanity.

It's worse than your scariest nightmare, where sleep is something you take a chance on doing, at the risk of never waking up. This life is a vicious circle that has gone on inside prisons for hundreds of years and will continue. For survival, you're caught up in a game that either side will cost you some large part of whatever is left of your human decency.

This brings to the forefront the whole issue of rehabilitation. Is it really possible, and is it recognized by society? Does society understand what they create in the men they wear down by time? The whole concept of punishment seems to teach offenders how to effectively "Not" be part of society, the "unmaking" of a man.

It's impossible to escape the ever-present feeling of punishment during the initial months of imprisonment. I remember the sleepless nights, the contemplation of suicide, and the humiliation I felt because I let myself, my family and my friends down. But as the days turned into weeks, then months and years, I began to get used to confinement. It was as if the scream of punishment had weakened to a faint whisper, one that takes some effort to hear. And so, doing time as punishment has lost it's meaning for me.

I'm learning many ways to cope with confinement but time is all I have left. I have learned my lesson and I will not commit another crime. It was proper punishment for me to come to prison but now I feel time is being wasted. I won't feel any different about crime the longer I stay in prison. I was hooked on drugs, now I'm not. My thought process was not working right, now it is. When is doing time an effective punishment when the lesson has been learned? I will always remember the punishment phase, but for me, that phase ended long ago.

Punishment for me is not the time I'm wasting in prison, costing the taxpayers so much money; it's the guilt I feel. Punishment was admitting to my family that I was not only a convict, but a liar too. I hid the fact I was a drug addict from the ones I loved most. Punishment was realizing that I was a failure and a convicted felon; I'd be branded the rest of my days. Punishment was knowing that I disappointed and humiliated everyone who believed in me.

I know I am only one man but I know of a man who spent his whole life in poverty. He is a man who believed that people should be free. He is a man who knows that all men are created equal. He was born to humble parents and never traveled further than two hundred miles from his home, yet he had an impact upon mankind that has never been equaled. His name is Jesus. It is true that I am only one man but can make a difference now that I am born again. I am a new man. It took being a loser to make me a winner.

I am currently an inmate at the Maine State Prison awaiting the judge's decision on a motion to get a new lawyer. I was arrested on possession of drugs on April 7, 2003 and put in the maximum-security unit on October 31, 2003. As far as anyone knows, I'm the only prisoner here that wasn't convicted of a crime. All because I was a member of the Maine chapter of Hells Angels, and for the same reason I've been denied bail. It's been a long 26 months, that's for sure.

My worst punishment came on February 1 8, 2004. My mother died of cancer and the federal government said I was too dangerous to go to her funeral. The second to the worst punishment I was forced to endure came on the evening following Thanksgiving of 2004. My wife had another man's baby on the six o'clock news.

Because of the love of Jesus, the love and support of my family and what's left of my friends, I have endured these hardships and stayed a winner. But my legal battle still wages on and on. As I stand today, I'm known only as number 57171, but with God's help I'll get out of this prison and make a difference in the new world I'll be living in. I'm praying to God that I win my case. I'm fighting with all I have. I'm expecting the worse but hoping for the best.

....

I ended up getting a twenty-one-year sentence. The United States Justice system is crooked as hell. I made a plea agreement with the prosecutor. For my guilty plea, I was told I would get a ten-year sentence and they would leave my son alone. But, when I got to sentencing, the judge sentenced me to twenty-one years. After all those years in prison, I've learned all about jails and prisons and how they are run. I've learned that the system doesn't spend taxpayer's money the way they should. They get money for programs that they don't even have. There isn't any rehabilitation in prison. The only ones that actually change are the ones that want to. A prisoner can be in prison for years and do nothing at all. I learned all I can. I have sixty-five certificates for classes I've taken. I took a college course through the mail. I stayed as busy as I possibly can in prison. I changed my life around but it had nothing to do with the prison system. If I didn't want to do anything, I wouldn't have been forced to do anything. I'm trying my best now to live well.

In this chapter, I'll still put the poems I wrote in prison and they will still be about the things that I had on my mind on that day. My poems have no theme to them. When I was asked to write a book of poems, I didn't know how to write one.

Kairos "Prison Ministry"

Hi, my name is Bill Leland. I went through the last weekend of Kairos, number thirteen. I want to welcome all of you to the Kairos family. As you know by now Kairos is run on Christian principles of love of God and respect for men. Through Kairos, I learned that every day I have an opportunity to make a positive difference in someone's life. It could be by a simple smile, a reassuring glance, or a kind word. And it may be with someone I don't even know. Take what you have learned here in the past few days and it will sustain you during times of challenge, frustration and even failure. It will comfort you during times of confusion, pain and loss. I hope God becomes a true, lifelong companion to all of you as He is for me. If you let Him, He will offer continual insight and wisdom in many areas of your life. We are blessed by Kairos members all over the world.

Kairos, through the love of all the volunteers, brought me hope in a hopeless place. In the past my personal introspection has given me some doubts with respect to my religious faith. I have questioned the importance of God and faith to a limited extent. However, that has all changed because God got His message to me through the Kairos program. I pray that He did the same for all of you. It seems there is Christian activity in a place where there might not be. It seems there is growth in a place where there isn't any room to grow. The message I got from my Kairos weekend was one of comfort and encouragement. I'm living my life inside this prison trying to bring others a sense of hope in a world where cynicism is the norm. I'd like to be an inspiration to others so they have the courage and foresight to seek that hope for themselves. Through Kairos, and Chaplain Matt, I've learned about God's purpose of faith, family, hope and forgiveness. Both have strengthened my beliefs in my religion. I want to thank Chaplain Matt and all the Kairos volunteers for the experience, it has helped me more than you can ever know!

Now you're fourth day starts. Your task must be to free yourselves from this prison by widening your circles of compassion to embrace all God's children. It's not easy in this environment. This prison can be lonely, fearful and a violent place. But remember, the real enemy is within, and that's where the 180-degree turn begins. If any of you need to talk, I'll be more than happy to talk with you. Maybe I can help, maybe I can't, but you are my brothers in Christ and I'm more than willing to do all I can.

When you leave the security and comfort of this room, don't forget each other. Acknowledge each other in passing, whether it's just a nod of your head after eye contact. You will both know that you are brothers in Christ. As much as you can in this cold environment, walk the walk Jesus did and talk the talk.

I know everyone wrote some names down and got rid of them in the water. For me some of the names keep popping into my head. I immediately pray to God to let me forgive and forget. The names come up less and less in my mind now and it sure feels good. I also feel alone and somewhat forgotten once in a while. I go back and read some of the letters from the volunteers around the world and the children, the loving feeling comes over me again and my day goes a lot better. I want you all to know that you have friends and brothers in Christ in here, talk to them, get closer to them, and pray with them. You'll be surprised how good you can feel about yourself and the time you spend in this prison can be a positive thing, not a negative one.

The love of God will help you through each day if you pray to Him every morning when you wake up. He will help you to adjust to all circumstances that disrupt your daily functions. You'll feel stress begin to subside. All this has worked for me in my fourth day. I'm praying it works for all of you. Congratulations and Good Luck. Who is the Church?

"Kairos 14"

We are the Church!

So, stay united as one and spread the Love and Word. There are so many out there that need the seed planted in them. You just may be the one to change someone's life for the better.

....

Every year, an outside ministry called Kairos comes into the prison for a week and teaches the Word of God. I took this class and I got baptized again. They asked me to talk to the class on the fourth day. This is the little speech that I gave them. I got a lot out of this class and it made me realize that I could make it through prison and it didn't matter how long the judge was going to sentence me to. But it still was a shock to hear the judge say 252 months in federal custody with 5 years-probation. If it wasn't for my faith, I don't know if I could have done all the time I did, especially all the times I was put into solitary confinement. I talked to God a lot when I was alone in "The Hole". It was the only thing that helped me through.

Memories

I'm co-existing with all the demons here,
my pen is my power so I keep it near.
My thoughts are my freedom in my mind,
I'm without outer emotions of any kind.

I'm not content and I'm to the point.
Life slips away in this joint.
Prison life is hard to understand,
Nobody here will give you a hand.

Life doesn't pass without some pain,
Turn your pain into your gain.
Learn from it to make you strong,
Then you'll know where you went wrong.

Do your best at a constant stride,
Never do anything you have to hide.
Keeping secrets will drive you insane,
Keep everything on an open plane.

Hold strong to the strength of reminiscing,
Never forget what you are missing.
Your memories will help you live,
That's all you'll have left to give.

Some memories will bring you pain,
And some can drive you insane.
I want to make memories new,
I want them to be with you.

Private Clown

In this prison I wear a disguise, but I hope you see the love in my eyes.
As days go by my love grows stronger, I'm so lonely I can't last much longer.
My love for you is etched in stone, I pray to God you are my own.
They hear me cry with walls so thin, I have to hold my love within.
Songs, poems and promises I want to say to you, but I'll have to wait till my time Is through.
I want to whisper sweet things in your ear, saying all the things You love to hear.
Please forgive me for making a mistake, I'm paying for it with this heartache.
I'm paying also for these lessons I've learned, and you know how I got burned.
Get a new life is what I should have done, cause I sure as hell wrecked this one.
I have scars that run real deep, but take it from me, they didn't come cheap.
I finally figured out what life's all about, and I never take the easy way out.
I'm taking my old life and leaving it behind, I'll get it out of my mind.
Sometimes I feel like I'm spinning my wheels, but you know how that feels.
I'm always giving myself a beating, and I'm the only one I'm cheating.
I feel like I've failed life's test, but I'm going to lay that to rest.
I've learned I have to change my ways, cause behind bars, I've spent too many days.
I really don't want any sympathy, nobody's paying for my mistakes but me.
I just want you to answer when I call, because I love you with my all.
I remember you used to think I was funny, and you loved it when I called you honey.
I loved to be your private clown, please forgive me for letting you down.

Will Get Burned

Read my words and be a believer, do your best to be a high achiever.
Value your freedom and never let it slip away, Live life to its fullest every day.
My life revolved around drugs and alcohol, I was so messed up and not thinking at all.
My home life couldn't have been worse, believe me when I say, "drugs are a curse."
For years now, I've been alone in this tiny cell, It sure has changed me, you can tell.
When you look into my eyes you will see, That I'm not the man I used to be.
Depressed and lonely is all I ever feel, because this prison life is very real.
I've lost everything I ever had, and now my life is extremely sad.
I wish you would learn from my mistakes, do your best in life no matter what it takes.
When you love someone, let them know, you can lose them as fast as melting snow.
You can never make up for what is lost, and eternal heartache is what it cost.
Not a day goes by that I don't regret my past, because these painful memories last and last.
I wish there was a way I could start over again, I would be a good man in a world full of sin.
It's taken my whole life but I did learn, to do what is right or you will get burned!

By
Billy Leland
"April 3,2005"

It's 6:15 a.m. and I've been awake most of the night because my sinuses are stuffed up bad and I can't breathe. When I lay awake nights like this my mind goes a hundred miles an hour. Being locked in this little cell always makes me think about what got me here. So, my way of dealing with what's on my mind is to write it down. I try to do that in the most creative way possible. What you just read is the result.

RAIN

I'm locked inside looking out at the rain, I watch as drops slide down the pane.
It's so dark and dreary tonight, I'm so lonely and it don't feel right.

Lately, I've been feeling a lot of pain, it hurts like walking in freezing
rain. I myself have a painful tale, It's as bad as winter's hail.

Why is it always cold and dark, And the pain always hits its mark?
When it rains my days aren't very nice, Making my heart as cold as ice.

How can rain make me feel this way?
I need to change the way I feel today!
I'm so alone with nothing to do,
Please listen to me and help me through.

I wasn't born to be alone, And I hurt down to the bone.
I'd be okay in any kind of weather, as long as you and I are together.

....

I can't even tell you how many hours I've spent staring out a window at the rain wishing I was out there
in it. I would give anything at that time to be free. It made me depressed and I wrote more on rainy days.

Prison Guard

I'm starting to see things,
my mind is playing tricks.
I'm starting to hear things,
now, they're getting their kicks.
They walk by every half hour,
They look at you as if you aren't there.
It's just a body count to them,
They show that they don't care.
They see you crying in your cell,
With nothing in here to do.
You politely ask for a book,
And all they do is laugh at you.
To them you're just a show,
How you hurt, they don't know.
Is it an act that they put on,
Or are their feelings really gone?
How can they treat people this way,
Knowing what goes on day after day?
When you can do this and it isn't hard,
That's when you know you're ready to be A PRISON GUARD!
By
Billy Leland
(Super-Max Solitary Confinement)

Beauty I See

I'm in a secret place in my mind,
A place that is so hard to find.
It's not the fancy cars and diamond rings, It's all of life's beautiful things.
I've learned a lesson that I think is funny, Happiness isn't having a lot of money.
It's watching a baby come to life with a cry, Or, standing on a mountain way up high.
I've seen the most beautiful sunset,
I was as happy as I could get.
I've taken time out to smell the flowers, And I've walked on a sandy beach for hours.
But there's some things my heart can't hide,
and that's how much I love to ride.
On motorcycles I feel so free, and that's what I was born to be.
I've seen the beauty of a raging waterfall, A crystal clear lake, but that's not all!
The feel of a warm summer breeze, lying in the sun as long as I please.
The sun has always made my life bright, I guess it's where love feels so right.
Walking on a beach hand in hand, Making love in the hot, soft sand.
To look into the most beautiful eyes, to share love under the blue skies.
To be out on an ocean cruise,
And know you have a love you can't let go. I love an old muscle car show,
That's a sign of beauty, I hope you know! The heart being as
pure as gold, Having someone when you're old.
The Rocky Mountains in Colorado,
is a beautiful place to know.
The Glacier National Park, Is the place to be after dark.
All of these things in beauty I see,
I'd love to have someone share them with me.

Lesson Plan

This prison has a lesson plan for me, One of humiliation and degradation.
They stripped me of my identity, and put me in segregation.
I was alone but was I forgotten?
Not knowing is a very bad thing.
I was scared, cold and lonely,
And wondering what tomorrow will bring.
You were in all my thoughts and dreams, You're the glue that held me together.
With you I can ride out the fiercest storm, I could survive in any kind of weather.
I force myself to eat, sleep and breathe, while thinking of your beautiful face.
I suffered through all kinds of beatings, praying to get out of this place.

I did learn a most valuable lesson, But, not the one they planned for me. I wouldn't let them break my spirit, I am the man God meant me to be.

By

Billy Leland (6-2-04)

Chapter Five

In this chapter I am going to put some religious poems I wrote while in Prison. I hope you enjoy them. It is only by the grace of God I survived all those years alone in prison.

TRUST GOD

There is a purpose for all of our heartaches,
Our Savior always knows what is best.
We learn our precious lessons,
In every sorrow, trial and test.
This prison life is very painful,
My past with its darkness is gone.
I've learned a lot about myself,
And a change is beginning to dawn.
Though all around me there is darkness,
And earthly things have flown,
My Savior whispers His promise,
Never to leave me alone.
I pray that He leads me to a lost soul,
And then teach me what to say.
Because friends of mine are lost in sin,
And cannot find their way.
I'll tell the world how Jesus saved me,
How He gave me a life brand new.
I know that if you trust Him,
All He gave me, He'll give to you.

I'm No Different

When the steel door locks to my cell,
I sit down and pick up my pen.
To keep my mind from going to Hell,
I write these poems again and again.

I never thought that I would write,
But I'm all alone with nothing to do.
So, I sit here under God's light,
Sharing my deepest thoughts with you.

I'm supposed to act like a tough man,
And being a poet doesn't fit that bill.
I'm just lonely and doing the best I can,
While being locked up against my will.

Being a prisoner is tough on me,
Because I can't show what I feel.
I hope the other inmates can't see,
That what I show isn't real.

They say it's important what others think,
Because you can get hurt in the yard.
You have to watch your back and don't blink,
And that's not easy, it's really hard.

I've learned that I have to put on an aire,
You can't be who you want to be.
Show true feelings and no one will care,
Hatred and contempt is all I see.

I've learned to keep all my feelings inside,
But I write them down all the time.
To all you readers, I won't hide,
I tell you how I feel in a rhyme.

I hope you can relate to what I say,

It all comes from my heart.
I live in bondage day after day,
And I'm begging for a new start.

I know I'm not a professional poet,
I just write what's on my mind.
If you're reading it you know it,
But in here I'm one of a kind.

I know others here hurt the way I do,
And nobody shows who they really are.
They all hide their feelings too,
So, I'm no different, by far.

God's Light

God gave me the gift to write,
This pen expresses my feelings right.
I never knew I would make words rhyme,
But now, I'm doing it all the time.

I hope some of them touch your heart,
And some help you get a new start.
Poems are always popping into my head,
As I sit her on an empty bed.

My words don't just pop out of the air,
I write things that I want to share.
Sometimes I have to hold back the tears,
As I write about my worst fears.

I fear loneliness and the blues,
So, my fears are what I use.
I was afraid my heart would stop beating,
When I found out my wife was cheating.

I thought I was going to the graveyard,
Living without love is just too hard.
So, when you read what I write,
Know that I'm living under God's light.

He's not a ghost

There's a very special time for you and me,
It comes from the Kairos Prison Ministry.
I attended one of their awesome weekends,
I came away with many new friends.

I believed in God but my heart was cold,
Kairos taught me with lessons so bold.
I always knew the way I felt was wrong,
And I've been away from God for too long.

I know He loves me now, that's very clear,
He's gotten me through rough times in here.
My cold heart was changed really fast,
And now my faith in Him will last.

I've learned to open up the door,
Jesus will come knocking for sure.
I let Him in and broke down my wall,
You just have to open up, that's all!

Jesus will prove to you He's not a ghost,
He's the one that loves you the most.
When you let Him in, you will see,
What kind of love that must be.

Christmas Day

There was a poor little baby wrapped in swaddling clothes lying in a manger,
That was over two thousand years ago and to some He's still a stranger.
Happy Birthday sweet Jesus, this is your time of year,
Thank you for being my Savior and keeping your love near.
It's said that every knee shall bow and every tongue confess,
And when I first heard these words my life was a mess.
Today is your birthday and it's a magical time of year,
I have learned what this means now and I shed a tear.
I've always tried to be a good man but somehow my life went astray,
But You have been sent to save me and now I know I'll be okay.
With my religion I played hide and seek until the day that I heard God speak,
I never thought that I was weak until I learned to be meek.
God gave a gift to the world, he sent His only son, Jesus,
He was sent to forgive our sins and this should please us.
He would die for our sins and all we have to do is believe,
We are all going to win and blessings we will receive.
As you celebrate with family and friends this Christmas season,
Don't take it for granted because Jesus is the reason.
We tend to take a lot of things for granted such as all the beautiful lights,
But look up in the sky for the star of Bethlehem on clear nights.
It was under this star that our Savior was born,
And I thank God even though I'm weary and worn.
Even though I'm in this prison, I don't want you worrying about me,
God has me under his wing and He's has set me free.

Patience in His love

Freedom is the only gift I wanted today,
But in this prison, I must stay.
I live my life behind this locked door,
I don't want to live like this anymore.

I feel abandoned, insecure and unworthy now,
God, take away these feelings somehow.
Take away the painful memories of my past,
And please give me a love that will last?

I thank God that Jesus was born today,
And died to take all my sins away.
He loves me and wants me to live,
He has so much love to give.

He left His Father's throne above,
Emptied Himself of all but love.
So free, so infinite His grace,
He came to earth to save or race.

Though darker and rougher is my way,
My troubles get harder day by day.
With patience in His love I will rest,
He has taught me what is best.

By My Side

I'm struggling, yes, it's part of living,
Stay with me and I'll go on giving.
Nothing is gained on beds of ease,
Struggling has brought me to my knees.

"I love you Lord Jesus", I often say,
Talk to me and I will obey.
Just tell me what you want me to do,
Then I'll show you my love is true.

Doing things my way It's a wonder I didn't die,
I yearned for things, in the end were lies.
Lord, increase my courage so I will reign,
I'll bare the burdens and endure the pain.

In this prison, I hear a lot of talk,
But very few walk the walk.
I bare a load of pain and sorrow,
And I pray for my tomorrow.

I trust my Lord, He's my faithful guide,
I know He's walking by my side.
In this prison, I am safe with You,
You're always with me no matter what I do.

His Loving Care

Come walk with me on the street called Straight,
That leads to Heaven through a narrow gate.
Come talk with me and You'll understand,
Why I'm headed to the promise land.

My new life is thanks to the blood of the lamb,
In a place where I'm accepted for who I am.
Tomorrow may never come so be prepared,
For eternity you will be spared.

Accept Jesus as your savior before it's too late,
Give your life to Him and come through the gate.
No matter if you're battered, bruised or frail,
The love of God will always prevail.

You'll have no more worries, no more fright,
The promise of God protects day and night.
He will keep you safe in the perils of life,
He'll deliver you from struggles and strife.

For He is the vine and I am His branch,
He's giving our life another chance.
His fruit I'll bare and His fruit I'll share,
Let Him nourish you with His loving care.

Pray

The sun never shines down on me,
I'm in a dark prison cell, I'm not free.
There is nothing but darkness all around,
Love is nowhere to be found.

I see nothing but pain and heartache,
It's amazing what some men can take.
Some men here are never getting out,
This is not what life should be about.

We make our home in a tiny cell,
In it, we don't live all that well.
The food here is barely fit to eat,
If you're not careful, you get beat.

We don't see life outside the prison wall,
This is a community of criminals, that's all.
The only way to make our future bright,
Is to look for God's Loving Light.

He gives us something to live for,
In a place where we feel so poor.
I get out of bed each day and pray,
I don't want to live here another day.

HUMAN TOUCH

Please listen when I tell you my story,
It's filled with love and glory.
In prison is where I can be found,
With pain, sorrow and tears all around.

I'm listening to Jesus's every word,
They're the most precious I've ever heard.
He made the blessing of the Lord known,
His wisdom, truth, and love are shown.

Before I knew Jesus, I wanted to die,
I'd lay in my lonely cell and cry.
God offers new life, what more could He give?
His only son died so that I may live.

He won't burden me with more than I can bare,
With Him, my pain, I will share.
I listen to Him when He comes to call,
With my heart, my live, my all.

When I thought I'd give up the fight,
I trusted God and saw the light.
I've learned to love His so much,
That I don't miss the human touch.

Are we all prisoners?

When looking at me through prison bars,
Don't forget about our Savior's scars.
He died on the cross for me and you,
You can't imagine what He went through.

He was sent here to save mankind,
He doesn't want to leave anyone behind.
All we have to do is hear His word,
And obey all that we have heard.

Was He a prison because of love?
You know He came from Heaven above.
Without him my live became insane,
His love takes away all of my pain.

The love of Jesus is so exciting,
And to everyone He's inviting.
He wants you to join Him in prayer,
He wants everyone out there.

He was resurrected from the ground,
And if you let him, He'll be around.
I feel so content when I'm in church,
Anywhere else and it hurts.

Without Jesus in my life I was so blind,
I was a prisoner in my own mind.
I can't remember ever feeling worse,
Now, my old self is in a hearse.

I've escaped through my prison bars,
And Jesus is healing all my scars.
I've buried the man I used to be,
Jesus opened my eyes so I could see.

Walking with Christ is the only way,
I want Him with me every day.
Even in this prison He set me free,
As long as He walks with me.

··········

Before I found Jesus and turned my life over to Him, I wanted to die. I didn't think I could last 21 years behind bars and living with every degenerate in the system. When I turned my life over to Jesus, I immediately felt free. I felt like I could do anything. I learned to pray and leave my life in His hands and whatever came my way I could count on Him to be there with me. I have faith now and I take one day at a time and leave it all up to Him. If something doesn't go my way, which it often didn't, I pray on it and deal with it. I think about Him carrying the heavy cross to His death and getting whipped all the way. I think about the crown of thorns on His head with the never-ending pain He suffered for me. It makes me think that what I'm going through is nothing compared to what He went through for me. I can endure anything now when I think of what He endured for me. I have no room to complain. I know now that I am going to live the best life I can and follow His ways. I'm not the man I used to be and I'm proud of that. I just want to be a simple man now. I want to live a life He would be proud of. I know I fall short of that every day. But I'm a work in progress. I'm trying and I'll continue to try every day. I'm a sinner still but not like I used to be. I'm more aware of it now and I do all I can to prevent it.

HE'S BY YOUR SIDE!

I hope my poems and stories will bring someone delight,
And bring them out of darkness into the light.
Even though I'm in prison and seeing darkness every day,
Through Jesus Christ I have found my way.

Wherever I am I feel God's presence there,
He makes my time of sorrow easier to bare.
With the Lord in my life I will reign,
I'll grow stronger while enduring the pain.

He has a voice that I've never heard,
But I know He loves me by His word.
I know that someday in Heaven, I will be,
And with His voice, He will speak to me.

If you let Him in your heart, I know what He'll do,
What He gives to me, He'll give to you.
You'll feel protected by His loving hand,
Never can an enemy follow or a traitor stand.

You'll never have to worry, He'll always be there,
You'll feel the warmth of His loving care.
Trust in Him because He's your faithful guide,
And you'll love knowing He's by your side.

THE TEST

In my mind, during the many sleepless nights in my lonely cell, I contemplate. Prison is a test for me. The hardest test in my life. I often wonder what I am doing here, and why I put myself in a position to be sent here. Why did I hurt all those who love and care about me? When I first got arrested, I thought that I would handle it all and fight these charges and win. I didn't know the system. The system always wins. I can't fight the United States of America alone. When they took me right from the streets to prison, I thought I could handle that and do a good job at being a prisoner. Once again, I didn't know what prison life was all about. Then the tests came, one after another, harder and harder. My standing among the other inmates, my self-respect, and then the violence. Being put in prison isn't the test. The test is how I react to living in the environment with others. Living on my own in solitary confinement is the hardest test. I'm not a follower and I never will be no matter how long I'm in prison. The tests make me realize that I have to walk tall and be proud of myself even though a lot of inmates look down on me because I'm a loner and don't want to fit in. I know there is no greater enemy than myself. I will not be a judge of others. I will not close my heart and my mind to someone because they are inmates. We all make mistakes. I'm no better than the next guy and besides, God forgives them, who am I to hold it against them?

In this prison, I am tested daily. The hardest part of the day for me is the hour before the bugle sounds off for our six-a.m. count. I am usually awake at five or before that. Sometimes I'm awake all night. I lay there dreading the sound of the bugle and the recording that comes over the intercom really loud telling all the inmates to stand up and turn on their overhead lights so we can be counted. It's within this hour that thoughts come tumbling into my mind, many of them are unsettling. I find my mind drifting into a stream of consciousness-type of wandering. Thoughts of freedom often get me depressed when I open my eyes only to find that I'm locked in this cold prison cell. I try to pull my mind back to this reality but being so tired and emotionally unbalanced, I only succeed for a moment or two only to have it drift away again. I become a watchman who waits for the morning. When anxiety comes, as it almost always does, I cast all my anxieties on Jesus.

As I grow in faith, the demons of the early morning have gotten quieter. They no longer scream at me, but they haven't taken a permanent hike either. May all prisoners who suffer from anxiety, and we all do, cast it on the Lord. We can be calm watchmen who feel God's comfort and security as we await the morning in the darkness of our cells. For all of you that haven't been in jail or prison, and feel you don't need the Lord, I pray for you. Don't wait until you've hit rock bottom before you turn to Him. He is always there for you.

I have opened up to Him and discussed my failed tests in life. I didn't want to let these tests beat me, so I had to give up trying to be in control. My way obviously wasn't working. My way got me to where I am today. I need God to give me the strength and show me how to live again. In the loneliness and darkest days of my life, God showed me His love by picking me up and giving me direction, always rewarding me with loving thoughts, peaceful feelings, and a need to live and thrive. On my own, in this prison, I couldn't find the strength to carry on.

Another important test for me is how I handle being away from my family and all I love for so long. I'm asked quite often by the guards, as well as a few other inmates how I'm doing. I say to them, "blessed". After all, I really am blessed and I know it. I am blessed to have such a wonderful family that loves me. Time does not hurt the love we have for each other, it only makes it grow stronger. From my seven months in three different county jails, and now my two years in the Maine State Prison, I have used my time writing and reading. I have read the whole Bible. I have studied the Bible. I've taken a seminary course and have a certificate as an Ordained Minister. There are many other things I've done in prison to kill this time. I am not one of the thousands of inmates that sit in front of a TV playing games or just laying around. I've participated in many programs in the education department, I've gone to many classes on drug and alcohol rehabilitation, I've participated in group counseling etc. These are tools that can aid in the rehabilitation of our souls. They are not the cure though. What is the cure is the Word of God. He heals and makes free all those who are bound. When I first came to prison, I had a lot of insane thoughts and beliefs. It was only through renewing my mind and reprograming my heart according to God's word, that I saw a change in me. Was this also a test?

I have wrestled with and overcame many issues that held me bound before. I have made drastic changes in my thinking and behavior. I know that I am not the evil man that the police and prosecutor want society to believe I am. God has been merciful in changing me, as I have renewed my mind. I don't claim to be all that I will become, but I am rehabilitated! This is what leads me to ask God, "When will I be released"? I come to the same conclusion each time. It is not for me to know at this time, it is God's will that will be done and I will accept whatever happens. I am waiting for God to perform as He promised that He would. I'm waiting patiently and in faith. If we knew every detail of things, there would be no need to trust God. He shall bring it to pass in His name.

Since coming to prison, I've experienced some treacherous and extremely problematic situations that include people trying to rip me off, set me up, and even trying to take my life. Both staff and inmates alike have put me in harm's way on many occasions, just as my own stupidity has caused me difficulties. As a result, I've been locked down in "The Hole", beat up and put through pure hell. But, all of us have made our mistakes along the way and have encountered the wrongs of others. These wrongs brought consequences that tore us apart inside with no solace or concern from those around us. I pass this test by knowing God is an ever-present help in my difficulties. He gives us the means to stand and hope in the midst of life's most oppressive storms.

I wrote this on June 19, 2005. At that time, I was a federal detainee at the Maine State Prison in the maximum-security Unit. I didn't know I was going to receive a twenty-one-year sentence in a couple of months and the real trouble would begin. I did know that no matter what I would receive for time the Lord would be with me. I didn't know the tests were going to get a lot harder. I just kept writing and writing.

What Happened to Justice?

Very early in the Bible, God laid out some laws. These laws are known to us as the "Ten Commandments". They were given to Moses and etched in stone. On Mount Sinai covered in smoke, because the Lord descended upon it in fire, the whole mountain quaked greatly. It is obvious that God takes law and justice very seriously. The commandments are amplified throughout the Bible by detailed code of right and wrong.

Only to the extent a nation obeys the laws of God is there an opportunity for an orderly society where men and women may pursue happiness, engage in fruitful labor, and receive the inspiration of worship. In this time of unprecedented technology, it has been forgotten that the Bible offers a stern, swift, fair and effective system of justice. The ignoring and compromising of the biblical law has caused America to pay a fearful price. Crime has become a way of life for and ever-growing army of law breakers. The streets of America have become a jungle. We live in a condition of terror, and fear immobilizes people. I'm afraid things are going to get worse before they get better. Until there is a vast law and order reform movements based on divine justice, things will not get better. We've let a lot of people in this country and gave them rights. These people don't believe in Jesus Christ. They want you to believe in their God. I'm afraid America is being torn apart.

The number of Americans and others from other countries incarcerated in federal and state prisons has soared to an unbelievable proportion; the largest prison population in the nation's history is right now. The end is nowhere in sight. As soon as they empty a bed in these places, they fill them again. Prisons across the nation are already grievously over-crowded and new facilities or expansions are on the drawing boards now. Costs are in the billions! Prisons are the biggest growth industry in America today.

Vast, expensive prisons are a relatively late invention of mankind, they did not begin to appear until the late 1200's in England. In the biblical times, there was no need for large prisons. Imprisonment wasn't used much for penalty. The secret for the wise ancients for avoiding prisons and dealing realistically with crime was two-fold, swift justice and restitution.

In the Old Testament, when someone committed a crime, they were not sent to prison to be fed and sheltered at the expense of taxpayers. God's law was clear. Exodus 21:1 NIV declares: "If a man shall steal an Ox, and four sheep, and kill it of sell it; he shall restore five Oxen for an Ox, and four sheep for a sheep". There are many examples in the Bible of restitution. With this system of restitution, the victim didn't lose, the taxpayer didn't lose, and the only loser was the criminal.

Lawbreakers were quickly brought before judges who meted out punishment, which intimately involved the criminal and his victim. There were no loopholes or such delaying tactics by clever lawyers as endless postponements and appeals. The only appeal, if he intended to mend his ways, was to God. What if a criminal couldn't repay? In that case he was required to sell himself as a bondservant to the person he had wronged or to another employer-master who would pay off his obligation, and he had to work for that person until the dept was paid off. Such was the "imprisonment" of the Bible. From Exodus to Revelation, the criminal was punished severely but evenhandedly. Under our contemporary system, those who pay the least for their crimes are criminals. Instead of penalizing the victim and the taxpayer, crime should be paid for by the criminals. We need less retribution and more restitution!

Suppose a man is convicted of committing a five-thousand-dollar robbery, and is sentenced to five years in prison with no restitution required, which happens all the time in this country. The money he stole is repaid by the victim or his insurance company, which results in higher premiums for everyone. The taxpayer, who had no part in the crime, pays all the legal charges, the cost of the investigation, the arrest and the trial. Then the pay to feed, house and clothe him. Keeping a man in prison costs the taxpayer's today in the vicinity of $40,000 a year. (At the time of her conviction for bank robbery, the bill to Californians for housing, the trial and hospitalization of Patty Hearst was in excess of $230,000.00) Moreover, by keeping a man in prison, the man's family will probably apply welfare, thus causing the taxpayer's an extra burden.

The result of the system is that the criminal is only inconvenienced while at the same time he is housed, clothed, fed and given medical attention. Is that justice? It's merely a form of comparatively mild retribution or punishment and it serves nobody well. This system totally ignores the victims and the taxpayers. If the criminal is fined, the state or the government keeps that money. If the criminal does have property that the has to forfeit, the money doesn't go to the victim. It goes to the state or the government.

In the old times, if the thief had been sentenced to repay the money he stole, three things would have resulted. First, the victim would be compensated. Second, the taxpayer would be relieved of the major part of the cost of the crime. Third, the lawbreaker would learn more and be more effectively rehabilitated by making restitution.

The rule of restitution should not apply only to those who steal with a gun, but to those who rob with a ball point pen or a computer. America, according to the Justice Department, is buckling under the weight of $75 billion a year stolen by white-collar crooks (far, far more than is stolen by armed criminals). Rarely, if ever, is that $75 billion repaid when the "businessman" in custom-tailored suits is convicted. Most of time fines aren't even demanded. After their relatively short prison sentences, they return to their mansions, still multi-millionaires. Just look at the case of Martha Stewart. Today she is still looked upon as a good citizen and celebrity.

America has to develop a creative alternative to prison and think about more drug counseling and rehabilitation on the streets. There is no rehabilitation in prison unless the prisoner wants to be rehabilitated. That can happen on the streets a lot cheaper than in a prison setting. The normal life of an inmate is sixteen hours a day of lusting, watching TV, sleeping or whatever the inmate wants to do to pass his or her time. For the most part, imprisonment should be limited to the most incorrigible and violent criminals. Society, obviously needs the protection and even those prisoners should be sentenced to the therapy of labor.

Penitentiaries should not be used for storage or warehouses for human beings at the expense of the taxpayer. Idleness breeds trouble and restlessness behind the walls. You can take that from me. For almost fifteen years I have been doing all I can so I wouldn't be idle. Prison reform takes place in America all the time but it's not the reform America needs. It needs to reevaluate its whole system.

The necessity is to reintroduce the Bible's bondservant concept. The entire apparatus of justice must be refocused. In most cases, those convicted of crimes should be sent to prison only if they refuse to take a job and compensate their victims. Inside prisons, inmates should be required to work meaningful jobs, and they should be paid prevailing wages, not the twelve-cents an hour the federal system pays now. What they earn should be shared by those they victimized and the prisoner's families (in order to help reduce the nation's astronomical welfare bill).

Private industries and governmental agencies should farm out as much work as possible to prisoners. Everly state governor should appoint a tough no-nonsense task force to determine in detail what profit-making businesses can be created in its prisons. The prisons should become anvils of labor, factories employing men instead of just babysitting them. We must be concerned by what kind of people inmates are going to be when they are released. Certainly, if they have worked productively, they will be better citizens. All inmates in our penal institutions, except the sick and infirm, should be made productive. The federal prison system today is closing jobs such as Unicor. Instead of cutting out these jobs, they should be creating more.

The need for upgrading education inside prisons is vast. Inmates should be taught realistic vocational or white-collar skills that will be in demand once they leave the institution. Here, at the Maine State Prison, some of these programs are in place, on paper anyway. In reality, very little reform goes on here and only a select few are allowed in the programs that they do have. If these programs were run the way they were designed on paper to run, they would do much to reduce the high rate of recidivism and would serve to rehabilitate ninety-five percent of the prisoners that are returning to society. But, as you can see by the recidivism rate here at the Maine State Prison, and the repeat offenders, it's not enough to have these programs in place just on paper.

Back to the Bible? The recidivism rate is at least two-thirds lower among Christians coming out of prison than it is non-Christians who are released. Jesus says in Mathew 25:36, NIV "I was in prison, and Ye came unto me". He was stressing helpfulness, sympathy, good works, compassion, brotherly love, and saying that visiting prisoners and winning their souls are the obligations of Christians. The Bible doesn't take the view that lawbreakers should be shunned or treated badly by Christians. The Bible takes the view that even though men and women have sinned and broken the law, they are still members of the human family. Their lives are precious.

Man was created by an intelligent, moral, spiritual, and intellectual God who gave each individual the power to choose. Man, therefor, is not the product of his environment. He is the product of his own choices. Until a man chooses what to change in his life and chooses to let God fill his heart, he will be lost. Crime stems from the human heart, until the hearts on men can be changed through Christ they will continue to kill, rape, steal, and embezzle. When the heart is changed the crime disappears. Time and again I have seen that the human heart can be changed, that great sinners can become great Christians once they have met the Lord and received the transforming experience of salvation. All men are created in the image of God and are capable of redemption by the blood of the son of God. No matter how ugly a man's life has been, no matter what crimes he's committed, if that man can be reached by the gospel and turned to Christ, he is a new creature.

Let's go back to the finger of God where law and justice were not idle matters, where imprisonment was only used for the incorrigible, and the ones that hurt others. It was used to keep society safe from the violent criminals. Let's get back on track and use more restitution and less retribution, this would stop penalizing the victim and the taxpayer. This methodology allowed people in biblical times to maintain an orderly society. There was a minimal amount of crime and taxes. Exactly the opposite characterizes our society today. Today's imprisonment is not working, let's get back to biblical times!

··········

SONS OF GOD

God has a plan for my life that includes a joy and usefulness that most people never know. I've been to the bottom, felt worthless and full of shame. I'm still in prison physically, that hasn't changed. But my condition, spirituality speaking, has been changed drastically. I repented and asked God to forgive my sins. I also asked Jesus Christ to come into my heart because I trust Him to save me. God granted me a full pardon and it's a permanent one. It's a pardon from all the guilt of my sins and the sentence of Hell that was on my soul.

There was a time, before I was saved, that I was not accepted by God. I had no righteousness, I was an unclean thing. But this has all changed now. I have, through Christ, a place of acceptance with God. The Father has bestowed on me to be called a Son of God. We, as saved Christians, are all called Sons of God. Nothing can ever change this. Our position in Christ and our place of acceptance with God is secure. It is permanent! So, in your mind know that you have a good solid footing with your walk with God. We, who are saved will never perish; we are safe in the Father's hands. If we had to be kept saved by our own power, we would be in trouble. But we are not kept by our own strength, will power, or good deeds. We are kept saved by the mighty power of God himself.

Behind these prison walls I have found relief from living aimlessly, with no purpose and an empty life. My life in prison is not as good as others might think. I'm lonely and I really miss my family and a few close friends. I'm no different than you, except that I have to hide my feelings, watch my back and put on a mask every time I leave the safety of my locked single man cell. But those who do know Christ as their Savior, even though they may be behind prison walls, can find greater fulfillment and joy in life than those on the "outside" and are unsaved. I feel I know more freedom and power behind bars now that I have Jesus in my life, than a person can ever know outside of prison if he is, at the same time, outside of Christ.

The world in general is not believer-friendly. It is hostile! Can you imagine the hostility, the hurt, anger and the resentment just being in prison causes? This attitude and the attitude of the world surely present a problem for anyone seeking to live a Christ-like life behind prison walls.

You can't bother yourself with the crimes that others committed. By ignoring this aspect of prison life, you will find that most of the other inmates are not friendly toward you. They won't allow you to participate in some things that you might ordinarily participate in. They also will assume that because you are a Christian, you have a "holier-than-thou" attitude toward them. Other inmates may want to test you to get you to lose your temper. They may try to get you to give into temptation. They want to prove, through you, that Christianity isn't real. Sometimes, I think that down deep, they are hoping to find what you have. But some inmates perhaps even guards, and other personnel will resent the happiness they see in your life as a Christian, because it convicts them of the wrongness of their lives. They will not feel good until they dragged you down. This is a struggle for me every day. I know there will always be problems for Christians in prisons. For me, most of my problems stem from the people around me. There are a lot of evil people in prison, but that's why they are here, right? I can't avoid them. It's a day-to-day struggle to not get disappointed and discouraged.

I know I have to be strong and sober and very careful as I walk through this prison. The Devil gives me all kinds of problems too, hoping to trip me up so that I lose any influence that I might have with the Lord and with my fellow prisoners. He will do all he can to stop me from being an effective tool for the Lord. He knows that once I lose my influence, it will take some time to get it back. In the meantime, those prisoners and others I come in contact with may be removed from my reach and they may never come in contact with someone who will tell them how to be saved. The Devil does not want them, but he doesn't want God to have them either.

It is easy for a person to get down-hearted in prison. There is also plenty of time to think, and if a person is not careful, he will think about the wrong things, things that will hurt him instead of things that would be healthy and helpful to him. Just remember this… "forget those things which are behind, and reach for those things which are ahead". Satan wants to burden you down with thoughts of sins that are past – sins that Jesus shed His blood for so that they could be forgiven, sins that God has already dealt with. You must not let the devil snare you in this way. Jesus got victory for me when he died on the cross. Who am I not to forgive myself for the sins of the past when God has forgiven me? You need to forget "those things, which are behind." Forget them!

The Bible calls self "Old Man", and our spirit is called "The New Man". These two "Men" are fighting with one another every day. Each of them wants to get the upper hand in our lives. You have to make sure your new man is fed better, given more attention, and kept stronger than your old man. Put off the old man which is corrupt according to the deceitful lusts and put on the new man which after God is created in righteousness and true holiness.

All in all, it may seem strange for you to read this, and at first difficult for you to believe. But as a prisoner, locked up behind bars, you have tremendous potential to serve the Lord Jesus Christ and make a difference in people's lives at this present time and for eternity. There are Christian prison inmates today who are accomplishing more for the Lord than many of their brothers and sisters in Christ who are not in prison. God can make your prison cell a powerful place, and even a pleasant place, because you are there and He lives with you.

It does not matter what your past life has been like, forget it! It doesn't matter how dirty or wicked and hurtful you have been, forget it! Now live your life in a way that pleases God. Set out every day with a firm goal in your heart. You are a "Son of God" and you are not going to sin today.

I'm not a mistake

I did some things that I'm ashamed of, and I'm paying for them dearly. I now realize there were a lot of people that used me. When it came time, they testified against me to save their own asses. I thought they all liked me and would never do anything like that. I must have been a fool! I wonder if they really hated me? That's okay if they do because I hated myself for letting them use me and me getting mixed up in their world. Drugs, alcohol and partying is all that was important. I learned that good people are sometimes capable of doing bad things, and allow stupidity to overcome rational thought.

As I have said before, I blindly followed the wrong crowd. But I'll never forget it. I'll live with that for the rest of my life. Even with endless talent and exceptional intellect, when we're unethical, we can lose everything we worked hard to achieve. I've lost everything I've ever owned, to include my house, vehicles, toys, and pets. I'm one of the more fortunate inmates, I didn't lose the love of my family and a few good friends. I've learned a lot from prison experience. Without the loving support of friends and family, life is meaningless. I think that me being in prison is hurting my family more than it hurts me.

I don't know how long I'll be in prison, but the time I've already served, twenty-six months, was enough time to think about my mistakes. I never want to spend another day in prison, but I do want to spend the rest of my life with the ones I love and trying to serve my community.

I've learned that it's not what we do occasionally that makes us who we are, it's what we do consistently. Good people sometimes do bad things. I'm no longer the same person I was in 2003. I made a mistake, but I'm not a mistake! I've also learned that the best way to see the good in others is to find it in ourselves.

When I was free, I wasn't sure who I really was. I used to say, "I don't know what I want to be when I grow up" all the time. Then I'd laugh about it. Now, that sounds so stupid to me and I'm ashamed of myself for even thinking that was funny. I was lost and didn't know what I wanted to do with my life but I was a grown up, I should have acted that way. I also said, "Those who die with the most toys, wins", that definitely isn't true and it's a stupid thing to say and believe. The truth is, those who die living in Christ wins. It doesn't matter how many possessions you have. You can be the richest man in the world and still go to hell when you die.

I guess I was doing what was expected of me, on the surface anyway. I was a husband, a father, and a good provider. Nobody saw what was going on inside me. Outwardly it appeared that I was succeeding at everything. I had a beautiful home, nice vehicles, horses, snowmobiles, ATV's, and money enough to do whatever I wanted. I had everything, but inside I felt like a failure and a fake. I wasn't working like a normal man, I was getting money illegally. This always weighed heavily on my conscience.

Now that I've had time to look at my life and examine my values and beliefs, I know what my priorities are. Family and true friends are far more important than material things. I never thought my life made a difference to anyone else. I often felt useless and alone, feelings I hid very well. This "Time Out" from free living has stopped me from wandering aimlessly, not knowing what I wanted. Now, I have set my life on course. I feel like I have direction and purpose. Even though I have a lot of regret for what I did to get this time-out, I am thankful for it. I now have the determination and self-esteem to accomplish my goals. I'm at peace with myself and can accept who I am, even though I may not succeed at every single thing. I know I'm not a superman! I'll still make small mistakes, but I'm not a mistake!

I want to thank God, everyone in my family, and the few friends that have stuck by me in the hardest times of my life. A special friend named Henry Burleigh, better known as Stick supported me monetarily and visited me whenever he could. A special thanks goes out to him.

I want to thank my mother, she is with God now. She was a big influence in my life. She's with me everyday in my heart. I want to try my best to make her proud of me.

For everyone in my life that I've caused any kind of pain, I'm deeply sorry! If there's a way I can make it up to you, please tell me somehow. It would ease the burden on my heart to make amends. I'm currently incarcerated at the Maine State Prison in the maximum-security unit where I have lived since October 31, 2003

....

At the time I wrote that letter, I thought I was going to go to trial and be found NOT GUILTY. I was dead wrong! I never went to trial and ended up pleading guilty. If I didn't, the government was going to go after my son. They knew I would plead guilty if they threatened to put my son in prison. God did that time with me. I don't know if I could have done all those years and faced all the things I faced without God in my life. My father died before I got out of prison too. He was one of my biggest supporters. I will always regret not being there for my Mom and Dad during their last days. My remaining family helped me tremendously to make it through those fourteen years. I love them with all my heart and will never be able to repay them for all they did. It hasn't been easy since I've been in the real world but I'm staying busy.

I'm doing all I can to make a new life, one God will be proud of. I miss my loved ones more than anything in the world but I know life goes on and losing people is all part of life. Building trust with the ones you love is hard but I think I'm doing good at that. I'm still a work in progress but I'm on the right path now and I feel good about myself, finally. I am not a rich man at all and I probably never will be. I just want to live the life of a simple man now.

BY MY SIDE

I'm struggling, yes, its all part of living,
But my love, I'll go on giving.
Nothing is gained on a bed of ease,
And God I'll always try to please.

"I love you Lord Jesus", I often say,
Talk to me and I will obey.
Just a sign telling me what to do,
I'll show you that my love is true.

I did things my way and should have to die,
I yearned for things that were a lie.
Lord, increase my courage so I can reign,
I bear all burdens and endure the pain.

In this prison, a lot of people talk,
And they don't walk the walk.
I'm living with so much pain and sorrow,
But I'll walk the walk tomorrow.

I trust you Lord to be my guide,
I know you're walking by my side.
I know that I am always safe with you,
You're with me no matter what I do.

TRUSTING HIS LOVE

I thought my life was ruined by sin,
And the world of drugs I was living in.
I used to think there was nothing I could do,
And in this prison my life was through.

Sins were all around me and I didn't think,
I got caught up in all the stink.
I closed my eyes to what was going on,
And now, everything I own is gone.

With God's help, I've had a change of heart,
Now my life has a brand-new start.
God has helped me to understand,
Jesus has provided His helping hand.

It's time I show this world a little spark,
Instead of living in the dark.
I can't make it to Heaven on my own,
Where no sorrow shall ever be known.

I'm following Jesus, it's the only way,
And it's a struggle day after day.
But I'm in prison glorifying His name,
Ever trusting His love, it's always the same.

MY MAKER

I love all of life's beautiful things,
Listening to a bird as she sings.
She gives me peace, I give her praise,
Living in this hell for so many days.

I have no one to love, as it seems,
And nothing but broken dreams.
When I sleep there's love in the making,
But all is lost as I am waking.

I'm waking broken hearted every morning,
I've lost all of love's adorning.
How I feel, no one can measure,
Losing love is a lost treasure.

My life is a swarm of foul destruction,
And drugs have been my seduction.
With promise of manhood so full and fair,
As it left me cold, lost and bare.

Now I'm a man that's badly bruised,
And one that has been surely used.
I've met the world's losers and forsaker,
And now, I'm ready to meet my maker.

WHAT A WORLD IT WOULD BE

I've spent a lifetime learning about living,
Life's not about taking, it's about giving.
We often forget about life's greatest treasures,
When we live our lives to collect material measures.
It's easy to say that it's better to give,
If only that was the creed to which we would live.
There's only one gift we all need to receive,
In order to receive it, we must simply believe.
We must believe in a God that's not seen or heard,
All the proof that we need, can be found in His word.
His Word is the Bible and His revelation,
Believe in His word and your gift is salvation.
God sent Jesus to earth as His only son,
He sent Him for us, so our fight can be won.
Jesus lived His life as the perfect teacher,
He was not only our friend, but also our teacher.
He taught us to respect and love one another,
He said love your enemies as you do your brother.
He set an example for the whole world to see,
If only we'd follow it, what a world it would be.

....

This poem was written by my youngest brother,
Mathew Leland

Chapter Six

What is prison like?

To describe prison life is a difficult task. Violent scenes from movies, television dramas, and newspaper reports have clouded the public's perception of what prison is really like. Prison is not like a country club, or is it like a dungeon, a cave, or a torture chamber. It is a lot worse than that. Unless you learn how to do time and you better learn fast. The seasoned inmates will use you for all your worth if you don't learn to live your own life in prison.

When I first entered prison, a guard told me that this prison is what you make of it. In a very narrow sense, that is true. Although I cannot make it feel like I'm on vacation, I can make it a place that I can survive. Another guard told me that prison is a learning experience. That is definitely true. However, the same can be said about a heart attack. They are both experiences we don't want. They both can be prevented if we worked at it. But you have to have early detection. Preventing prison, you have to live a good life and obey the laws. I took things for granted and broke the laws with wreckless abandon.

Every new prisoner portrays a false image of what he considers toughness. This "mask" he wears is to hide the fact that he is scared. He really doesn't know how to act yet. He knows he cannot show kindness, because kindness is considered a weakness. To be weak in this environment will bring on infinite pain and suffering. It is impossible to be gentle in a world where nothing is gentle. One must play a role, act a part for the benefit of the hateful eyes of those who would rather spit on you than smile at you.

Try to understand the chill of walking by another inmate's cell and see clotting puddles of blood from his slashed wrists of one who couldn't take it any longer. The first thing I thought of is, wow, I didn't know there was that much blood in the human body. You become numb to emotions after so long in prison and seeing and hearing the things you do. Try watching someone's mind snap under the strain until he becomes a human vegetable from the heavy dosages of anti-depressants forced upon him. At that point, he is easy prey for the homosexuals.

Up until my incarceration, my concept of a homosexual was one of a weak, feminine man who has womanly characteristics. I imagined that they would keep quiet about their sexual preferences in hopes of avoiding getting beaten by "Gay Bashers". I found out that in prison it is quite different. The biggest and most muscle-bound man can just as easily be gay. He doesn't request your sexual company, to the weak ones, he demands it. If they resist, they have to fight. Even for the Non-Gay convict, a trip to the shower means he will be showering at the same time as other men. Some prisons don't have stalls and the ones that do don't have shower curtains. Of course, there are some prisons that have both. If you are lucky, you might get sent to one of those. It is not uncommon to be the object of another man's masturbation fantasy while lathering up. It's like living in a fish bowl. We can't even sit on a toilet without being observed.

The daily and constant attack on one's soul forces him to turn off his emotional process. To be a prisoner is to be completely stripped of your identity, to become a faceless number among many. Whenever you are called for anything, they call your prison number. It is a total denial of self. You lose who you really are as a man if you are not very careful. You may never find yourself again after so many years as a prisoner.

So, you ask, "What is prison like?" Prison is like going to sleep at night wondering who, if anyone, is missing you. It is hearing a favorite song on the radio that transports you to the exact time, place, and feeling to when she last said, "I Love You". Then you look around your prison cell and want to die.

One would rather be transported to Hell, a distant prison, than to be ambushed by memories of such manner, especially knowing she's with another man now. Prison is patiently waiting for mail-call the way an alcoholic might be waiting for happy hour. It is hardening of the heart to hide who you really are from the contamination of this sick society. Your guilt or innocence is no longer the issue, only survival. Prison is a place where another inmate can use you to take all his frustrations out and not be punished severely for it. After all, what are they going to do to him? Lock him up? If he already has life in prison, he has nothing to lose. He can do whatever he wants.

Welcome to the real prison life. Be smart, keep your eyes open, your mouth shut, be strong, stay away from the wrong crowd, and get used to being treated like a faceless number. Expect nothing good come from anyone, including the staff. Hope for the best but expect the worst and you won't be disappointed. If you are lucky, you might make it through your sentence fairly intact. Good Luck.

....

A decade after I wrote this, I got out of prison. It was very hard to get thrust into a new world everything has changed. I didn't have a credit score, they didn't have them when I went to prison. I didn't have a place of my own and couldn't get one. I worked a job for ten dollars and hour for the first six months. It was a job in a concrete place. It was hard work. I started driving truck after that for thirteen dollars an hour. I'm still driving truck today. I got laid off for a few months in the winter. Unemployment is almost impossible to collect now. You can't speak to anyone live. It's all on a computer recording. If you don't know much about technology, like me, you are screwed. Times get rough. I'm sitting here learning to write this on a laptop. Typing is not my specialty. I'm doing it though. It just takes a lot of time. But it's winter here in Maine and I'm warm at the kitchen table. It's a hell of a lot better than prison.

YOU CAN HEAR

Prison life is a mountain that I must climb, with its sharp rocks and deep ridges.
The pathways here are dark and dangerous, they're like crossing broken bridges.

In the middle of the night my soul cries out, and my heart aches from being all alone,

Storm clouds are raging today, and darkness overshadows the season,
Anger rises up and threatens us all, with no warning or reason.

In my heart the sun still shines, you're love in me will remain,
I can feel your presence near, and it warms me in this rain.

Knowing that you stand by me, you'll pick me up when I fall,
I walk these dark and dangerous paths, behind this prison wall.

As you are with me my heart is calm, I just go with the flow,
I'm like a brook moving swiftly along, because it's your love that I know.

My feelings cry out like an angry wolf, and most often bring a tear,
My thoughts are transmitted directly to you, and I know that YOU CAN HEAR.

....

Prison is a place where heartbreak is a constant. But I don't blame women for leaving us. What kind of life is it for them out there, when the ones that are supposed to be loving them and taking care of them are far away in a prison cell? We got ourselves in here, and they pay a price too. It's in here I learned to true meaning of the phrase, "You don't know what you've got till it's gone". We take so much of our lives for granted. I will never take a thing for granted again. NO! Not even walking in the rain. I've learned my lesson the hard way about love and life. I'm hoping it's not too late to enjoy them both one day.

THE PAIN OF PRISON

Don't take it for granted that you're free, you could end up behind bars like me.
I used to be a rambling man, and now I can barely move in this can.
While in this hellhole my Mom passed away, I didn't want to live after that day.
I felt so guilty and all alone, I should have been with her at home.
A few months after I came to jail my wife was cheating, my heart took a beating.
That was hard to know her love wasn't real, I hated the way that made me feel.
She had another man's baby on TV, she sure as hell didn't care about me.
I had to watch it on the eleven o'clock news, I had the painful prison blues.
My heart has been dragged through the dirt, you don't know how that hurt.
For many years I've lost my freedom, I only have family now and Lord, I need em.
When my heart was broken, the real tears would fall, I need someone to call.
Prison is a sad and lonely place, all you see is hate on everyone's face.
The thoughts of love I have inside, to survive in here I have to hide.
Sometimes I feel like I'm going to burst, when my heart aches at its worst.
A lot of things here are sad but true, and there's nothing one person can do.
Prison life is so full of pain, it's so easy to lose yourself and go insane.
I hurt so bad and I know why, it's because my life is passing me by.
When it comes to pain it isn't fair, and I've had more than my share.
Writing about this pain is easy for me, it just comes naturally.
Not a day goes by that I don't feel pain, on my heart it will leave a stain.

My World
By
Billy Leland

This is a short story about life
At the
Maine State Prison
(August 15, 2005)

I've written a lot of short stories. I've only put a few of them in this book. I don't know if that's what you want to read or not. I hope you like them. I hope I can open up your eyes to life in prison. There are a lot of misconceptions about prison. Most people in the free world don't even want to think about prison unless one of their loved ones go there. It's then that the shock hits them about how our justice system runs these prisons. Everything I write about is what I've seen for myself and what I've been through. None of it is fiction!

There is no way the memories of the years of punishment in my world can be erased from my life. But despite all that has happened, I'm making it and I am still alive and sane. My world has put me in some severe circumstances and on the edge of death a few times. The life I live today is full of monotonous and restrictions. I ask myself, "Is there a meaning in all of this and in the end will it be possible to find joy, and satisfaction in such a hard life?" I look back and I'm very uneasy about my wasted years. I wish my life had a destination, some star to reach for, or a purpose. There must be a purpose, God keeps me here. I should have been dead many times. But I'm still here and I don't know when I'm getting out. I'm here still searching. All my life I've had an obscure feeling I was searching for something but I never knew what.

The world I live in now is only satisfying in my dreams. My reality is absent of all delight. Deep insatiable longings and vague unhappiness fill my days. Sometimes I feel as if this place is beating me down and I feel broken, blow after blow, disaster after disaster, until my spirit seems to break under the pressure. In my dreams I feel like I am guarding something. Is it life itself? This world is dark and cold with a lot of pain, but most of all it's filled with fear. I see it in a lot of other's faces. I am not afraid of my world. I can live through anything. I fear not being free and I have no idea when I will be released.

I'm a lonely man now looking out of my small cell window with very sad eyes. I look out to see what I can of the free world with a burning desire to be a part of it. I still have a radiance of hope to be free, but it's getting weaker as the days turn into weeks, weeks into months, and months into years. It baffles me how the United States government can take one of its citizens off the street and put him in prison without stepping foot into a court room. Who has the authority to do that in a country that prides itself on being free? Freedom is just a lie in America!

At night as I sleep alone in deep silence, I suffer torments of yearning and I wake up with wet cheeks from the tears that I cry in solitude. Nobody in my world now cares anyway. But to show the tears is to show weakness. I rise day after day to greet the dawn as I stand looking out this little window into the window of my mind. It's in my mind where I find peace and happiness. It's in my mind where I know I'll find love again. I know I'll try to make it the best love I can this time. No more taking it for granted.

My world is filled with waiting, just waiting and waiting. I hate waiting, to me it's the worst thing on earth, especially waiting for the unknown. Even hope is pain when you're waiting because it never comes alone. It's always in the company of fear and doubt. How well I remember my fear when the first cell door slammed shut behind me. It was as if I died and it was permanent. The world as I knew it vanished behind me and I entered into a life of limbo. I feel like I am lost in a nightmare. There is something unforgettable about the steel door as it as it clangs shut behind you while you wait and wait, always waiting, never knowing what will happen next. You know whatever it is it will not be nice.

Once again, it's another night in this cursed cell. It's so full of horrible memories with its frustrations, disappointments, and humiliations that live on night after night. I often wonder who will live in this cell after I'm gone. Whoever he is, he will not have pleasant dreams. Demons live in this cell! But still I'm here waiting and waiting, always waiting in my world.

My world is also overflowing with despair and depression. What do I know about depression and despair you ask? I can tell you by experience that despair is not merely acute depression. Despair is more than the sum of many terrible parts. Depression is purgatory and despair is hell!

In my world I feel like I'm drifting away on strange currents from the free spirit that I was. Do you have any idea how it feels to lose your freedom? I feel incomplete, lost and lonelier than I thought humanly possible. Nothing in my world looks the same or is the same. I'm looking for pieces of myself where there are none. I wish with all my heart that I could turn back time so I could get one more shot to get it right. All that is here is emptiness. I look back to the horror of the journey that got me to this empty land and I cry. How did I let something like this happen? I have so much regret for the mistakes I've made. I wish I could tell everyone how sorry I am and start over.

I sit here day after day trying to piece the insanity of my past days, months and years together into some comprehensible form. But it is awful hard to justify any of this. I try to communicate the experiences of my past times into words but they're painfully inadequate. If you could hear my experiences, it would be an unending echo of the scream of total terror. If you could feel my experiences, it would be that of acid as it eats at your flesh without any relief. I'm lost, confused, tired, angry and profoundly sad and lonely. My body is in so much pain but my soul is in despair.

I believe the tremendous sadness and emptiness is due to the loss of critical elements in my life, the loss of security, the loss of identity, the loss of dignity, but most of all the loss of love. I've had so many painful experiences over a short period of time. There is still a great deal of sadness that accompanies the crying but that is understandable, don't you think? I know now that the tears that I have been fighting not to show are my strong allies in releasing some of the pain.

Along with the feeling of emptiness, sadness and a cold heart, time feels like it's all messed up. It goes so slow at times that I feel like I'm in a state of nothingness. What a terrible feeling. I have a hard time trying to find things to do to kill this terrible time. It's sad when you think about it. Time is all we have and it goes by so fast in the free world, yet, so slow in prison. I wish for it to go fast, in essence, I am wishing my life away.

In my world I scream constantly but silently. The panic feels like it's too much to cope with, but cope I must if I am to survive. This deep sadness in me forces me to hold back tears hoping the feeling will go away before someone sees me. Inside, I long to be held and rocked like a child would be. There is so much pain when my nights are filled with those awful nightmares and old memories that linger and haunt. But here I am still waiting, waiting and needing something so desperately. That something is the feeling of being loved in a place so full of hate. Twenty-four hours of hate, seven days a week. The hate never ends. I know there is such a thing as love and tenderness but it has been so long since I've experienced it that I can't remember what it's like. I can see it out there at the foot of the rainbow or maybe beyond in the vast blue distance. In my world, the end of the rainbow is bottomless and you can fall forever. The blue distance is a void that can swallow you and your efforts at happiness into its emptiness. To tell you that you have to be careful in my world is an understatement.

I'm a man alone and the best I can do is hold on and wait for better times. There's no stardom, no wealth, not much of anything to hold on to except my dreams. I don't know if the better times are ever going to come for me now. I sometimes think that I'm going to die in this God forsaken place. But, for now, I keep holding on while waiting and waiting in this empty time, this empty cell.

I look out of my tiny, cold cell window and see a star as it falls to earth through the darkness of night like God striking a match across the ceiling of the sky. Like the falling star, my life will flare and die. But for now, I'm holding on to that light. I take my stand for life, for this is my place on earth and in time. Do not expect me to quit, to move over or to give up hope. Like a tree, I have to be tough, in the sense of being strong and enduring. The fight I fight is within, but I must always win or chaos will come again. I have at last unraveled all the mysteries of my life. I am a fallen angel who needs love to stand back up.

When you look into the window of my world, you'll see me looking out with sad eyes and features of stone. (PRAY FOR ME)

(I'M IN SOLITARY CONEFINEMENT)

•••••••••••

266

The hardest times I've ever had are the times I've spent in solitary confinement. It didn't matter to me that I was beat up and had broken bones. The physical pain is nothing compared to the emotional pain I felt. The physical pain heals, and I fight and fight my emotions. If you've never been in situations like I have been, you can't imagine how it feels when all you can do is think about your life and how you screwed it up. All you can think about is your kids and how you won't be there for them. The worst part is when the ones you love the most get old, get sick and die while you're behind bars and can't see them, comfort them and tell them you love them. My worst fears all came true while I was in prison, I lost so much and can never get it back. The most precious gift of all, Time. It's gone now, and I need to use what little time I have left to find happiness in a world so full of hate. Time, I need to learn the new world I'm released into. There just isn't enough time for me now.

SHATTERED LIFE

Did you ever drop a glass and see if shatter in a hundred pieces? I watched my life self-destruct in that same way. There are so many pieces of my life gone and some are gone forever. My marriage was shattered by the destructive lifestyle of drugs and alcohol. When I look back at the time I spent with my wife, partying with others was the only thing we had in common. We were always drinking and doing drugs. I don't know what my wife was like sober. She was always either smoking pot, using cocaine or drinking. My life with her is just an endless blur of endless partying. We didn't do much else together. Don't get me wrong, I'm not blaming her for a thing. I know it's all my fault.

I have also lost my freedom. The biggest part of my life shattered when I got locked behind these walls. Prison is a lonely, painful and bare place. Loss of freedom, for me anyway, is the most painful aspect of my shattered life. Being away from my children and the rest of my family is devastating. I also miss the few friends that I have left. Going to prison has a way of weeding out casual acquaintances from real friends.

Prison is the fastest way to harden the heart too. It makes you forget what real feeling are. It's a place where you can never truly relax. You always have to be alert and on guard. Other prisoners are predators and guards treat you like you're an animal and like to lock you in a cage. The guards think you are just put here to obey. They don't care if you get rehabilitated so you can go back into society and stay out of prison. I see so many inmates get out of prison with no skills, nowhere to live, nobody that cares about them and they return to prison quickly. When someone returns to prison the authorities keep track of the number and that is called "Recidivism".

Don't they know that they can lock a dog into a closet for years, and throw food in there just to keep it alive but who would want to be the one to open the door to let it out in the end? This is what I see happening to human beings all the time, every day.

I know I've done some things wrong in my life but I don't deserve to be locked away for so long. I've paid my dept to society and I've learned my lesson. I've learned from every mistake I've every made. I'm trying to get out of this shithole and put the pieces of my shattered life back together again. I have found healing and I'm growing in my faith. I know that now I can go back into society and be a productive member and pay the taxes to the government that they so badly want. I'm praying to God that I have another chance to get back into society to be with my family and pick up the pieces of my life that I lost. I don't belong locked in a tiny cage for many years to come. It will only be a waste of my life.

I have had some major adjustments to overcome just to live inside this prison. I made my peace with it and I've accepted the fact that I might be here even longer. Every day I spend after today will be a day of my life wasted. I'm not going to learn the lesson any better than I have already learned it. In here I had the chance to start a new relationship with God. I learned that I did not have to be afraid to give my life to God and accept that He had control over it. After all, look what happened to my life when I was in control. I learned that He is patient and forgiving. There is no easy and fast way to find healing and peace. For me, there is only the daily journey of getting back up after I fall. I ask for God's forgiveness and ask Him to let me learn to forgive myself again. Most of all I have learned to let the Holy Spirit guide me.

I am not always anxious about what is coming my way next. It may be something special from God, but if it's not, I know I can make it through whatever it is because He is with me. I know that my life will not be perfect and pain free forever just because I know Christ. It means that in spite of the difficulties and pain that exists here on earth, there is joy, peace and a reason to celebrate when living in the love of God.

When I was in the Piscataquis County Jail I repented and invited Christ into my life and into my heart. Slowly the Holy Spirit is changing me. The emptiness I felt inside for most of my life is gone now. I was always looking for something but I wasn't quite sure what that was until now. I have a joy that I have never felt before.

I was moved to the Maine State Prison and held in the maximum-security unit to await going to trial. A trial the government and my lawyer both knew would never take place. Because I'm a founding member of the Hells Angel motorcycle club, I was denied bail. I attended as many chapel services as I could at the prison. The other big-time drug dealers, murderers, and thieves look at me like I've lost my mind. But the Lord is guiding me and has allowed this to happen. I don't fit the profile that other inmates think I should fit anymore. I am a new man now and they don't understand. Instead of depending on myself to get by in life, I proclaim God's presence in my life and have confidence the He'll meet all my needs. His plan for me is far more gracious than anything I can dream up. He will never leave me or forsake me, I would have! I was a broken man when I turned to Jesus, that is when God does His best work. Without Christ I would still be lost in my sin. Now I can do all things through Him who strengthen me. He has helped me pick up the pieces of my shattered life.

....

This was also written over a decade ago. I wasted many more years after this in prison. It costs the taxpayers forty-thousand dollars to keep me in prison a year. That's not including medical expenses. I figure the taxpayers spent over five-hundred thousand dollars more than they had to, to rehabilitate me and make me pay for the crimes I committed. It's America's way. Don't you get fed up with paying so much in taxes just so the government can waste it?

They should let the non-violent prisoners, and the ones not a threat to society out of prison and make them go to work. Prisoners are America's biggest business.

CONVICTED ON LIES

Can one man control another man's fate?
Can he say you will die on a certain date?
Yes, he can, I hope you know,
It could be you on death row.

Just try to imagine if it was you,
Waiting for the governor to pull through.
Would you walk quietly down the hall,
Knowing this will be your last fall?

What would you eat for your last meal,
Can you imagine how you would feel?
I think I would go out of my head,
Knowing that I would soon be dead.

In prison, there is death in the air,
And nobody out there seems to care.
Family and friends are at the prison to pray,
Hoping the governor will grant a stay.

How can a judge play God and kill someone?
It's still murder when you kill someone's son.
Who gives a judge the right to say who dies?
He just may be convicted on lies.

PRISON FLOWERS

Outside my window in my prison cell,
Roses are blooming and looking very well,
So, flowers really do grow in Hell
I thought it was just a rumor I was told,
But these flowers are growing big and bold,
To this warden, they are like gold.
They are growing everywhere, far and wide,
The warden doesn't want them to hide,
He's growing them with pride.
To grow them, sometimes we're hurried,
In the headlines they are scurried,
And the warden isn't worried.
Over the garden, the warden has gloated,
The flowers have his ego so bloated,
I'd laugh if it exploded.
They're on a prison ground surrounded by razor wire,
Just to see them you'd have to fly higher,
They have made the warden out to be a liar.
They do have beauty and a really nice scent,
Inmate benefit fund pays the rent,
That's why we get all hellbent.
This whole program is one big scam,
Try to get in it and the door will slam,
All the money it generates is for the man.

....

YOU'VE BEEN RELEASED

From this lonely cell I can see the sunrise.
It's like a flame burning in my eyes.
That portrait is painted in my mind,
As I awake with no love of any kind.

This is how I wake up every day,
But today, I feel like I'll be okay.
Even though I'm in a world of sin,
I have enough faith to win.

I will survive and this is the only way,
Or in a bed of blood I will lay.
Death is not anything to fear,
If you are keeping Jesus near.

Living among enemies, day after day,
Keep the faith and you'll be okay.
With Jesus you are never alone,
He'll be there bringing you home.

It's okay to cry, but don't be weak,
Always be strong and meek.
You'll be free when you're deceased,
Then you'll know you've been released!

HATE

In my heart, I've always been a lover,
And to show it, I can't wait.
Pain and heartache are all I feel now,
All there is in prison is hate.

I see people get beaten almost every day,
In a place with hate it gets real.
Then one day the haters came for me,
Then in me, hate was all I could feel.

After that, hate filled my heart,
And now, I don't want to forgive.
Hate wasn't there from the start,
It's a product of where I live.

Living with hate in your heart is a bad feeling,
When you let it build up inside.
The burning hate gets your insides reeling,
And then your enemies can't hide.

You'll hunt them down at your will,
No more listening to them lie.
You wait for the right time to kill,
And in that cell, you will die.

PAT DOWN

I got strip searched today,
I got searched twice yesterday.
Once on the way to chow,
What are they looking for now?

All I'm doing is going up to eat,
What would I hide in my feet?
The see me walking in the halls,
And they pat down my balls.

I'm in maximum security all day,
I couldn't smuggle anything anyway.
When I see them coming, I frown,
They just love to pat me down.

I did try to bring back sugar today,
They caught me and threw it away.
I'm not making a very good thief,
All it docs is cause me grief.

I get caught and have to throw away food,
That puts me in a very bad mood.
The guards throw a lot of food away,
We should take it out of their pay.

TO MY FAMILY

I Still can't figure out what I'm doing here,
October thirty first I'll be here a year.
Things are horrible and I hate to say,
We are all criminals on display.
Men are coming to this place every day,
Proving that crime really doesn't pay.
I'm doing time and it's ruining my life,
I've lost everything to include my wife.
There are days I wish I were dying,
And on those days, I end up crying.
I've more than learned my lesson now,
I'd like to help someone else somehow.
How I wish I never came to this place,
I see the hurt on my family's face.
Nobody knows how I'm hurting inside,
Because here, those feelings I must hide.
Now, I don't even know who I am anymore,
I lost myself when I walked through the door.
I know I'm your son, father, cousin or brother,
And I'll always love you like no other.
I'm sorry if I have hurt you along the way,
I'm locked in this tiny cell and I must pay.
I have no idea if I'll will ever be free,
But I'll feel better if you forgive me.
I hope that when you go to bed tonight,
You will know that now I'm doing right.

TWENTY DAYS IN THE HOLE

On April nineteenth, two thousand and four,
I couldn't think of anything I had to live for.
I feel empty in side now, my freedom they stole,
I've been twenty days now locked in this hole.

There's nothing to see, not even any sunlight,
This kind of life will never seem right.
I woke up full of sorrow, lonely and blue,
And my thoughts turned directly to you.

I'm lucky to have my Bible on the night stand,
It wasn't long before it was in my hand.
I began to read about You're undying love,
And how You're my savior so high above.

Thank you for saving my life this way,
If it wasn't for you, I was going to die today.
I was sure I didn't have anything to live for,
I didn't want to live like this anymore.

But now, you've given me the will to live,
Knowing you have so much love to give.
I don't know why you saved a wretch like me,
But I'm glad you gave me love I can see.

DARKNESS

I am hungry and thirsty,
My life is passing by.
Every day I cry out,
And ask the good Lord why.

I'm living in darkness,
With a terrible affliction.
A thing that brings so much pain,
This thing is my addiction.

Please come and rescue me,
From what is certain death.
Save me from this brutal attack,
So, I can take another breath.

I use the strength I get from you,
And know that I'm not rushed.
Your unfailing love stays with me,
And the waves of pain are hushed.

Lord, now I owe you my life,
For letting me win this fight.
You've brought me out of darkness,
And back into the light.

LIVING ON BORROWED TIME

It felt all wrong the day I'd arrive,
My head ached from the long bumpy drive.
I had fallen asleep and panicked when I awoke,
Armed guards, guarded towers made me choke.

I prayed for the strength to live through this distress,
While my name is added to this prison address.
"Unload!!" a loud voice shouted, his bellow filled the air,
"This is your new home and we have clothes for you to wear."

My feet hit the ground and my head began to spin,
This harsh reality reminded me of the trouble I was in.
"They got me bad", one inmate cried, "I don't deserve to be here."
"Shut up!!", the guard yelled, "and welcome home dear."

They say justice is blind and now I see the truth,
We're just warehoused here and robbed of our youth.
I can't help thinking that being treated this way is a crime,
And I know now that I'm living on borrowed time.

··········

I'll never forget the first day I arrived at the federal prison. The bus ride was four hours long and I was handcuffed and shackled. It was extremely uncomfortable.

FIND A WAY

I sit down and put earplugs in my ears,
I've been doing this for so many years.
In my locker, I get my pen and notebook,
And now, nobody gives me a funny look.

It's like everyone here expects it from me,
They know what I write and some come to see.
Some people nicknamed me the poet man,
And can't believe I can write as much as I can.

I sit in this plastic chair and write hour after hour,
It's well after midnight before I get my shower.
I climb in an uncomfortable bed after a long day,
Wishing for once to sleep the night away.

I toss and I turn and I sleep a little bit,
Every day I wake up in here feeling like shit.
I drag my ass out of bed to start another day,
And to make it through I have to find a way.

I pray to God I will die one night in my sleep,
And when I'm gone no one will weep.
Just know that I don't want to live like this today,
But once again, I know I will find a way.

CLOSE THE DISTANCE

Sometimes I sit here and I'm moved to tears,
Because I finally found you after all these years.
It seems like I've been searching for you for eternity,
And now, you'll be there for me when I'm free.

It's still hard to believe but I know it's true,
I'll never love anyone the way I love you.
I would walk through fire just to see your smile,
I'll be with you forever in just a little while.

Every time I hear your sexy voice it is so nice,
Being with you will be like being in paradise.
I know that when you are truly in love with someone,
You are always smiling and having so much fun.

That's exactly the way I feel about you right now,
I'm going to make you very happy somehow.
Because I couldn't stand to see you with another man,
To keep you I will do everything that I can.

I love you my sweet angel, unconditionally, no strings,
A wedding and reception are, unnecessary things.
I gladly give you my heart with no resistance,
All I want to do now is close the distance.

I WAS HER SUGAR DADDY

A beautiful young girl came chasing after me,
I was on meth and I was as high as can be.
I was a fool and wasn't sure what I was thinking,
Every day doing drugs, partying and drinking.

I must have had a mid-life crisis come along,
I let her seduce me even though it was wrong.
She was beautiful and made me feel young at heart,
I knew I was just her sugar daddy from the start.

Life with her was doing drugs and committing crimes,
I was stupid and thought those were good times.
Because of her, I ruined a really good life,
She talked me into leaving a really good wife.

I'm not the same man that made those stupid mistakes,
She wants you to hate me and she's doing whatever it takes.
I haven't heard people talking about me for a lot of years,
But soon I'll be free and that renews their fears.

The difference is, I've paid dearly for what I've done,
While they got off scot free and continued having fun.
They are going to try to deny everything when I write my book,
But you will know the truth as soon as you take a look.

Some of the things in my book will be embarrassing to me,
I was a stupid man and I'm sure you will agree.
I bought this girl jewelry made of diamonds and gold,
And I knew that for her, I was too old.

I bought here a snowmobile, four-wheeler, and even a horse,
A car, a truck and a lot of nice clothes, of course.
A few times I brought her back stage to her favorite band,
She used me and that I understand.

But now she is married with a family of her own,
Why doesn't she grow up and leave me alone?
I haven't even been released from this prison yet,
Karma might catch up to her, I bet.

....

I expect there are some people out there that don't want to see me come home. I really don't blame them. I've owned up to what I've done and paid one hell of a price for it. They have gotten away with what they've done by using me. I've often wondered over the years what they had on my wife to get her to do a Grand Jury testimony on me. All of them have had the luxury of living well and telling lies about me to get them to look good. I don't know why they'd hate me so bad for telling my side of the story. After all, doesn't everyone know that there are two sides to every story? Nobody had to fight to stay alive like I did when inmates heard the rumors and lies about me. Because of their lies, I have had many fights and in them I have gotten broken bones, teeth knocked our and many scars. They didn't know how I had to be in there because of what they said out here. As a matter of fact, when they heard that I got a twenty-one-year sentence they though that I was never going to get out to tell anyone that they were the real rats. They thought their secret was safe. They never dreamt that I would get out of prison and write a book to tell my story. "The Fall of an Angel"

I'm coming home to you

I can't sleep my love, I'm just too excited,
To share my love with the only woman I've invited.
Sweetheart, you don't realize what you've done for me,
You've made me the happiest man before I'm free.

You're my angel that touched me like nobody else could,
I know you'll love me like nobody else would.
I can feel your love and hear it in your voice,
You're stuck with me and it was your choice.

I hope you know I'm still a little bad boy inside,
I'll show you now that I have nothing to hide.
I might ask you to wear just a sundress in the car,
I'd take you for a ride but won't go very far.

You never know what goes through my mind,
But it will be excitement that you will find.
I hope you're never bored when you're with me,
You can do anything because you are free.

I will always love you with my heart and soul,
To love you forever is my goal.
I won't try to control you and tell you what to do,
I am content just to be coming home to you.

SMOTHER YOU

I'll do my best to live up to your expectation,
Being with you will feel like I'm on vacation.
A vacation in Heaven after what I've been through,
I just can't wait to hold and kiss you.

I will do all I can to leave you satisfied,
Kiss away every happy tear that you cried.
I'll always be there if you want me to stay,
I'll drive every doubt in your mind away.

You'll soon know that nobody loves you more,
And I'm the man you've been looking for.
I'll do my best to give you laughter and fun,
To show you that for me, you are the only one.

I'll be there with you soon and you will see,
That you are the only woman for me.
You are the love of my life and that is best,
I don't even want to talk to the rest.

I want to live the rest of my life with you,
Be with you in Heaven when this life is through.
Not a day will go by that I won't tell you this,
Or hold you tight and smother you with a kiss.

I'D BE TOO OLD

I've made some enemies along the way,
Some people still talk about me today.
There are some people out there calling me names,
The ones who are still playing their games.

They say things about me to avert everyone's eyes,
What comes out of their mouths are all lies.
They are the ones who testified against me,
Apparently thinking that I would never be free.

I've made it now and I'm close to getting out,
You'll soon see what the truth is all about.
They talked about me and they had their fun,
The truth will be told and I am the one.

Don't worry if you hear people talk shit about me,
Their names will be in my book and you will see.
Everything I write will be the truth in my book,
I have all the paperwork if you want to look.

They want eyes off themselves so they lie about me,
Wait until you see how freaked out some will be.
None of them thought my story would ever be told,
They thought I'd die in prison or I'd be too old.

I CAN KEEP THIS WIFE

I want to walk with you through the soft beach sand,
Tell you I love you as I hold your hand.
We get bac, to the camper and I cook you lunch,
Then we start kissing a whole bunch.
Then I lay a big soft blanket down in the dirt,
And I enjoy my favorite dessert.
In the sunshine we go for a swim in a lake,
We get out after we've had all we can take.
We take a shower and get on some riding clothes,
I bring you to a place where nobody knows.
We fill the Harley's saddlebags with our gear,
It will be after dark when we get back here.
A beautiful ride on the Harley and we don't get wet,
And we get to watch the most awesome sunset.
We sip our drinks on a mountain way up high,
We kiss passionately under a beautiful sky.
She kissed me and thanked me for everything,
But I wasn't done, I gave her a diamond ring.
She knows that I screwed up marriages before,
She also knows that I'm not that man anymore.
The ring fit on her finger perfectly,
And she said that she would marry me.
I told her I love her with all my heart,
And I'm ready for a brand-new start.
I'm strong now and nobody can make me weak,
And the happy tears rolled down her cheek.
I held her and I kissed her happy tears away,
She told me that this was the most perfect day.
We got on the bike after we lost daylight,
I told her she was also in for a perfect night.
She held me close and we enjoyed the ride,
And the pain disappeared that I had inside.
When she said yes, the pain was quickly gone,
With the love of my life, I will move on.
I am going to be happy for the rest of my life,
I know in my heart, I can keep this wife.

....

As the years went by and I didn't have a woman. I wrote hundreds of poems about the woman I wanted to find. These poems are about the woman I want. At the time, I didn't know a name but I had a face in mind. I know what kind of woman I want and I'm praying to God that I find her. I kept writing these kinds of poems and my daughter put them on Facebook. She was asked who the poems were for and when she told them that I am not writing them for anyone, people didn't understand how I could write poems like that and not have a girlfriend. It was easy for me because I've been living in my own mind for well over a decade. I lived on fantasies and dreams for so long. I knew what I wanted to say to the right woman. I want to write those poems for her.

LIVE AND HAVE FUN

It's easy for someone to tell me to let it all go,
Because the Hell I've been through, they don't know.
When you're locked in a prison and nothing you can do,
The cowards out there constantly bad mouth you.

I know a lot of people so I always hear about it,
For fourteen-years I've had to take their shit.
Rumors make their way inside and cause me to fight,
Nobody there, cares if the rumors aren't right.

For all those years while the rats were having fun,
I had to fight because I'm not one to run.
Don't tell me to forget about it and move on,
Not after all the shit I've gone through for so long.

When the "Fall of an Angel" is published, I'll let it go,
I want the truth told so everyone will know.
It's easy for people to tell me to just let it be,
But they couldn't do it either if they were me.

Most people couldn't imagine what I've been through,
Writing that book now, is all I want to do.
I don't want to get out there and hurt anyone,
It's my turn now to live life and have fun.

....

"I wrote my book and it has done well and it has done what I said it would do."

LOVE TURNS TO HATE

She made love to me just before my arrest,
She said she loved me and I was the best.
When I was gone, she shed a lot of tears,
She said she'd wait for me for ten years.

But just a little over three months went by,
She was having sex with another guy.
How did her love turn to hate so fast?
And why can't she leave it in the past?

I'm just trying to get on with my life,
Besides, she's now someone else's wife.
I wonder what kind of wife she could be,
If she is still focused on me?

Why does she care what I write in a rhyme?
I'm only doing it to kill this time.
She should just ignore these things I write,
Because with her, I'm not going to fight.

She's got her life and I've got to make mine,
If I never see her again that will be fine.
We both made mistakes and she must agree,
How did her love turn to hate for me?

BLAME

After my arrest, she blamed everything on me,
But she was happy the way things used to be.
Over the years I've grown accustomed to taking the blame,
Too bad other people couldn't do the same.

It wasn't long after everything in my life went south,
That I was the one that she would bad mouth.
Fourteen-years later and she's still doing it,
Why does she still give a shit?

I committed crimes and was put in a prison cell,
While she was out there living very well.
After I got arrested, she was gone in a blur,
And forgot about everything I've done for her.

I loved her, but she was just using me,
I was her sugar daddy and too stupid to see.
I was the laughing stock for the whole town,
You will see how the whole thing went down.

I'm not going to worry about making anyone mad,
They didn't care about the hard time I've had.
I lost everything I owned when I took the blame,
Suffered through extreme heartache, loneliness and shame.

MY FIRST WIFE

I'm broke again, I don't even have a dime,
And I'm quickly running out of time.
There's one thing I've always dreamt I'd do,
But now I know I'm too old for you.

What's even worse than me committing a crime,
Is that I can't turn back the time.
I don't know if I ever had a chance with you,
Or should I accept that, that dream is through?

Now my body is too broken from the ages,
Along with the fourteen-years of living in cages.
I'm going to keep my head up and swallow my pride,
Knowing I'll never have you as my bride.

I was never anything but a diamond in the rough,
Some tried to smooth my edges but it was too tough.
Everyone eventually gives up on me,
I'm not the man they need me to be.

I don't know why they messed with me from the start,
It's not my intention to break their heart.
I just you could have been my first wife,
I would have been happy for the rest of my life.

REPEAT THEIR TIME

I paid dearly for my crime,
But 21-years is too much time.
Killers hardly ever get that much,
Or even the pedophiles that touch.

I see them come and go,
And society doesn't even know.
I have to got to drug classes,
They don't, they sit on their asses.

They just play games and wait,
They don't have to rehabilitate.
There's no class for them here,
So, children still have to fear.

They'll return to do what they did,
Pictures of adults having sex with a kid.
While I'm here doing so much time,
They go back and repeat their crime.

....

I had to take drug and alcohol classes while I was a federal detainee at the Maine State Prison, I had to take drug and alcohol classes at the federal prison in Schuylkill, PA. and Fort Dix, New Jersey. I was transported to Danbury, Connecticut and had to do a nine month long residential care drug course call RDAP, "Residential Drug Abuse Program" I had to take these courses the whole time I was in prison even though I only have a conspiracy crime. Pedophiles DO NOT have to take one hour of counseling in the federal system.

MAYBE I'M THE ONE

You jump into my truck and say you're ready to go,
We drive down the road blasting the radio.
I'm so happy you're with me, I'm singing to you,
Being with you is all I want to do.

I know that the love you have inside hasn't died,
That smile on your face shows me you're satisfied.
A song comes on and we sing as one,
Like teenagers again going parking and having fun.

If our grandkids could see us, they'd laugh at you and me,
They'd think we are as crazy as could be.
Neither one of us is ready for the rocking chair,
We still have a lot of life and love to share.

Words are like weapons and they hurt sometimes,
I want to show you love with my rhymes.
This is my way to reach you from so far away,
I want you to keep me in your heart today.

Maybe I'm the one man that can make your life complete,
The memories I have of you are so sweet.
Maybe I'm the one man that can make your dreams come true,
Just give me the chance to show you what I can do.

I'LL BE THERE

I know there's things about me wearing on your mind,
But you'll find that I am one of a kind.
I want to be with you for the rest of my years,
If you cry, they will be happy tears.

I'll be with you until death do us part,
I'll love you with every beat of my heart.
You are the woman that I'll always need,
For your love, I would gladly plead.

The searching for me came to an end,
You are my lover and my friend.
I'm so happy that you want me as your man,
I've been alone since my sentence began.

I was searching for a home for this heart of mine,
I've been dying of loneliness for a long time.
It's so hard and the nights seem so long,
I fought really hard to stay strong.

I wanted a woman to call my own,
Now, neither one of us will be alone.
Were you waiting for someone to love too?
I'll be there when my sentence is through.

THE MAN WHO FOUGHT

If I care about you, I'd give you my last dime,
I'd be there for you all the time.
I'll pick you up whenever you're feeling down,
I'll be the best friend you ever found.

I'll work for you as hard as I must,
I'll be the man that you know you can trust,
Nothing can make my love for you go wrong,
I've been working on this for so long.

I may not be as young as I used to be,
But I'm strong and soon you will see.
I'm as solid now as a new brick wall,
I'll pick you up whenever you fall.

I've learned just how I want to live,
Only for you do I have love to give.
You are my woman for the rest of my life,
And someday you are going to be my wife.

I know you've heard me being talked about,
But that's the man who's life ran out.
Nobody knows who I really am today,
I'm the man who fought to find his way.

A GOOD WIFE

I don't do anything that I hate anymore,
I'm good enough now to come to your door.
I've paid for my crime and I've nothing to hide,
I would be proud with you by my side.

I can be the man that you've wanted to see,
That's always the man that I've wanted to be.
I'll give you more love than you've ever known,
I'll show you more than I've ever shown.

My heart tells me you're the one for me,
And this time it's for eternity.
I trust you and know you won't break my heart,
I can believe in you though we are far apart.

Someday, I see me with a beautiful wedding band,
And a matching one on you little hand.
My good time dreams of us have just begun,
My heart tells me that you are the one.

For many years, I held onto what was already gone,
And I've always hurt too much to hold on.
Then, all of a sudden, you came into my life,
I'm thinking you would make me a good wife.

HE THANKED ME

I watched another inmate as he walked by,
He's a good guy that had a tear in his eye.
He went down the Isle and laid in his bed,
He pulled the covers up over his head.

I walked down and asked if he was okay,
He said today was his worst day.
He had just called his wife on the phone,
When she answered, she wasn't alone.

He heard the laughter of another guy,
He asked her about him and she didn't lie.
His marriage is over now for sure,
And this guy doesn't want to live anymore.

I stayed there talking to him for a while,
I was finally able to get him to smile.
I told him he's a young, good looking guy,
For him, girls would fall out of the sky.

I said, "Look at me man, I'm old and fat,
I'd love to be where you're at.
You'll get a beautiful woman when you're free".
He smiled at me and thanked me.

I KNOW WHAT I WAS THINKING

Others have their way of coping and I've got mine,
Leave me alone and I'll be just fine.
These days I'm so used to being alone,
And killing all these years on my own.

I have come to terms for losing it all,
I've apologized for causing teardrops to fall.
I wonder if you think about me now and then,
I often wonder how things might have been.

I know I was a poor excuse for a man,
I would change it all right now if I can.
I'm sorry for the promises I've broken,
And all the hurtful words I've spoken.

I'm hoping that when I'm no longer around,
You remember me by the words I've written down.
I know I'm close to the end of the line,
These are the words that are truly mine.

I've said a lot of things I didn't mean before,
When I was doing coke, meth and more.
I said the stupidest things when I was drinking,
But now I know just what I'm thinking.

MORE TO LIFE THAN THIS

I honestly thought that I would never see the day,
I'd come home after they locked me away.
I cringed when I heard the slamming of that steel door,
At that time, I thought my life was over for sure.

I went from one life to another in just one minute,
I knew this one had a lot of hate in it.
I have learned so much after fourteen years,
And come face to face with my worst fears.

I lived in another world and everything now is gone,
I really didn't want to move on.
Moving on for me was to a life filled with unknown,
But it didn't take long before I was shown.

I learned that everyone can bleed just like me,
From then on, fighting was the way it will be.
I've finally made it through, but I can't lie,
Right now, only God knows why.

I'm hoping that when I finally get there with you,
He'll give me a sign showing me what to do.
I know there's more to my life than this,
There's nothing here that I'm going to miss.

I LEAVE IT UP TO YOU

If you don't like me, go ahead and take your shot,
Don't hold back either, give it all you've got.
If you are lucky, you might knock me down,
But I'm getting up off the ground.

To keep me there it will take someone bigger than you,
And when we're done, you won't look brand new.
What are you waiting for, did you change your mind?
Are you wondering how I deal with your kind?

I told you, I don't give a shit if you like me,
I'll show you why you should leave me be.
Quit running your mouth and take the first swing,
Apparently, you haven't learned a damn thing.

You act like a tough guy but I am not afraid,
Come on, back up all the noise you made.
I'm at least twenty years older than you,
Come on, show me what you can do.

Listen, I'm tired of talking to you man,
Just try to hit me if you think you can.
Either way, we're going to end this here and now,
I'm going to leave it up to you as to how.

LOVE OUTSIDE THIS GATE

Nobody is awake yet and I'm sitting here writing like this,
Just wishing and dreaming about a tender kiss.
I can't sleep and once again, it's still dark outside,
I just toss and turn with my eyes open wide.

Even though this is the quietest part of the day,
My worrying is stopping me from sleeping anyway.
Starting over at my age is going to be hard to do,
I thank God I have friends like you.

I don't want to be a burden on anyone out there,
But all I have left is love to share.
I won't feel right until I can pay my own way,
That is what I'm worried about again today.

I wish I didn't have to worry about that anymore,
It's getting worse the closer I get to the door.
I dream about it when I do get to sleep,
I'm lucky I have friends to help me get on my feet.

I was amazed to see how many people that really care,
Some of them hardly know me and yet, they still share.
For so many long years, I've lived with nothing but hate,
But I guess there's still love outside this gate.

HELP

I'm sitting here thinking about love and affection,
When all I see here is hate in every direction.
I'm sick of it all and I've definitely had my fill,
It's a wonder I think of love and affection still.

But, I'm still the man my mom and dad raised,
They showed me love and affection in many ways.
Even when I was running wild and breaking the law,
They were the best parents I ever saw.

I have changed but there will always be a part of me,
Who'll remain the loving man I was taught to be.
I have had the best of intentions all along,
I made some mistakes and it all went wrong.

Some people may think I'm a loser right now,
I've paid my dues and I'm going to be a winner somehow.
I'm at the bottom now with nothing left to lose,
And there's nothing inside me left to abuse.

I've been hurt as bad as I possible can over the years,
And there's now way I can produce any more tears.
The other end of the spectrum is my one true love,
I'm going to get help from the good Lord above.

NO FEARS

It's five o'clock in the morning and it's snowing,
It's coming down hard and the wind is blowing.
I'm bored and lonely and didn't sleep very good,
I didn't get released on Dec. 1st like I should.

I'm mad, discusted and I'm getting depressed,
I couldn't sleep so I got up and got dressed.
They just got done the five o'clock count in here,
I got counted almost fifteen hundred times this year.

When they count, they do their damn best to be loud,
They really like it when they wake up the whole crowd.
It's just one more thing that I try not to get to me,
It's just the way some ignorant guards will always be.

I'm going to the commissary this morning out in the snow,
I'll wait outside for an hour because there's nowhere to go.
I just made a coffee to warm me up inside.
While I dream about going for a snowmobile ride.

I'd ride a snowmobile from here to home if I could,
If they would release me today like they should.
After living in these shitholes for almost fifteen years,
I'd drive anything home with no fears.

TAXPAYER'S MONEY

It's snowing outside so most of the staff are late,
It gets really irritating for us to have to wait.
I've gone through this every winter with the staff,
With these government workers, I have to laugh.

You shouldn't laugh though, they're getting over on you,
They will always get paid no matter what they do.
Bad weather and they don't show up at all,
The sissies must be afraid they will fall.

Most of them drive a four-wheel drive car,
And none of them live too far.
They miss a lot of work for no good reason,
Their vehicles can get here in any season.

They miss work knowing they'll get paid anyway,
There's a lot of taxpayer's money being wasted today.
They get the best of benefits and the highest salary,
Yet, they are the laziest workers I ever did see.

When they don't show up, we are locked down all day,
Shortage of staff because they couldn't make their way.
Now, taxpayer money is going to a ton of overtime,
It's such easy money, they don't have to commit a crime.

TAKE MY WORD

I don't have the words to accurately describe the things I see,
With the hundreds of different guys walking by me.
I wish I could accurately describe the things I hear,
A lot of different languages that are not clear.

You would have to be here to really understand the smell,
I wouldn't wish this on you because this is hell.
The sights, the smell and the noise 24 hours a day,
I try to get away for it but there's just no way.

Some days you want to kill someone because it is so bad,
But there's nothing you can do about it and it's sad.
It gets on my nerves enough to tear me apart,
I want to kill someone for laughing when they fart.

After all these years, there are some things that still get to me,
But I keep reminding myself that soon I'll be free.
I should have been released already so I'm really irritated,
Because it seems like forever that I have waited.

I'm just so tired of putting up with all of this shit,
I don't have the words to explain so that you will get it.
You'd have to see, smell and hear all the things I have heard,
It really can drive a man crazy, just take my word.

MY STORY

I will be the one still standing tall,
I never gave up, I fought it all.
There's still a lot of fight left in me,
When I'm free, you will see.

I got sentenced and they got it in their head,
I'd never get out, I would be dead.
I'm very close to walking out the door,
And they aren't comfortable anymore.

They are the ones with something to hide,
They thought I wasn't going to tell my side.
I made it now and my time is here,
You talked about me, you have something to fear.

You are not who you portray yourself to be,
And the truth won't set you free.
No more living behind made up alibis,
No more hiding behind your lies.

I don't care what you think of me,
The truth is going to set me free.
I've been in prison and growing old,
It's my turn to get my story told.

THE TRUTH IS COMING OUT

All that is left for me now is the unknown,
There is so much that I'll have to be shown.
I've been out of circulation and the world evolved,
And a prison sentence is the only thing I solved.

I did the time and paid society its dues,
By the people I cared about, I got used.
It's over now and they better leave me alone,
Who they are, I'm going to be let known.

While they are out there enjoying the fact they're free,
I was rotting in prison and they forgot about me.
They've had their fun spreading rumors and lies,
It's going to be my turn to watch as their ass fries.

I've had to fight many times over what's been said,
The truth is coming out and they made their bed.
Some people think I should let it all die now,
They think I should just forget about it somehow.

But I can never forget these past fourteen years,
The bloodshed, the heartache and the tears.
They were out there happy and didn't care about me,
The truth is coming out now for the world to see.

STILL ALONE TODAY

I'm a distraction until someone else comes along,
I'm easy because I've been in prison for so long.
She's lonely as hell and she starts writing to me,
I'm a prisoner so she knows where I'll be.

Her man cheated on her and broke her heart,
Her writing to me was how she had to start.
She fell in love just long enough to get her through,
She got over him and knew what she wanted to do.

I was good for her self-esteem and to make her forget,
The first guy to come along now and she was all set.
I'm glad I could help her through what she went through,
But to me, that was a shitty thing for her to do.

She wrote to me for years telling me that we were best friends,
And we were lovers until our time on earth ends.
Then her best friend's husband is available and she's gone,
Now, there's nothing left between us and that's wrong.

Whiles she's happy out there with her brand-new start,
She could care less what she did to my heart.
Time is healing me but it's still a long way away,
I'm still cold and alone in this prison today.

A STAND IN

I keep telling myself that I've got nothing to lose,
So, a woman comes along and I don't refuse.
That's the chance I take because of a lonely heart,
But I know it's just going to fall apart.

In her letters she makes everything sound just right,
While she sleeps with another guy at night.
To her, I'm just a game for her to play,
I'm not going anywhere, I'm in prison today.

So, she keeps telling me that she's crazy about me,
I'm no fool, it was easy for me to see.
Because little by little she kept pulling away,
She even tried to blame it on me today.

She didn't tell me she changed her mind,
And she's leaving what we had far behind.
Long before she admitted it, I knew she was gone,
She had a lover and she was moving on.

She must have thought I was stupid and couldn't see,
But I knew she wasn't crazy about me.
I put myself in the position to be the victim of,
A stand in until she could find real love.

LINK IN A CHAIN

Some things I can't get used to even if I try,
I keep getting betrayed and I don't know why.
I've always tried to be a good man and a good friend,
Most of the ones I've befriended go on to pretend.

Until someone else comes along, they are fine with me,
Then all of a sudden, they show me how it will be.
Some of them used me to get out of trouble with the law,
They told on me, everything they heard or saw.

Others just used me to get over a broken heart,
I'm glad I could help them get a new start.
I just wish they didn't tell me that they love me,
Or tell me how nice our life together will be.

They made a lot of promises with no intention to keep,
Making me dream about them when I sleep.
I feel like a fool for opening up my heart,
But they are not faithful when we are apart.

I've written thousands and thousands of wasted pages,
In the fourteen years that seem like ages.
I've learned the hard way that I'm just a link in a chain,
I'm glad I could help them get over their pain.

ANOTHER GUY

She came into my life to say,
I could find a better way.
She said I won't be alone,
I will never be on my own.

I was convinced she would stay,
But she's nowhere around today.
She made me open my heart once more,
Only to walk out the door.

She comes to me in my dreams,
Proving nothing is how it seems.
She taught me not to make a plan,
Because she had another man.

Now, I won't take another chance,
Until after our first dance.
Because if she can't hold me,
She'll act like she's free.

She can't take me in prison like this,
She needs a man there to kiss.
She doesn't want me anymore,
Another guy opened his door.

WHAT DOESN'T KILL YOU

I've got the only key to my heart that is made,
My heart still has on its band aid.
And not I've built some walls very high,
You can't break it again if you try.

You succeeded once to steal my heart away,
But I'm protecting it very well today.
When I get out, I am going to live well,
Even though you put me through hell.

And now because of you, I made a rule,
Nobody will make me feel like a fool.
I'll make friends now but nothing more,
My heart can't take anymore.

If you're married, stay away from me,
I'm not the fool you'd make me out to be.
Before I make another mistake, I'll be alone,
I can live just fine on my own.

There isn't anything that I can't do through,
I'm not so desperate that I need you.
What doesn't kill you makes you stronger,
And I won't be in prison my longer.

I'M GOING TO SHOW YOU

In prison there is no way to unwind,
There are so many things on my mind.
It's hard on me to live this way,
Fighting hour after hour, day after day.
I'll make a promise I intend to keep,
Alone again, you'll never sleep.
I'm going to be living with you,
When this sentence is through.
I'm the man you're looking for,
I'll come knocking at your door.
I'll kiss you like you've never been kissed,
Show you the love you've missed.
It's been fourteen lonely years for me,
I'll show you how the rest of our lives will be.
I promise our love will never grow old,
In my arms, you'll never be cold.
I know I won't have any regrets,
Our love will be as good as it gets.
No words to say how much I love you,
I'll just show you in everything I do.

....

It doesn't matter if you have no intentions of breaking anyone's heart, it happens because we can't tell what will happen in the future. We never know when someone will come along that will take us by storm. Someone may sweep you off your feet when you are not looking for anyone. I understand that completely. Just know that when you write to a prisoner, it is very exciting to him or her. It gets their hopes up of being loved and cared about in a place where there is no love.

IN HER DREAMS

"GET UP, GET UP!! IT'S INSPECTION TIME!!
THIS IS PRISON, YOU COMMITTED A CRIME.
INSPECTION READY FROM SEVEN TO FOUR,
WE'RE NOT MESSING WITH YOU ANYMORE!!"

"WE'RE TIRED OF YOU GUYS SMOKING THAT K2,
WE'RE COMING DOWN HARD ON YOU."
I woke up and thought I was dreaming,
I looked up and saw some bitch screaming.

She was yelling out all kinds of threats,
She is about as ugly as it gets.
She said she was shutting of our TV,
And improvements she better sec.

"There better be nothing on your locker tops,
And hanging clothes off you bed, stops!
You better sweep and mop the floor,
And nothing hidden under your bed anymore."

She can scream and threaten all she wants to,
These guys do whatever they want to do.
Personally, I don't give a shit how much she screams,
It's only going to make a difference in her dreams.

YOU RESCUED ME

You came to me when I was hurtin",
You rescued me for certain.
I was lost and all alone,
You brought me back on your own.

There was nothing as far as I could see,
Then you came and rescued me.
I was ready to give up and die,
I didn't have any reason to try.

Everything I worked for was gone,
Everyone I know has moved on.
There was nothing out there for me,
That's how I thought it would be.

I didn't have anything to live for,
Didn't have any fight left anymore.
I didn't have a woman out there,
So, if I died, I didn't care.

I was as low as any man can go,
You really did rescue me you know.
You've taken me out of this prison cell,
And because of you I'm doing well.

I'M NOT THE MAN I WAS BEFORE

After you read this, you can decide,
Whether I told the truth, or I lied.
You entered my life by writing me a letter,
You said you could make my life better.

I told you about my lonely broken heart,
You said we could both have a new start.
That you'd wait no matter how long it takes,
You knew about all of my mistakes.

You knew I was I was tired of being alone,
You fooled me by the love you've shown.
You said your love was growing stronger,
And I wouldn't be lonely any longer.

I told you how good you're making me feel,
You said your love for me is real.
You wanted to be my lover and my best friend,
And you'll be there until my life would end.

You made me tell you my most intimate fantasy,
You said you wanted the same thing as me.
Then you emailed me and you said good-bye,
Just like that you had another guy.

That's how my side of the story goes,
But you are the only one that knows.
Twist my story if you want to try,
But we both know I didn't lie.

You hurt me and it made me mad,
For quite a while, I was sad.
I didn't think you'd do that to me,
It was something I didn't see.

After all the time that has gone by,
I realized you told me a lie.
You wanted our relationship fast,
Yet, he's part of your past.

You were best friends with this guy's wife,
For years he's been in your life.
And all this time you were lying to me,
All along it was him you wanted to see.

How in the hell can you call me a friend?
Then know that our relationship would end.
I'm glad I'm not the man I was before,
Back then I would have called you a whore.

FORGIVE ME

Come on, can't you give me a break?
I've already paid dearly for my mistake.
How long will this be held over my head?
Can't you just forgive me instead?

I've suffered for it way more than I should,
I would take it all back if I could.
For fourteen years I've lived with sorrow,
I'll live with it again tomorrow.

I know, to you, this might sound strange,
But I've worked my ass off to change.
I'm not the same man as I was before,
I've got my priorities straight once more.

Every minute of every hour of every day,
A very heavy price I was made to pay.
My heart remains broken and I don't feel whole,
And the pain reaches down to my soul.

If I haven't suffered enough for you,
Tell me what else you want me to do.
Until you forgive me, I'm not going to heal,
I hope you understand the way I feel?

READY TO SNUGGLE

I'm a man without a home to call his own anymore,
But I'll make Maine my home that's for sure.
So, whenever anyone asks me about going home now,
It always manages to break my heart somehow.

I've had a home ever since I was a young man,
I'll make another home for myself as soon as I can.
The only one I have to take care of now is me,
But I hope that's not the way it will always be.

I hope to find someone who wants a new start,
Someone who will open up her heart.
There is a lot of life left in me to live,
And a lot of love inside me to give.

I wish that someday we can make a home together,
One filled with happiness that will last forever.
I think it will happen, I just don't know when,
I know I'll be one happy camper then.

It's been so long since I've felt affection,
I live with hate in every direction.
I'm sick of all the arguments and fights,
I'm ready to snuggle and hold you tight.

I'LL NEVER MAKE IT

OH GOD, I hope you hear my plea,
I need to know that you're still near me.
This pain is almost more than I can bare,
Give me a sign that you're still there.

I can't sleep and I've lost my way,
Without you, I won't make it another day.
This is such a cold, long and lonely night,
I'm so tired that I'm running out of fight.

Let me sleep Lord, so I can get some rest,
To survive here I have to be my best.
All of these years I've been waiting patiently,
Wondering if this will be the day you take me.

I've made it through the hardest years somehow,
I need you more than ever now.
I may have all these prison battles won,
But a new life for me has begun.

I think of all the heartaches, pain and cost,
I'm returning to everything that I lost.
There's a whole new world out there to see,
And I'll never make it without you with me.

YOUR FORGIVESS

I want to thank you for being so forgiving,
I have changed my way of living.
I'll always regret some things from my past,
I know those memories won't fade fast.

I still can't believe I was so stupid and naïve,
To let some of the ones I love leave.
Drugs distorted my way of seeing things,
I've suffered from the heartache that brings.

Many times, I couldn't see straight,
Doing lines and drinking, I couldn't wait.
Many nights I should have gone to bed,
For days I stayed awake doing drugs instead.

I'm mad at myself because I'm not a stupid man,
I couldn't stop the drugs from doing what they can.
If you think you're in control because you're strong,
Think again, you are dead wrong!

Drugs and alcohol have the power to control you,
Making you do things you wouldn't normally do.
I've beat it and I am the man you see today,
Your forgiveness helped my find my way.

ONE MORE CHANCE

Don't believe the rumors about me that you've heard,
Trust me, at least until I break my word.
That will never happen as long as I'm alive,
This endless love for you is my drive.

My heart pounds when I look at your face,
I stare at your picture in this lonely place.
You touch me way down deep in my heart,
It's slowly killing me that we are apart.

My love is deeper than the ocean, higher than the sky,
And nothing in the world can make it die.
I've been gone a long time but I know how I feel,
In my heart, I know this love is real.

If I had to live without you, I'd rather be dead,
It's my heart sending these words to my head.
I'm trying to write this to you with a steady hand,
I'm trembling inside hoping you will understand.

You can believe every word that I've said,
And every word that I've written that you've read.
I've only got one more chance with this old heart,
Please baby, don't tear it apart.

HOLD ON TO ME

I'll be there soon and you can hold on to me,
I will take care of you for the world to see.
I want to wake up each morning looking at you,
For me, that is a dream come true.

You can hold on to me and I'll always be around,
When all your feelings are coming unwound.
Hold on to me when you're feeling cold,
I'll keep you warm as we grow old.

You don't know if you can hold on to you your dreams,
When a lot of things in life goes wrong it seems.
Tell me all your troubles holding on to me,
Together we'll solve them, whatever they may be.

Tell me your secrets and show me your pain,
You'll never have to worry about it again.
When everything comes unraveled that you believed,
Hold on to me and you'll feel relieved.

I'll hold on to you forever if you want me to,
I'll take your troubles and pain away from you.
Hold on to me and look into my eyes,
Nothing can hurt you no matter how hard it tries.

YOU'RE THE BEST

I know that sometimes dealing with me is rough,
Saying I'm sorry, just don't seem to be enough.
I hope you know I love you unconditionally,
I'm proud of you for putting up with me.

It's okay that we don't always see eye to eye,
We never will, no matter how hard we try.
We are two strong willed people that's for sure,
But nobody in the world truly loves you more.

It's natural that we don't have the same things in mind,
But we can leave all our differences behind.
You and I can just agree to disagree today,
And we'll both come out winners in a way.

With me, it will mean learning which subjects or taboo,
Stay away from them and I won't argue with you.
And you will know that what I say is not always right,
But on some subjects, I will argue and fight.

But nothing can take away my love and affection,
And me wanting to go in the right direction.
Just remember, I love you and think that you're the best,
You and I can work through all the rest.

SLEEP UNTIL TEN

An inmate just yelled, "HEY, W.V.!!",
Three damn times, just as loud as can be.
Whoever W.V. is, he didn't answer this guy,
He doesn't live in this unit, that's why.

I opened my eyes and its half past six,
I want to kill some of these ignorant pricks.
I wake up mad nine out of ten days,
So mad sometimes I'm in a haze.

I lay here deciding if I want to fight,
But I just lay here in the morning light.
I asked somebody what W.V. means,
They can't say their real names it seems.

I hear nicknames like Big Money, and Triple D.,
But West Virginia is W.V.
It's pretty bad when they're called by a state,
Calling me "Maine" I would really hate.

But these guys are so stupid they can't spell,
So, using initials for them, works out well.
But they shouldn't scream it again and again,
This is Sunday, I'd like to sleep until ten.

I'M NOT THE SAME PERSON

I've often wondered if there was a way out,
Or if this is what my life will always be about.
When people see me, they'll think about this sentence,
Not that I've already paid my pentence.

They will always use this sentence to define me,
That's the guy who went to prison you see.
They'll never forget I pled guilty to a crime,
Even though I've done so much time.

They will always hang it over my head,
And not the man I am today instead.
They don't care who I am today,
They'll still talk about me anyway.

Those people don't have a life of their own,
They spend all their time on a phone.
If they weren't spending time talking about me,
Somebody else they would be.

I'm not the same person I was anymore,
I was an easy going, trusting guy before.
Prison didn't make a better person out of me,
It made me the man you soon will see.

NO JOKE!

OH NO! Son of a bitch! Not again today,
It was dark, I opened my eyes anyway.
I thought to myself, "What the hell?",
That is the most awful smell!

I took one earplug out of my ear,
But I honestly didn't want to hear.
Sure enough, I heard a long, gross loud fart,
And a minute later another guy would start.

I reached up and opened the window by my head,
Sucked in the fresh air as I lay in my bed.
I'm so tired of waking up that way,
Now, I feel like killing someone today.

Unless you experience this, you can't understand this,
You've never smelled anything like this shit.
If you've ever smelled a sewer line that broke,
It's worse than that, this is no joke.

I'm not squeamish but It makes my stomach upset,
Now, I'm as close to throwing up as I can get.
Just now, I heard another guy fart real loud,
I pray, "Dear God, please get me out of this crowd?"

THE REAL ME

I look in the mirror and what do I see?
I don't like the guy looking back at me.
First of all, I have some long hair,
I guess I'm lucky, at my age, it's still there.

My eyes are small and a dull bluish green,
The whites aren't the whitest I've ever seen.
My nose has been broken and it's not straight,
I need my teeth fixed but that can wait.

I've got some new scars on my forehead,
To cover some scars, I grew a beard instead.
One of the biggest changes came inevitably,
I wear glasses now so I can see.

When you get old, the first thing to go is your sight,
All the scars are from a fight.
Believe me, I don't want to fight at my age,
But I live with animals in a cage.

I've done really well to make it this far,
Soon I'll be out there where you are.
I wish I could change some of the things I see,
But then, it wouldn't be the real me.

DRUGS

I was 33 years old when I started using coke,
No, not the cola, the stuff that's no joke.
I knew that using cocaine was a serious crime,
But I got hooked and wanted it all the time.

It took over my life and made everyone sad,
I ended up losing everything I had.
Doing coke was more important than my wife,
And it changed the way I looked at life.

Before that, everyone thought that I was a good man,
It changed me the way that drugs can.
After a while, I started doing meth too,
Wow! I was surprised what that could do.

I made me forget about everyone else but me,
Other drug addicts were the only ones I'd see.
I ignored the ones that I loved the most,
When I was high, I'd disappear like a ghost.

Nobody knew if I was even in the state,
I was doing things I know they would hate.
Drugs always take you away from the ones you love,
But you can go back with help from the Lord above.

I MADE IT SOMEHOW

It's January first, two thousand, and seventeen,
I sit here writing like you have never seen.
This year is going to be a special year for me,
I'm going to be going back into society.

My son has proposed to his beautiful girl,
It's about time he gives marriage a whirl.
It's about time he stops being wild,
And he better give me another grandchild.

I'm happy now because I already have three,
I can't wait until they get to know me.
It is going to be hard to make up for lost time,
But I'll teach them not to commit a crime.

I'm going to stick close to family and good friends,
My time living with hate and discontent ends.
I'm looking forward to getting back out there,
And being around people that I know care.

Now, I don't mind saying Happy New Year,
Because I am happy that this is my last year here.
Hopefully, a lot of really good things happen to me now,
Because I feel like I have made it somehow.

A WOMAN LIKE YOU

I tried to hold on but I had to let go,
Everyone has to move on, I know.
A man not there will lose his wife,
She too, has to get on with her life.

I wasn't there to walk my daughter down the isle,
I had to fight back tears and force a smile.
I was in a prison, not just out of town,
If I let the tears fall, I will drown.

I had to sell my house and my land,
And put into a position I didn't understand.
Everything I owned had to be sold,
As I was put into a cage to grow old.

I lost hope because I was so far down,
I knew I'd die if I couldn't turn it around.
I'm a man who's world was torn in two,
I couldn't have been more lonely and blue.

I tried so hard to hold on to everything I had,
But I had to let go and my life turned bad.
And its almost over now, I made it through,
Now, I'm looking for a woman like you.

I'M NOT GOD'S GIFT

Today is the first day of the new year,
My release date is very near.
I want to build my new world around you,
To make you happy, is all I want to do.

My past life is over and done,
With you, I want to start a new one.
This time I won't do anything wrong,
Because my love for you is so strong.

There will never be a need to explore,
Because you are all I want and more.
But before you make up your mind,
I don't want you to go into this blind.

Everything I have is what you can see,
All I have to offer you is me.
We will be starting at the bottom of the hill,
But we'll get to the top, I know we will.

With a little luck, I know we'll be okay,
If you say yes, my luck starts today.
I'm not God's gift to you, I know,
But I'll love you and never let you go.

LIFETIME OF LOVE

All I want to do is make love to you,
I need someone to hold on to.
I've been alone for an awful long time,
When I saw you, I heard bells chime.

Do you believe in love in first sight?
If you do, be with me tonight.
You are right for me, I feel it in my heart,
I never want us to be apart.

Come to me and let go of all your fears,
Be with me for the rest of my years.
I know this love is going to work out right,
And with you, I'm never going to fight.

I'm done fighting, I will be your lover,
Together we've got a lot of ground to cover.
Age is just a number, I'm still young at heart,
Out new life together will soon start.

I have two strong arms and a heart of gold,
You are the one I long to hold.
I don't want just a brief love affair,
I have a lifetime of love to share.

BITE YOU IN THE ASS

They don't know that you're playing my game,
What they don't know is a damn shame.
They get on a computer or phone and talk about me,
They're nervous because soon I'll be free.

They don't know what I've been through since I got burned,
They don't have a clue about what I've learned.
While I spent all those years locked in a cage,
The whole world has come into the digital age.

This can be a good thing but it can also be bad,
People use it in ways that are sad.
When I was younger and someone talked about you,
It would spread by mouth to one or two.

Somebody types something now and away it goes,
It doesn't take long and everybody knows.
If it goes viral it will go all around the earth,
It's so easy to give lies and rumors birth.

What a lot of dumbasses fail to understand,
That they better have the proof at hand.
Telling lies about someone doesn't take balls of brass,
But be prepared when it comes back and bites you in the ass.

MY WORST FEARS

I'm just tell you short stories about my prison time,
In almost all of these stupid rhymes.
There are some people who don't want my story told,
But hearing all the rumors about me is getting old.

Nobody has to read it if they don't want to,
It's my right to write about what I went through.
The only thing mightier than the sword is the pen,
So, I write about what happened back then.

They have locked me up over five hundred miles away,
But they can't stop me from writing today.
I'm still just an old-fashioned analog man,
Writing about my life the best way I can.

I have no way in here to get onto the internet,
The ones mad at me haven't seen anything yet.
Wait until I get to use modern technology,
They'll wish they never talked about me.

They're fine with me locked up while they're out there,
But my turn will come, and it's only fair.
I have been silenced now for fourteen years,
And I have had to suffer through my worst fears.

STAY IN THE GAME

There are a lot of guys here that will stab you in the back,
A few white, more Spanish but mostly black.
In this place you always have to stay on your toes,
And it is a lot harder than anyone knows.

It is hard on your nerves to stay wound up so tight,
Never relaxing, always ready for a fight.
Guarding against homemade shanks or locks in a sock,
Or out in the yard getting hit with a rock.

In this prison, fights are very rarely one on one,
But I don't back down and I never run.
I've been going through this shit for too long,
And the good Lord has kept me strong.

In a lot of these poems I have said before,
I don't want to fight anymore.
It doesn't mean I won't if I am not left alone,
Don't force me to show you what I've been shown.

I have had to learn my lesson from the hard way, for sure,
I don't give a shit about fighting fair anymore.
That side of me died and I'll never be the same,
I had to kill him so I could stay in the game.

ACCEPT MY APOLOGY

Just when you think you don't have anything to live for,
Someone comes into your life and shows you more.
You were blaming yourself for everything that went wrong,
You cried and stayed depressed for too long.

You stayed hidden so nobody would see you that way,
You didn't want to hear what anyone had to say.
They would come over and ask how you're feeling tonight,
You knew they didn't care, they were just being polite.

In a way you would never expect will touch you.
You might think you do, but you really don't know this guy,
He's not very proud of himself because he lived a lie.

But now, everything he says comes from his heart,
He has nothing to lose, his world was torn apart.
Because you have a heart too, you can relate,
You've also been through some things that you hate.

He's open and honest with his words after his fall,
That's why you can relate to him after all.
He knows what a man you loved dearly did to you,
He hates it now but he did the same thing too.

It's something he'll never forgive himself for,
But he'll never do it again that's for sure.
To help you, he will do whatever it takes,
Do not blame yourself for others mistakes.

I know it's hard when you think you don't want to live,
In reality, you still have a lot of love left to give.
You're hurting but there's still love deep inside of you,
And one day someone will come along to love you too.

You know that I'm the guy that's in this rhyme,
I hurt a woman just like you at one time.
So, I bare my heart and soul for you to read,
And I hope I'm giving you what you need.

The words that will help you get your life back on track,
And the understanding to never look back.
Be proud of yourself whatever you do,
He'll never find anybody better than you.

I'd like to think I was forgiven for what I've done,
I've suffered dearly, but I'm not the only one.
If you're reading this and I've hurt you,
Please accept my apology and know it's true.

....

Over the years, I know I've hurt some people and broke some hearts. I didn't do it on purpose. I hope that
If you are reading this and I hurt you in any way, you know that I'm sorry.

I'm not that person anymore.

DR. JECKYL AND MR. HYDE

I'll caress your soft skin with my fingertips,
I'll slowly and passionately kiss your soft lips.
I'll lick your neck and gently nibble your ears,
Tell you I love you and relieve all your fears.

Nobody will ever hurt you while I'm around,
They'll find themselves six feet underground.
I can be Dr. Jeckyl or Mr. Hyde,
I can be a big teddy bear with you by my side.

But when someone tries to hurt the ones I care about,
That's when I let the other side of me out.
It has been known to happen in the blink of an eye,
So, if someone wants to hurt us, they can try.

I'd much rather be a lover than a fighter,
My circle of friends would be much tighter.
When I'm free, I'll do my best to avoid strife,
I've had enough of that in my life.

If you're not a friend of mine just leave me alone,
And try to live a good life on your own.
But don't forget Dr. Jeckyl and Mr. Hyde,
I don't want to show you my violent side.

YOU FIT THAT BILL

I have to smile now, I don't have a choice,
Everytime I hear your sexy voice.
I dream of Heaven but I still live in Hell,
But after hearing your voice I feel well.

You helped me pick myself up off the ground,
When you talk to me, I love every sound.
I don't say anything that I don't mean,
So. on me you can always lean.

Soon, I'm going to be there for you to touch,
And I hope you want to, very much.
It's time we both let the healing begin,
I think that together we both can win.

I'm glad I saw all your comments on Facebook,
Finding you single, was all it took.
I had my little girl look into you for me,
You are perfect as far as she could see.

My daughter only wants the best for her dad,
She knows that for years I've been hurting bad.
She knows what kind of woman I'm looking for,
And she said you fit that bill for sure.

DEAD END ROADS

I've been down my share of dead-end roads,
And I've carried some really heavy loads.
I've had some rough, dangerous mountains to climb,
And now, I've wasted too much time.

I hit rock bottom in life and I was beat,
There were days I couldn't get on my feet.
I was alone and sick and I wanted to die,
Only God was there making me try.

I didn't want to do all the time ahead of me,
I was tired of seeing all the things I see.
I hate the dreams I've been having every night,
And I hate it every time I have to fight.

Over these long, lonely years, I have learned,
And a brand-new life, I have earned.
I can't stop this feeling I have for you,
Right now, it helps to get me through.

I've made some decisions that were not the best,
The heartache it has caused has to be put to rest.
There are no secrets that I will not confess,
There will be no lies to get me into a mess.
I've been alone in hell for fourteen lonely years,
And the last thing I want to do is cause more tears.
I hope you don't expect too much of me,
My life on the street is a mystery to see.

There's so much I don't know about the world today,
I can't make you happy until I find my way.
I'll be very happy if you agree to go out with me,
It will be nice to see what our life together could be.

The first time I saw you, my knees got weak,
You were so beautiful, I could hardly speak.
There was something inside of me that was awaken,
I was praying to God that you weren't taken.

I am ready to go down a different road now,
I hope that you will be with me somehow.
You are going to be the last love I'm trying,
And there will be no more trying.

I just want to live my live as a simple man,
And show you my love the best way I can.
I've gotten rid of my heavy loads,
And I'm not going down any dead-end roads.

....

Change is hard, but I'm more than ready for it. I know the unknown is scary but after what I've been through, nothing is scary to me. I need to find a woman to spend the rest of my life with.

WE WON'T BE ALONE

The ties that once bound you are now broken away,
It's my turn to give you love and affection starting today.
I'm a man that will love you and never let you down,
We can stay home or go out on the town.

With me, you'll never feel like you are bound,
You will have the freedom that you've found.
I trust you with my heart because I know who you are,
I have plans for our relationship going very far.

I'm not feeling whole but your love is the answer,
You're smart and beautiful, are you a dancer?
I'll hold you tight as we dance across the floor,
We won't feel lonely and blue anymore.

Now, after what seems like a hundred lonely years,
And the pain and heartache of a million tears;
There's a feeling that I have that I just can't hide,
I know I'll be happy with you by my side.

Soon, I won't have to send you letters through the mail,
I'll be knocking on your door when I get out of jail.
I'm not always going to call you on the phone,
I want to come over so we won't always be alone.

TORN

I used to be hell on wheels,
I know how being close to death feels.
Wait until you see all my scars someday,
My poor body had hell to pay.

I wasn't afraid of anything at all,
I'm recovering fast from this fall.
Today, I'm praying for the damage I've done,
Strong bones, yet, I've broken every one.

I've driven around this country a time or two,
Sone almost anything a man can do.
You wouldn't believe the hell I've raised,
If it could be done, I'd find the ways.

From the outside, it looked like I had it all,
I've always felt like I was up against the wall.
I was making a great deal of money at one time,
I worked very hard at hiding the crime.

The more money I made, the more I'd need,
Everyone around me, I would feed.
The scars are from all the reckless things I tried,
I was torn and didn't care if I lived or died.

WORLD OF ILLUSION

There's so much pain in my life's path,
And many a sad road I have crossed.
I worked so hard for all I had,
And now all I had is lost!

All my life I either laughed or cried,
And I had a lot of fears.
It seems that no matter how hard I tried,
I've had to shed way too many tears.

Am I living in a world full of illusion?
I'm trying to break free and succeed.
It's hard to do here in seclusion,
And with the pain inside, I bleed.

I am tired of living and being caged,
And to them, I'm on a stage.
Looking in a mirror, I sure have aged,
Wasting these years puts me in a rage.

In this lonely world of illusion,
No hope have I found.
Many lies and a maze of confusion,
As I look all around.

CLOSE TO THE END

I keep telling myself that it could be worse,
I could be leaving here is a hearse.
I've seen plenty of guys leave that way,
I thought I would too, one day.

Through all the things I've survived,
On days that were good, I thrived.
I started having more good times than bad,
I have a better attitude than I had.

Fights were getting further apart,
I've learned to live with a broken heart.
Then as the years slowly passed me by,
I found myself actually wanting to try.

Instead of wanting to be six feet in the ground,
I was slowly turning my life around.
There is a light at the end of the tunnel I see,
It happened after seven years in here for me.

That was the time I really started to write,
Since then, I write, every single night.
And now that I am so close to the end,
I enjoy writing these for you my friend.

MY REAL FRIENDS

Over the years, I've lived with this trend,
Years go by and I don't hear from a friend.
I've seen this happen so many times before,
They contact you when you're close to the door.

Where were they when I needed them the most,
They disappeared like Casper the friendly ghost.
All these years I've been struggling to get by,
And there were times I didn't want to try.

Those were the times I felt so alone,
I have a few real friends and they've shown.
Henry Burleigh, who I have always called "Stick",
He bought me medication when I was sick.

Another real friend is Kenny Bradford, I call him "Doc",
And he's as solid as a rock.
Then there's my friend Tim Theriault the minister,
He's given up his ways that were sinister.

The three of them helped me all the way through,
I loved them right to death too.
For the rest of my life they will be my friends,
And they will be until my life ends.

MY WORST CRIME

I'm the one that caused my heart so much misery,
I can't blame anyone but me.
The decisions I made tore my whole world apart,
Caused me so much pain in my heart.

I turned my life into a damned mess,
There's nothing in my life now that I won't confess.
I won't tell lies to anyone no matter what anymore,
I will never again open up that door.

I've had a million hours to think about nothing but me,
And feel sorrow for the man I used to be.
I wish I could undo some of the things I've done,
If I could, I'd give anything under the sun.

It was never my intention to hurt anyone's lives,
But I was an asshole just ask my ex-wives.
I have felt really bad about that for years,
I hate myself for making women shed tears.

If I could talk to them, this is what I'd say,
"I'm more sorry than you know for hurting you that way.
I would give anything to be able to turn back time,
Because hurting you was my worst crime."

ANIMAL

I'm sitting here alone and I'm really discusted,
I got into a fight and my nose got busted.
I did the best I could to straighten it,
It's a little crooked but I don't give a shit.

I'm mad as hell because both my eyes turned black,
For two days I got away with it by turning my back.
But, as I knew I would, I eventually got caught,
They put me in the hole for not telling who I fought.

Now, here I sit again and I'm lonely as hell,
Time goes by so slow in this cold, little cell.
I just about had to beg for some paper and pen,
The guards are some cold-hearted men.

It seems like they get off on other people's misery,
But I don't care, I don't let them get to me.
I just sit here writing to kill this lonely time,
Telling the truth while trying to make it rhyme.

As the hours turn to days and weeks go by,
I can't hold everyone in, no matter how hard I try.
As the months passed, my anger turned to rage,
They're turning me into an animal in this damned cage.

GONE TOO LONG

I want to make it easy for you to love me,
By being the man you want me to be.
Because if I'm a man that's good enough for you,
I'm the man that Mom and Dad wanted too.

After all these years, that makes me feel good,
I'm finally being the man that I should be.
A man that will always be honest, open and true,
The man that loves nobody but you.

You would never love the man that I was before,
I didn't even respect myself anymore.
Nobody should've believed a word I have spoken,
I should have died for the hearts I've broken.

I hated myself for what I put them through,
Drinking and doing drugs was all I knew.
I thought I was going to die and go straight to hell,
But instead, I ended up in a prison cell.

Tomorrow I'm going to be released after 14 years,
I'd be lying if I said I didn't have any fears.
I'm afraid, but it doesn't mean I'm not strong,
It just means I've been gone for too long.

I MOVED ON

Your time has come to shine,
Your love is mixed with mine.
When you're tired and feeling small,
I will not let your teardrops fall.

I'll hold you tight when times get rough,
And I will always be enough.
You will have your dreams come truc,
And I'll always be with you.

I will wash all your troubles away,
You won't be lonely even for a day.
You won't need anyone but me,
This is the way it will always be.

Why are you with this other guy,
He will only make you cry.
He'll bring you nothing but heartache,
But I don't know how long it will take.

Right now, you think everything is good,
Everything is going the way it should.
But what you have now will be gone,
You didn't believe me, so I moved on.

TALK ABOUT ME

I heard that there is a lot of people talking,
They see me, they better keep on walking.
They'll find out that I'm not the same man,
And they can talk as much as they can.

After fourteen years on the inside,
I've learned to tame my wild side.
I always loved being a rolling stone,
Trying to tame the world on my own.

I rode my Harley from town to town,
There is nothing that kept me down.
I was on a road that would never end,
And I was lost, my friend.

From everyone I loved I drifted away,
And I was getting worse day by day.
A storm was coming that I wouldn't survive,
I got a prison sentence that kept me alive.

I brought out the fighter that lies in me,
And I fought everyone I could see.
Now I'm close to walking out the door,
They won't talk about me again, for sure.

AS DISGUSTED AS ME

Disappointment has set in hard today,
I'm depressed and it won't go away.
My heart is filled with sorrow,
I know I'll still be here tomorrow.

I was supposed to be in Maine yesterday,
Yet, with regret, here I stay.
I know that my granddaughter is sad,
And that makes me very mad.

March first my family was expecting me,
All of them I long to see.
It has been so long since I've been free,
They are all at home waiting for me.

I don't know why they are making me wait so long,
Keeping me any longer is just wrong.
It's not justice what they are doing to me,
I'm not a threat to society.

The bureau of prisons doesn't care,
They certainly don't do things fair.
If you could see the ones they do set free,
You would be as disgusted as me.

CHAPTER SIX

This is my Mom and Dad, Francis and Shirley Leland. The best parents in the world.

These are pictures of my Mom and Dad. The one above is me at 17 years old with my mom. The one on the left is my daughter Tianna with my dad. The two above are my father a little while before he died. I lost both of them while I was in prison.

Since my mom and dad died, the six of us are the matriarchs of the Leland family. My brother Butch, Bobby, my sister Tammy, brother Bud and youngest brother Matt. I'm the one with long hair and the wild Harley Davidson sweatshirt.

This is my older brother Mark "Butch" Leland. He is only ten months older than I am. He was a big part of me surviving in prison. He supported me the whole time I was in there and he helped me get on my feet when I got out of prison. I love you Butch. Thank you very much.

This is a picture of my son Derek, His wife Debby and his son Brage. Derek and his family live in California.

I'm very proud of my son. I wish he lived in Maine though. I've only seen my awesome grandson once when he was just a few months old. I do get videos and pictures all the time now. I've written poems about my whole family and I'll put them in this chapter. I love you Son.

This is a picture of my daughter Tianna, my son in law Ryan and my granddaughter Kiaira. I met Ryan once while I was in prison and at the same time got to see my granddaughter. She was two years old at the time. I lived in a camper in her back yard the first winter I was out of prison. I got to know Ryan and Kiaira and I love them with all my heart. Thank you, Tianna for all you guys have done for me.

The top picture is my daughter Lynda and I, on bottom are three of my grandkids and Derek, Lynda's boyfriend and father of my two grandsons, Atreyu and Ziya, my granddaughter Kiaira and I. This was the first time I met my grandsons and only about the fourth or fifth time seeing my granddaughter. At this time, I was wearing an ankle monitor because I was on house arrest for six months.

This is a picture of my bother Bobby and his wife Milly. Bobby never missed a month sending me money while I was in prison all those years. It's because of his love and support I did so well in there. I will never be able to thank him and his wife enough for all they did for me. I love you guys with all my heart. Thank you very much for all you've done for me. I hope you know that I would do anything in the world for either of you. If you ever need anything, I will always be there for you.

This is my sister Tammy Leland Kennedy, she is my only sister and I couldn't love her anymore than I do right now and I always will. She has always been there for me and I will always be in her dept too.

This is a picture of me and my brother Bud. His real name is Thomas but we haven't called him that in so long, hardly anyone knows his real name. It's the same way as my brother Butch. His real name is Mark but nobody knows that either. Bud also stood by me while I was in prison and got me a job where he works when I got out.

This picture is a picture of the first family cookout I got to go to when I was released. On the left is my youngest brother Matt and on the right is my sister Tammy. I don't get to see either one of them as much as I'd like to. I've been working for a concrete company in Old Town, Maine. I've been working many hours to try to get on my feet. It's not easy starting over in today's world. Everything is so expensive now. That's one thing that surprised me the most. I work my butt off and it seems like I can't get ahead. Everyone is so busy we don't get together like we used to back before I came to prison.

On these next pages, I am going to show you how many relatives I had pass away while I was in prison. It seems like at least once a year for the first six or seven years I was getting news of one of my relatives dying. It was heartbreaking every time I heard the news. I never got over the pain of losing each and every one them. I have so much regret and sorrow still today. Nothing seems the same out here without them. We were a very close family and had family get togethers all the time. I love and deeply miss all of them and wish I could have been here with them. Just before I went to prison, my mother's sister Florence died, and just ten months after I was arrested and put in jail, WITH NO BAIL, my mother died and I wasn't allowed to go to the wake or the funeral. We have a very inhumane and unjust Justice Department!

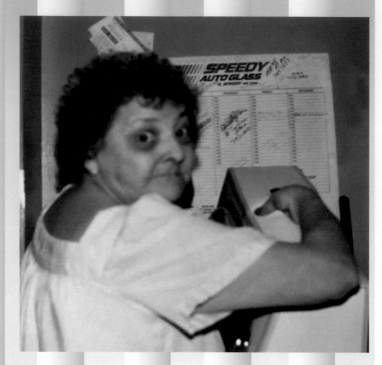

This is the last picture I have of my aunt. It wasn't long after this was taken that she passed away. She was an awesome aunt. She was always visiting or babysitting me and my brothers. I will surely miss her and have fond memories of her for the rest of my life. Losing her inspired some of the poems I wrote. I couldn't show pain or even sadness if the places where I was at. It would be a sign of weakness for sure. You have gotten this far in my book, then you know what weakness does for a person in prison. I love you aunt Florence and miss you so much. I have some really good memories of you and I can't thank you enough for the love you always showed me, even when I raised so much hell and frustrated you when you were babysitting me.

This is a picture of my sister in law Kathy, hugging our cousin Hugh Hicks "Junior". He was a great guy and God took him away from all of us way too early. He wasn't very old when he had a fatal heart attack. He was a very thoughtful and lovable guy. Everyone hugged Junior. You couldn't help it, when you saw him you just wanted to hug him. I love and miss him very much and when I heard the news about his death, I was in solitary confinement once again and I cried. At that time in my life, I thought it was all over for me. My Mom and my aunt already died and now Junior. It was getting bad. I couldn't be with anyone of them and I loved them dearly and still do. I know that someday I will see them all again. The only consolation I have in losing the ones I love, is they all knew that I loved them. I told them so every time I saw them. I enjoyed going to Junior's house and I enjoyed every time he came up to our house. I will never forget our card games and hunting trips with Junior. He always had a great sense of humor and made everyone laugh. Nobody ever felt uncomfortable around him.

This is a picture of my aunt Betty with her two sons, Billy on the left and Ricky on the right. Betty was a great aunt and I was very close to her. She lived about two and a half hours south of my house and when I traveled, I would never go by without stopping in. I loved her with all my heart and I still do. It hurt like hell when I heard about her passing away. It seemed like the hits just kept coming and coming. Junior was her brother, and they were very close also. I know how much the family was hurting when they passed. I was alone in prison grieving by myself. I couldn't talk to anyone and nobody would care if I did say anything. I kept all of the pain to myself and wrote the poems that you are reading to get my feelings out. I never dreamt anyone would be reading my poems. I didn't think they would want to. I'm still shocked that I am writing a whole book about prison and poems. I just hope you like them. Someone asked me to write a book and make it about fiction. I wouldn't know where to start. I just write the things I feel and the things I've been through. I write to stay sane and pass the time. I don't know how I would have come out of prison, or if I would have come out, if I didn't write.

This is a picture of my nephew Shawn and my cousin Oscar in the Kenduskeag River Race in Bangor, Maine. Oscar passed away at a very young age. Oscar and I hung out together quite a bit. We grew up together. His mother is Florence, my aunt. I was very surprised to hear about his death. He was so young. I can remember the day I found out he died. I was walking the track and my name was called over the intercom to come to the office in the church. I knew it wasn't good news. The only time we're called there is when someone in your family dies. That's the way we are told when the prison gets a call like that. I went there as fast as I can.

Oscar and I when we were a little younger. We went out and sang quite a bit. We were not very good but we had an awesome time. We hung out together as much as we could. He was an awesome cook too. I loved everything he made, especially his homemade cinnamon rolls. They were definitely my favorite. He would come to my house and stay and nobody else had to cook. I miss him dearly too. Rest in peace buddy. Someday we'll sing together again.

Love and Respect to you always.

This is a picture of my cousins Diana and Brenda. They are sisters and the best cousins I could ever ask for. I love them. They both wrote to me the whole time I was in prison. But Diana died of cancer a few years before I was released. I was devastated by the news of her death. I couldn't believe so many of the ones I loved were passing away and I never got the chance to be with them. I will never forget any of them and I will go on loving them until the end of time. I know that I will see them all again in Heaven.

I'm sorry, but this is one of my favorite memories of my cousin Pammy. I know the picture is not very clear but I had to put this one in this book because Pammy had a stroke while I was in prison and she is in a vegetable state in a nursing home in Portland, Maine. I went to see her as soon as I could after I got out of prison. Even though her body is alive, she isn't. She doesn't know anyone and she can't do anything for herself. She has been in this state for over ten years and I can't believe it. It is cruel and inhumane. If she was an animal, we could put her to sleep peacefully. I am so sad over her. I have prayed many times that God take her home. I hope you don't thing I'm cruel. If you could see her in that bed, you would agree.

This is a picture of the camper I lived in behind my daughter's house. I had an ankle bracelet on because I was on house arrest. The only places I could go were to work and to church and AA meetings. Everyone asked me how I could live in a small camper in the winter in Maine. I just told them that I have lived in places much worse than this for fourteen years and this camper felt like a mansion to me. It had a refrigerator, microwave, heat and everything I need. Here it is, almost three years since I left prison and I still live in a camper. It's not the same one though. This one is a Ford and it has a V10 in it. I love it. I can move it anywhere I want to. It is also very quiet and I don't have any drama in my little home. I'm a simple man.

True Friends

When a person goes to prison and he's down and out and need a friend the most, is when he or she finds out who their true friends really are. I was in for a rude awakening. I found out the hard way that I didn't really have that many real friends. Here are pictures of the people that I know I can trust.

This is Henry Burleigh, he's one of the best guys in the world. He helped me so much while I was in prison. He bought me medication, a new pair of boots and anything else I needed. He sent me a book called "Another bite at the apple." It is a book about the 2255 motion. The 2255 motion is a federal prisoner's last chance to get his sentence reduced or his case turned over.

This is Henry Burleigh again. Nobody calls him Henry, his name to everyone is STICK. He has a wooden leg, so we call him Stick. He's holding the first book I wrote called, "The Fall of an Angel." Stick is a little rough around the edges but he is one of the most loyal people you will ever meet. I am blessed to be able to call him a friend. If you read this whole book, you will have read a poem with his name in it. Well, here's a face to the name. Yes, he always has a look like that on his face, especially after reading my first book.

This is a picture of me with a really loyal friend, Kenny Bradford – "DOC". Right from the beginning this man fought for me. He made tee shirts, hats that said "Free Billy" and sold them to give me some money for my lawyers. His woman, Bea Flannery wrote a ten-thousand-dollar check to my lawyer to get started on my defense. If you read The Fall of an Angel, you will see just what that lawyer did to me. You can't find a more loyal and true friend than Doc. Love and Respect to you always Doc. We've got many rides to go on together my friend. The past is in the past. We are living for the future now my friend and the best revenge is "LIVING WELL."

This is one of the best friends I've ever had. We've been through a lot together in what Tim would call his "WILDER DAYS". He is a true friend and he always will be. He's turned his life around and I'm very proud of him. He's a deacon at a church now and I love and respect him right to death. Tim was another one that stood by me and supported me the whole time I was locked up. God bless you my friend. I'll always hold you to the highest esteem. Much love and respect.

These are two men that I am very proud to call my friends. Grizz Galipeau and Rod Whitten. Grizz was there for me from the very beginning and I met Rod while I was a detainee at the Maine State Prison. I love both of these guy right to death too. I'll always be here for you both. Much Love and Respect to you both.

These two pictures are of me and Debby McCallister. She is the best female friend I have ever had and I love her, I always will. She has never wavered about me, she has always believed in me. Whenever anyone talked shit about me and she heard it, she put them in their place. She didn't care if they were seven feet tall. She's not afraid to speak her mind. Love you Deb.

The man on the last page was a good friend of mine too. His name is Cliff Blood. He dies just a few weeks after I went to see him and give him a signed copy of my first book. He was as true a friend as you can find. RIP my friend. Much Love and Respect to you always.

This is my great friend, Fred Peavey. He is responsible for all of my knowledge on a computer and phone. He has helped me more than I could ever imagine and has never asked for a thing in return. Just today he helped me download all of these pictures. He set an office up in his home and gave me unconditional access. I love you buddy, thank you for all you do.

This is a picture of my good friend "skeeter". We are standing in front of my father's 2003 pickup truck. When I got out of prison, I completely restored the truck in memory of my father. Skeeter and Doc did the bodywork and painted it and I'm really happy with the way it came out. It's the best looking 2003 I've seen. Thank you, Skeeter, you are a true and loyal friend. They don't come any better than you my friend. Love and Respect to you always.

This is a picture of one of the most loyal friends I've ever had. He's a long time member of the Hells Angels in New York City. I loved this guy and was proud to be his brother in the club. It hurt very much to lose such a good true friend while I was in prison. I love you brother. Love and Respect to you always. RIP my friend. We'll ride together again someday.

This is me standing on the concrete mixer I drove for Owen J. Folsom's concrete in Old Town, Maine. I started driving for them after I had my ankle monitor taken off. I can't thank them enough for hiring me. It was a blessing. I am getting on my feet now. I'm laid off for three months because it's winter here in Maine. It is giving me time to write my book.

This is the first and only time I've seen my grandson. This is a picture of me and my son and my grandson. We were at a restaurant in Old Town, Maine and I was a really happy man that day. I love getting the pictures and videos my son sends me.

Francis and Shirley Leland

I don't know where I'd be without the two of you,
You were the best parents through and through.
You showed me what unconditional love means,
Because any other love is not what it seems.

You showed me love in every way you could,
It didn't matter if I was bad or good.
You taught me what was right and wrong,
And taught me to stand tall and be strong.

When I screwed up and got myself into trouble,
You both rushed to my rescue on the double.
After my arrest God took my Mom away from me,
I cried so hard alone, so no one could see.

Dad, for the next twelve years, you were my rock,
Then God took you too, and I went into shock.
I'm filled with regret, heartache, sorrow and shame,
Nothing in my life will ever be the same.

I know that I've said that a hundred times,
You've read it a lot in these rhymes.
But unfortunately, I know that it's true,
Because I will never be able to hug you.

Kiaira

Today I am thinking about you again,
It's hard to believe you are turning ten.
I look at all your pictures and I see,
That you look a little bit like me.

I'm sorry sweetheart, I'm not there with you,
And not doing the things a grampa should do.
I feel like I committed another crime,
Because I've only seen you one time.

You came to see me when you were only two,
You don't understand how much I love you.
It was really hard seeing you that day,
I cried watching you walk away.

I knew I was going to miss watching you grow,
And the extent of my love you wouldn't know.
I hope that you don't think that I don't care,
I love you and I'll show you when I'm there.

Honey, my time in this prison is almost through,
When it's over I will never leave you.
Please forgive your old grandpa sweetheart,
For us having such a late start.

Mom

I've heard inmates say that time is a cure,
But after fourteen years I am sure.
I know that it is not true,
Because time is all I do.

My heart has always been broken you see,
Because I'm not with my family.
I pray to be home with you someday,
I broke the law and now I pay.

Don't forget Mom, no matter what you do,
I will always love you.
I am more sorry than I can say,
That I can't be there with you today.

I know that you are not feeling well,
I'll be there when I get out of this hell.
I hope you start feeling better soon,
I love you to the stars and moon.

I asked God to take care of you,
I wish there was more that I could do.
Believe every word of this verse,
You are the best mom in the universe.

Tammy Theresa Leland Kennedy

There's something that I want to say to you,
When I was there, I didn't know how to.
I had my feelings locked up inside,
And now, I write them so they don't hide.

You are the best sister anyone ever had,
I didn't tell you that enough and I feel bad.
I know I should have said it a lot more,
Because of that, I've always been sure.

I want to say, I love and miss you every day,
I'm praying that I'll be with you again someday.
But I don't know if I'm ever getting out of here,
Not knowing, fills me full of fear.

The unknown is the worst thing for me,
But I'll always dream about being free.
They can't keep my locked up in my mind,
Because freedom is what I'll always find.

Thank you, Theresa, for always being there,
I know you love me and truly care.
Just knowing that helps me get through,
And I will always love you too.

My Son

There's a man that I love, one that makes me real proud,
He works and plays really hard, and likes his vehicles loud.

He has a woman that he loves very much, Debby is her name,
They have a son named Brage, and they love to play games.

I watched this guy grow from an infant to a boy,
We did a lot of things together that brought me joy.

Then the spoiled little boy became a real man,
And now he's in California doing the best he can.

I was locked in a prison and it kept us apart,
But I have always loved him with all my heart.

I love and miss this man more than he'll ever know,
I thank God everyday that I got to watch him grow.

I want him to be happy and have a lot of fun,
There's nobody as happy as I am to call him MY Son.

I Love You – Derek
"My thoughts and prayers are always with you"

Daddy, I love you!

I'm trapped in this lonely prison,
Locked in a one-man cell.
They say that I'm a dangerous man,
My true feelings, no one can tell.

I have tattoos all over me,
And a special one on my back.
Most people are leaving me alone,
I'm trying to get my life on track.

Every week on visiting day,
With my family all here.
We embrace with a big hug,
I kiss them holding back a tear.

I know my children love me,
And they know I love them too.
My daughter puts her arms around me,
And says, "Daddy, I Love You,"

No matter how tough you may act,
Or how well you play the part.
Those four little words,
Can melt the coldest heart.

TO MY FRIENDS

I miss all of you with all my heart,
You are my loyal and true friends.
I'm locked in this small cage right now,
I'll see you when this nightmare ends.

I hope to God that when I'm free,
We will have the chance to hang together.
You are the ones I long to see,
Our friendship will last forever.

I've learned a very painful lesson,
That a true friend is hard to find.
I am a very lucky man to have you,
Because you all are one of a kind.

The letters and cards I get from you,
Sure do bring me pleasure.
No matter what happens in my life,
Our friendship I'll always treasure,

I have always heard this old wives' tale,
"You can count your true friends on one hand."
Coming to prison you will find that it's true,
So many so called "friends, just don't understand.

This poem is dedicated to the prisoners who have died at the Maine State Prison and nobody came to get their bodies. They are buried in a small graveyard at "The Farm." I have seen a couple of inmates die alone and be buried quietly and forgotten. I will never forget!

Jesus knows Your Name

I know you made mistakes in your life,
And you have reaped what you have sowed.
You did your time like all the rest,
You paid more than you owed.
You not only suffered in these cells,
You paid the ultimate price,
Living like this seems like hell,
But dying in prison can't be nice.
Remember, you're a new man now,
You will never be the same.
This prison knows your number,
But Jesus knows your name.
I am still locked in this lonely cell,
But you have been set free.
You're saved by the blood of the lamb,
Someday it will be me.
You spent your life behind these bars,
But Jesus has loosed your chain.
Now you're looking down on me,
You see, I'm still in the game.
Your name is written in the book of life,
Your number is on the cross in white.
Your Angel is watching over you now,
You're in Heaven and it's OH SO BRIGHT!
Whatever you do, don't look back,
Everything here is the same,
The government knows your number,
But Jesus knows your name.
I will never forget any of you,
Even at the end of my own game.
This prison also calls me by a number,
But I know Jesus knows my name.

REST IN PEACE!

. . . .

I've written hundreds more poems than this. I hope you enjoyed reading them. This is what I did to survive the prison life. I tried to stay out of fights. But I soon learned that when you back down, other inmates will do all they can to take advantage of you. I also tried to talk to some instead of fight but I got sucker punched and ganged up on. So, instead of letting the hatred consume me and making me kill one of the idiots, I wrote about my experiences and let the anger out. I wrote about all the pain I held inside. I'm sure if I didn't do time my way, I would have been in there for life for killing others. I never thought I was capable of killing someone until I spent time in those places. I found out that I am capable of it. I just didn't want to spend the rest of my life behind bars. These poems kept me from losing what was left of my mind. To you some of them might seem stupid, but to me, they are the events I had to live through. Stay out of trouble and remember, everyone can be convicted of "Conspiracy" in this country. It is so easy to do. If you know of someone who committed a crime and you don't report it, you conspire to commit that crime. Love and Respect to you all and thank you for reading my book.

Is this my country?

I'm standing here leaning against the window pane,
Daydreaming as I stare out at the pouring rain.
I'm feeling sad and depressed as I watch it pour,
I shouldn't be locked in this prison anymore.

I try not to dwell on the 21 years the judge gave me,
While I see men who hurt children being set free.
Career criminals have gotten a lot less time,
And this is my first federal crime.

I lean against the window and I just stare,
Wondering how a justice system can be so unfair.
I can understand now how everyone hates,
The screwed up government of the United States,

When they put people in prison with no evidence at all,
This country is heading for a big downfall.
Our government employees commit the most crimes,
It's going to collapse, it's just a matter of time.

The politicians all end up being the same way,
It's about their personal greed at the end of the day.
But I'm still the one in prison staring out at the rain,
Watching the whole United States go insane.

ABOUT THE AUTHOR

I'm not a young man anymore. I have learned many lessons in my life the hard way. Today I sit here on a laptop computer that I just learned how to use two weeks ago. I drink my coffee out of the same cup that I had in prison for over ten years. It is a constant reminder where I've been. I don't dwell on the past but I will never forget it. I know that revenge is not mine and the best revenge is "LIVING WELL". I try my best to not hurt anyone physically or emotionally. I apologize to anyone that I've hurt. I'm just trying to complete my goals in life before I die and to find happiness in a world so full of greed and chaos. The United States is divided now and our government has gone astray. The current government does not care about the people, they have their own agenda.

You don't have to agree with me. I'm not into politics at all, I won't argue with anyone about it. What I am into is how the government is taking so much of my hard-earned money and using it for their benefit. Politicians give themselves a raise with my tax dollars and they certainly don't earn it. They are already way overpaid for the work they do and they take more time off from work than any other job in America would allow and they get paid for it. These same politicians passed a law stating that everyone had to have Health Insurance. If you don't it's a crime. They don't care about us. They don't care if the insurance is so expensive. Their insurance is paid for by us, the American working people. We struggle while they get all the benefits. The lawmakers said we can live in Maine on twelve dollars an hour but they make hundreds of dollars an hour. They say poverty level is seventeen thousand a year or less. Yet, they are paid hundreds of thousands a year on the money that the real working people have to give our government. They don't do their jobs! We bust our ass and some of us get our hands dirty every single day and can hardly afford to put food on the table after we pay our bills. They get free gas cards, also paid by us while they allow gas companies to charge us as much as they want to. When will the people of America take our country back?

I was sent to prison for 21 years by "The United States of America." It said that on every motion the federal prosecutor filed against me. In my opinion, I am a saint compared to what the politicians get away with. It makes it awful hard for me to get ahead. Yet, they all ride around in limos and eat meals that cost hundreds of dollars on taxpayer's money. Who is the real criminal in America today? Is this really our country? "WE THE PEOPLE" has been thrown out the window in today's America.

This is only my opinion and I am the author. I still have my first amendment rights for now, until they find a way of taking them away from me too. I watch the news and depending on what station I watch, is what one party says against the other. I am no longer proud to say I am an American. I live in the woods in Maine and have a clean, class one drivers license. I could have gotten a good job delivering heating oil but the government says I can't have a hazardous material driver's license anymore because I am a felon. What gives the government the right to do something like that in a country that is supposed to be free. Who do they think I am going to harm bringing them heating oil? There are many more restrictions on me now also. Today I got my first unemployment check and the United States bank took money out of me for a process fee. The unemployment money comes on a debit card now and the bank is owned by them. If you think for a second you are a free person, think again. You pay dearly to live In the United States if you have a job. Stop paying to live here and see how long you stay out of federal prison. I'll stop voicing my opinion now. I just wanted to tell you about the author who isn't a real writer. I'm just a simple man trying my best to make my way in life.

I don't want much anymore, just love and happiness. May God bless you today and every day. I am only on this earth for a short period of time, my soul will be with the ones I love for eternity by living well and doing the right thing. I pray the same for each and every one of you.

I'm living the life of a simple man now. I'm enjoying life and I see the most beautiful sights all the time now. I don't take anything for granted either. I look at things a lot differently. I thank God for letting me go to the places I go and see the things I see. I have my dad with me wherever I go. I'm leaning on his truck. It's the only thing I have left of him and I cherish it. If I had my wish, I'd wish each and every one of you can find true love and happiness in your lives. Life is too short and too precious to spend it with people that don't treat you right. My love and respect goes out to all of you. Take good care of yourselves and always tell the ones you love how much you love them. Never miss a chance, you never know when it will be too late. God bless you all.

Printed in the United States
by Baker & Taylor Publisher Services